CRIMINAL LITIGATION

CRIMINAL LITIGATION

John Holtam, LLB (Southampton), Solicitor

2001

Published by
Jordan Publishing Limited
21 St Thomas Street
Bristol BS1 6JS

British Library Cataloguing-in-Publication Data
A catalogue record for this book is available from the British Library.

ISSN 1352–4542
ISBN 0 85308 719 9

Printed in Great Britain by Hobbs The Printers Ltd of Southampton

PREFACE

This book has been written primarily for use by students on the Legal Practice Course. The content and depth of subject covered are determined by the requirements of the course. The aim of the book is to provide the framework upon which the criminal litigation course is built. Because students are expected to carry out their own research in some aspects of the course and will receive further tuition in others, the book is not intended as a standard textbook on the subject.

Each chapter contains suggestions on further reading. These are intended as examples of primary and secondary sources to which the reader should refer to follow up a subject.

Although I am responsible for this edition of the Resource Book, I remain indebted to John Clegg (now District Judge Clegg) for his valuable contributions in previous years. I am also grateful to Sarah De-Maine for her help and assistance with this edition of the book.

The Criminal Justice and Court Services Act 2000 renames probation orders, community service orders and combination orders as 'community rehabilitation orders', 'community punishment orders' and 'community punishment and rehabilitation orders' respectively. It introduces a number of new sentencing powers – disqualification orders, exclusion orders and restraining orders. It also makes important changes in the law relating to breaches of community orders and abolishes the sentence of detention in a young offenders' institution, lowering the minimum age for imprisonment from 21 to 18.

At the time of going to press, most of the changes made by the 2000 Act were not in force and have not been incorporated into the text. I have endeavoured to state the law as at 31 May 2001.

JOHN HOLTAM
Guildford

CONTENTS

TABLE OF CASES

References in the right-hand column are to paragraph numbers.

TABLE OF STATUTES

References in the right-hand column are to paragraph numbers and Appendices.

TABLE OF STATUTORY INSTRUMENTS, CIRCULARS AND GUIDANCE

References in the right-hand column are to paragraph numbers and Appendices.

TABLE OF EUROPEAN CONVENTIONS

References in the right-hand column are to paragraph numbers.

TABLE OF ABBREVIATIONS

CPS   Crown Prosecution Service
CPO   community punishment order
DVLA   Driver and Vehicle Licensing Authority
PCC(S)A 2000   Powers of Criminal Courts (Sentencing) Act 2000
PDH   plea and directions hearing
PH   preparatory hearing
PTR   pre-trial review
RDCO   recovery of defence costs order
TIC   (offences) taken into consideration

Chapter 1

INTRODUCTION TO CRIMINAL PROCEDURE

1.1 THE SOLICITOR'S ROLE

Solicitors are involved at every stage of the prosecution of a criminal offence, from police investigation to trial. Solicitors (and their unqualified representatives) are frequently called upon to advise suspects being held in the police station before they are charged. Difficult decisions have to be made with the client. Should police questions be answered? Should the client agree to stand on an identification parade?

Following the commencement of criminal proceedings, a solicitor may be involved in applying for a representation order for a client and in trying to secure his release from custody on bail. Criminal proceedings in a magistrates' court will usually be prosecuted and defended by solicitors, although barristers sometimes appear. If a case is to be dealt with in the Crown Court, most solicitors have limited rights of audience. Their major role is in preparing the case for trial and briefing a barrister (counsel) to represent the client.

Finally, where necessary, a solicitor will advise a client on rights of appeal, will prepare the appeal and, usually, will brief a barrister to represent the client at the appeal hearing.

This chapter provides an introduction to the criminal justice system and covers the basic information required to understand the progress of a criminal case from investigation to trial.

1.2 CLASSIFICATION OF CRIMINAL OFFENCES

Criminal offences are divided into three categories:

(1) summary offences;
(2) offences triable either way;
(3) offences triable only on indictment.

Summary offences may be tried only in a magistrates' court.

Offences triable either way may be tried in a magistrates' court or in the Crown Court before a judge and jury. The place of trial will be determined at a mode of trial hearing in a magistrates' court.

Offences triable only on indictment must be tried in the Crown Court.

1.3 THE COURTS AND COURT PERSONNEL

1.3.1 Magistrates' courts

Business

The prosecution of all criminal offences starts in the magistrates' court even if the case will ultimately be tried in the Crown Court. The functions of a magistrates' court include:

(1) to issue search and arrest warrants;
(2) to issue warrants of further detention under the Police and Criminal Evidence Act 1984;
(3) to issue summonses to defendants to appear before the court to answer a criminal charge;
(4) to try summary offences and some either way offences;
(5) to hold committal proceedings in respect of either way offences (not related to indictable only offences) which are to be tried in the Crown Court;
(6) to send indictable only offences (and related either way and summary offences) to the Crown Court for trial;
(7) to deal with applications for a representation order;
(8) to deal with applications for bail.

Personnel

Most magistrates are not legally qualified. Between two and four magistrates will usually sit in court. The magistrates are advised on points of law, practice and procedure by the clerk to the justices. The clerk should not advise magistrates on questions of fact. In some courts, a legally qualified magistrate known as a district judge (magistrates' court) (formerly known as a stipendiary magistrate) will sit alone.

1.3.2 Youth courts

Youth courts are courts set up to deal with defendants who are under 18 years of age. Lay magistrates and district judges (magistrates' court) sit in youth courts. (See Chapter 10.)

1.3.3 The Crown Court

Business

The functions of the Crown Court include:

(1) to try and to sentence offences triable only on indictment and either way offences committed for trial by a magistrates' court;
(2) to determine questions of bail and representation;
(3) to hear appeals against conviction and/or sentence from a magistrates' court and youth court.

Personnel

The judges of the Crown Court are recorders, circuit judges and High Court judges. The judge sits with a jury on not guilty pleas and with magistrates when dealing with appeals from a magistrates' court.

1.3.4 High Court (Queen's Bench Division)

Business

The Queen's Bench Division of the High Court hears appeals on points of law from magistrates' courts and youth courts and appeals on law from re-hearings in the Crown Court (appeals by way of case stated). It also has power to quash a decision by making a quashing order, to order the court to try a case by making a mandatory order, or to stop a court hearing a case by making a prohibiting order.

Personnel

The judges are judges of the Queen's Bench Division of the High Court chosen on an ad hoc basis.

1.3.5 The Court of Appeal

Business

The Court of Appeal (Criminal Division) hears appeals against conviction and/or sentence from the Crown Court.

Personnel

The judges in the Court of Appeal will be drawn from the Lord Chief Justice, Lords Justices of Appeal and High Court judges.

1.3.6 The House of Lords

Business

The House of Lords is the final appeal court. It hears appeals from the Court of Appeal and High Court but only where a point of law of general public importance is involved.

Personnel

The judges in the House of Lords are five Lords of Appeal.

1.4 THE PROSECUTION AND THE DEFENCE

1.4.1 The prosecution

Once the police have instituted proceedings, full responsibility for the prosecution will pass to the Crown Prosecution Service (CPS). The CPS will review the evidence and surrounding circumstances of each case and decide whether and how the prosecution should proceed. In appropriate cases the CPS can discontinue proceedings. There is a Code for Crown Prosecutors (October 2000) which gives guidelines on discontinuance and other matters.

Joint charging standards have been drawn up by the police and the CPS. The purpose of joint charging standards is to make sure that the most appropriate charge is selected, in the light of the evidence which can be proved, at the earliest possible opportunity. To date, three joint charging standards have been published: Offences Against the Person (26 April 1996), Public Order Offences (26 April 1996) and Driving Offences (March 1996).

1.4.2 The defence

A defendant has the right to conduct his own defence (*R v Woodward* [1944] KB 118; see also the European Convention on Human Rights, Article 6(3), and **1.8**). There are restrictions on cross-examination by defendants in person (see **4.3.2**). A defendant may, however, be represented by a solicitor whom he will pay privately, or who will be paid under a representation order. If the services of a barrister (counsel) are needed, the solicitor instructs a barrister. The defendant cannot instruct a barrister direct.

A solicitor has a right of audience in a magistrates' court. For most solicitors, rights of audience in the Crown Court are limited to:

(1) applications in chambers, for example bail applications;

(2) appeals against conviction and/or sentence from a magistrates' court, provided a member of the solicitor's firm conducted the proceedings in the magistrates' court;

(3) on committal by a magistrates' court to the Crown Court for sentence, provided a member of the solicitor's firm conducted the hearing in the magistrates' court;

(4) preliminary hearings in the Crown Court where the defendant has been sent for trial for an indictable defence.

Thus, solicitors cannot normally conduct a trial by jury in the Crown Court. However, in certain Crown Courts, solicitors enjoy extended rights of audience, including the right to conduct some jury trials (*Practice Direction (Solicitors: Audience in Crown Court)* [1988] 1 WLR 1427). A number of solicitors have now been granted full rights of audience in the Crown Court and higher appeal courts.

1.4.3 Criminal Defence Service

The Criminal Defence Service was created by the Access to Justice Act 1999 (ss 12–18 and Sch 3) and came into force on 2 April 2001. The purpose of the Criminal Defence Service is to 'secure the provision of advice, assistance and representation, according to the interests of justice, to people suspected of a criminal offence, or facing criminal proceedings' (*Legal Services Commission Manual* (Sweet & Maxwell, 1D-004)).

The Legal Services Commission funds the Criminal Defence Service and secures the provision of advice, assistance and representation under a General Criminal Contract with solicitors in private practice, or by providing them through salaried public defenders. All contractors are expected to meet quality assurance standards and provide the full range of services from arrest until the case is completed. Only those solicitors with a General Criminal Contract with the Legal Services Commission are able to undertake publicly funded defence work.

The following advice and assistance may be granted without reference to the financial resources of the individual:

- advocacy assistance before a magistrates' court or Crown Court;
- advice and assistance (including advocacy assistance) provided by a solicitor acting as a court duty solicitor;
- police station advice and assistance to a client who is arrested and held at a police station or who is a volunteer;

- advocacy assistance on an application for a warrant of further detention or for an extension to such a warrant (Criminal Defence Service (General) (No 2) Regulations 2001).

Where a representation order is requested an applicant will need to satisfy the interests of justice test set out in Access to Justice Act 1999, Sch 3 (see **3.3.2**).

1.5 AN OVERVIEW OF CRIMINAL PROCEDURE

See **Appendix 1(A)** for a flowchart giving an overview of criminal procedure.

1.5.1 Police investigations

Police investigation includes arrest, search and the detention and questioning of a suspect (see Chapter 2).

1.5.2 Commencement of criminal proceedings

The commencement of criminal proceedings will be by way of charge or summons. A charge is normally used when a suspect has been arrested and taken to the police station. A summons is normally used for relatively minor offences that may not involve arrest at all (eg motoring offences). The summons will be served by post and will notify the defendant of the date, time and place of the hearing (see Chapter 3).

1.5.3 Magistrates' courts

All cases begin in a magistrates' court. At the initial hearing, questions of adjournments, representation and bail are likely to arise (see Chapter 3).

If the offence before the court is a summary offence, it must be dealt with by a magistrates' court. The defendant will plead guilty or not guilty and on conviction will be sentenced (see Chapter 5).

If the offence is an either way offence (which is not related to an indictable only offence), the prosecution begins with the plea before venue hearing before the magistrates. If the defendant refuses to indicate a plea, or indicates a not guilty plea, the magistrates will proceed to mode of trial, to determine whether the case should be dealt with by a magistrates' court or by the Crown Court (see Chapter 6). If the offence proceeds in the magistrates' court and the defendant is convicted, then the magistrates may commit him to the Crown Court for sentencing in certain circumstances (see Chapter 9). If the case is to proceed to the Crown Court, there will be committal proceedings in the magistrates' court. At committal, the defence can require the prosecution to show that there is a case to answer. Alternatively, the defence may not dispute that there is a case to answer. If so, the committal may be a formality (see Chapter 7). Following committal, the defendant will be tried by judge and jury. Following conviction, the defendant is sentenced by a judge.

If the offence is an indictable only offence, the magistrates must send the defendant to the Crown Court to be tried. The magistrates must also send related summary only and either way offences to the Crown Court (see Chapter 7).

1.5.4 Disclosure of prosecution evidence

In all cases, the defendant has a statutory right to receive a copy of certain documents such as his custody record and the record of an identification parade.

However, if he is merely charged with a summary offence, the defendant has no further general right to see the prosecution evidence before it is presented at the trial. This may make it more difficult for the defence lawyer to prepare the defence. However, the prosecution is usually prepared to disclose its evidence on a voluntary basis.

If the defendant is charged with an either way offence, then prior to the mode of trial decision, he has a right to receive either a summary or a copy of the prosecution witness statements, under the Magistrates' Courts (Advance Information) Rules 1985.

If the defendant's case is to be committed to the Crown Court, the prosecution must serve copies of its evidence on the defence before the case is committed from the magistrates' court to the Crown Court.

If the defendant's case is sent to the Crown Court for trial, the prosecution must serve copies of its evidence on the defence at the Crown Court.

These rules are dealt with in more detail at **6.2** and in Chapter 7.

1.5.5 Appeal

There are rights of appeal against conviction and/or sentence from the magistrates' court and the Crown Court (see Chapter 11).

1.6 SUBSTANTIVE CRIMINAL LAW

This book has been designed as a constituent part of the Legal Practice Course. As such, it will not generally address questions of substantive criminal law. However, an outline knowledge of the offences which have been used to illustrate points of practice, procedure and evidence is necessary. It is also necessary to know how each offence is classified for trial purposes and the maximum penalties that can be imposed on conviction. The offences which are illustrated in this book are summarised below.

1.6.1 Theft

(1) Classification – triable either way.
(2) Theft is an arrestable offence within the meaning of the Police and Criminal Evidence Act 1984, s 24 (see Chapter 2).
(3) Maximum penalties – Crown Court: 7 years' imprisonment and/or unlimited fine. Magistrates' court: 6 months' imprisonment and/or £5,000 fine. If theft of a motor vehicle: discretionary disqualification from driving.
(4) Definition – Theft Act 1968, s 1:

> 'Dishonest appropriation of property belonging to another with the intention of permanently depriving the other of it.'

1.6.2 Burglary

(1) Classification – triable either way if involving theft or intention to steal, unless burglary of a dwelling and any person in the dwelling is subjected to violence or the threat of it, in which case triable only on indictment.

(2) Burglary is an arrestable offence within the meaning of the Police and Criminal Evidence Act 1984, s 24 (see Chapter 2).

(3) Maximum penalties – Crown Court: 14 years' imprisonment and/or unlimited fine (maximum 10 years if not of a dwelling). Magistrates' court: 6 months' imprisonment and/or £5,000 fine.

(4) There is a minimum sentence of 3 years' imprisonment for the third conviction of burglary of a dwelling. The court need not impose the minimum term if it is of the opinion that there are particular circumstances which:

    (a) relate to any of the offences or the offender; and

    (b) would make the prescribed minimum sentence unjust in all the circumstances (Powers of Criminal Courts (Sentencing) Act 2000 (PCC(S)A 2000), ss 111–115).

(5) Definition – Theft Act 1968, s 9:

'(1) A person is guilty of burglary if –

    (a) he enters any building or part of a building as a trespasser and with intent to commit any such offence as is mentioned in subsection (2) below; or

    (b) having entered any building or part of a building as a trespasser he steals or attempts to steal anything in the building or that part of it or inflicts or attempts to inflict on any person therein any grievous bodily harm.

(2) The offences referred to in subsection (1)(a) above are offences of stealing anything in the building or part of a building in question, of inflicting on any person therein any grievous bodily harm or raping any person therein, and of doing unlawful damage to the building or anything therein.'

1.6.3 Robbery

(1) Classification – triable only on indictment.

(2) Robbery is an arrestable offence within the meaning of the Police and Criminal Evidence Act 1984, s 24 (see Chapter 2).

(3) Maximum penalties – life imprisonment and/or unlimited fine.

(4) Definition – Theft Act 1968, s 8(1):

'A person is guilty of robbery if he steals and immediately before or at the time of doing so, and in order to do so, he uses force on any person or puts or seeks to put any person in fear of being then and there subjected to force.'

1.6.4 Taking a conveyance

(1) Classification – summary only.

(2) Taking a conveyance is an arrestable offence within the meaning of the Police and Criminal Evidence Act 1984, s 24 (see Chapter 2).

(3) Maximum penalties – 6 months' imprisonment and/or £5,000 fine. Discretionary disqualification.

(4) Definition – Theft Act 1968, s 12:

'(1) Subject to subsection … (6) below, a person shall be guilty of an offence if, without having the consent of the owner or other lawful authority, he takes any conveyance for his own or another's use or, knowing that any conveyance has been taken without such authority, drives it or allows himself to be carried in or on it …

(6)   A person does not commit an offence under this section by anything done in the belief that he has lawful authority to do it or that he would have the owner's consent if the owner knew of his doing it and the circumstances of it.'

1.6.5 Aggravated vehicle-taking

(1)   Classification – either way unless the aggravating feature is damage to the vehicle or other property in a sum not exceeding £5,000, in which case summary only.

(2)   Aggravated vehicle-taking is an arrestable offence within the meaning of the Police and Criminal Evidence Act 1984, s 24 (see Chapter 2).

(3)   Maximum penalties – Crown Court: 2 years' imprisonment and/or unlimited fine (5 years' imprisonment if accident caused death to a person). Magistrates' court: 6 months' imprisonment and/or £5,000 fine. In the Crown Court and magistrates' court, obligatory endorsement of driving licence, obligatory disqualification from driving or 3–11 penalty points (if disqualification is avoided but not endorsement).

(4)   Definition – Theft Act 1968, s 12A(1) (inserted by the Aggravated Vehicle Taking Act 1991):

'A person is guilty of aggravated taking of a vehicle if –

(a)   he commits an offence under s 12(1) [Taking a Conveyance] in relation to a mechanically propelled vehicle,

AND

(b)   [after the s 12(1) offence is committed and before the vehicle is recovered the vehicle was driven dangerously on a road or other public place or an accident occurred and injury to a person or damage to property arose or that damage was caused to the vehicle.]'

1.6.6 Driving without insurance

(1)   Classification – summary only.

(2)   This offence is not an arrestable offence within the meaning of the Police and Criminal Evidence Act 1984, s 24 (see Chapter 2).

(3)   Maximum penalties – £5,000 fine. Obligatory endorsement of driving licence, discretionary disqualification from driving or 6–8 penalty points.

(4)   Definition – Road Traffic Act 1988, s 143(a):

'A person must not use a motor vehicle on a road unless there is in force in relation to the use of the vehicle by that person a policy of insurance …'

(5)   If the prosecution proves that the defendant used a motor vehicle on a road, the burden shifts to the defendant to establish that he was insured (Magistrates' Courts Act 1980, s 101; *R v Edwards* [1975] QB 27).

1.6.7 Assault occasioning actual bodily harm

(1)   Classification – either way.

(2) The offence is an arrestable offence within the meaning of the Police and Criminal Evidence Act 1984, s 24 (see Chapter 2).

(3) Maximum penalties – Crown Court: 5 years' imprisonment and/or unlimited fine. Magistrates' court: 6 months' imprisonment and/or £5,000 fine.

(4) Definition – Offences Against the Person Act 1861, s 47:

'... assault occasioning actual bodily harm.'

Any injury can be classified as actual bodily harm. However, the Crown Prosecution Service *Charging Standards* document (issued in April 1996) makes it clear that a s 47 charge is not appropriate if the injuries amount to no more than 'grazes, scratches, abrasions, minor bruising, superficial cuts or a black eye'. For such minor injuries, the appropriate charge is common assault. A verdict of assault occasioning actual bodily harm may be returned on proof of an assault together with proof that actual bodily harm was occasioned by the assault. The prosecution do not have to prove that the defendant intended to cause some actual bodily harm or was reckless as to whether such harm would be caused (*R v Savage (Susan); DPP v Parmenter (Philip Mark)* [1991] 4 All ER 698).

1.6.8 Wounding or inflicting grievous bodily harm

(1) Classification – either way

(2) The offence is an arrestable offence within the Police and Criminal Evidence Act 1984, s 24 (see Chapter 2).

(3) Maximum penalties

Crown Court: 5 years' imprisonment and/or unlimited fine.

Magistrates' court: 6 months' imprisonment and/or £5000 fine.

(4) Definition – Offences Against the Person Act 1861, s 20:

'Whosoever shall unlawfully and maliciously wound or inflict grievous bodily harm upon any other person, either with or without any weapon or instrument, shall be guilty of [an offence], and being convicted thereof shall be liable to [imprisonment for not more than 5 years].'

A wound requires the breaking of two layers of skin. In theory, even trivial wounds may qualify, but the *Charging Standards* urge that minor wounds should not, in practice, be charged under s 20. Grievous bodily harm means really serious harm (*DPP v Smith* [1961] AC 290). The *Charging Standards* list examples of injuries which should normally be prosecuted under s 20, for example, injury resulting in permanent disability or permanent loss of sensory function; injury which results in more than minor permanent, visible disfigurement; broken or displaced limbs or bones, including fractured skull; compound fractures, broken cheek bone, jaw, ribs, etc; injuries which cause substantial loss of blood, usually necessitating a transfusion; and injuries resulting in lengthy treatment or incapacity.

The prosecution must prove that either the defendant intended, or actually foresaw, that the act would cause some harm. It is not necessary to prove that the defendant intended or foresaw that the unlawful act might cause the physical harm described in s 20. It is enough that the defendant foresaw that some physical harm to some person, albeit of a minor character, might result (*R v Savage; DPP v Parmenter*).

1.6.9 Fear or provocation of violence

(1) Classification – summary only.

(2) The offence is not an arrestable offence within the meaning of the Police and Criminal Evidence Act 1984, s 24 (see Chapter 2). The police do, however, have power to arrest without a warrant for the offence (Public Order Act 1986, s 4(3)).

(3) Maximum penalties – 6 months' imprisonment and/or £5,000 fine.

(4) Definition – Public Order Act 1986, s 4:

'(1) A person is guilty of an offence if he –

(a) uses towards another person threatening, abusive or insulting words or behaviour, or

(b) distributes or displays to another person any writing, sign or other visible representation which is threatening, abusive or insulting,

with intent to cause that person to believe that immediate unlawful violence will be used against him or another by any person, or to provoke the immediate use of unlawful violence by that person or another, or whereby that person is likely to believe that such violence will be used or it is likely that such violence will be provoked.

(2) An offence under this section may be committed in a public or a private place, except that no offence is committed where the words or behaviour are used, or the writing, sign or other visible representation is distributed or displayed, by a person inside a dwelling and the other person is also inside that or another dwelling.'

1.6.10 Intentionally causing harassment, alarm or distress

(1) Classification – summary only.

(2) The offence is not an arrestable offence within the meaning of the Police and Criminal Evidence Act 1984, s 24. The police do, however, have power to arrest without a warrant for the offence (Public Order Act 1986, s 4A(4)).

(3) Maximum penalties – 6 months' imprisonment and/or £5,000 fine.

(4) Definition – Public Order Act 1986, s 4A:

'(1) A person is guilty of an offence if, with intent to cause a person harassment, alarm or distress, he –

(a) uses threatening, abusive or insulting words or behaviour, or disorderly behaviour, or

(b) displays any writing, sign or other visible representation which is threatening, abusive or insulting, thereby causing that person harassment, alarm or distress.

(2) An offence under this section may be committed in a public or a private place, except that no offence is committed where the words or behaviour are used, or the writing, sign or other visible representation is displayed, by a person inside a dwelling and the person who is harassed, alarmed or distressed is also inside that or another dwelling.

(3) It is a defence for the accused to prove –

(a) that he was inside a dwelling and had no reason to believe that the behaviour used, or the writing, sign or other visible representation displayed, would be heard or seen by a person outside that or any other dwelling, or

(b) that his conduct was reasonable.'

1.6.11 Harassment, alarm or distress

(1) Classification – summary only.
(2) The offence is not an arrestable offence within the meaning of the Police and Criminal Evidence Act 1984, s 24. The police are given the power to arrest without warrant in certain circumstances laid down in the Public Order Act 1976, s 5(4).
(3) Maximum penalties – £1,000 fine.
(4) Definition – Public Order Act 1986, s 5:

'(1) A person is guilty of an offence if he –

(a) uses threatening, abusive or insulting words or behaviour, or disorderly behaviour, or

(b) displays any writing, sign or other visible representation which is threatening, abusive or insulting, within the hearing or sight of a person likely to be caused harassment, alarm or distress thereby.

(2) An offence under this section may be committed in a public or a private place, except that no offence is committed where the words or behaviour are used, or the writing, sign or other visible representation is displayed, by a person inside a dwelling and the other person is also inside that or another dwelling.'

1.6.12 Dangerous driving

(1) Classification – either way.
(2) This is not an arrestable offence within the meaning of the Police and Criminal Evidence Act 1984, s 24 (see Chapter 2).
(3) Maximum penalties – Crown Court: 2 years' imprisonment and/or unlimited fine. Magistrates' court: 6 months' imprisonment and/or £5,000 fine.

In either court, the offence carries obligatory endorsement of driving licence, obligatory disqualification from driving or 3–11 penalty points (if disqualification is avoided but not endorsement); compulsory re-testing before recommencement of driving.

(4) Definition – Road Traffic Act 1988, ss 2 and 2A (as amended by the Road Traffic Act 1991):

'2. A person who drives a mechanically propelled vehicle dangerously on a road or other public place is guilty of an offence.

2A. Meaning of dangerous driving

(1) For the purpose ... of section ... 2 above a person is to be regarded as driving dangerously if (and subject to subsection (2) below, only if) –

(a) the way he drives falls far below what would be expected of a competent and careful driver, and

(b) it would be obvious to a competent and careful driver that driving in that way would be dangerous.

(2)   A person is also to be regarded as driving dangerously for the purpose … of section … 2 above if it would be obvious to a competent and careful driver that driving the vehicle in its current state would be dangerous.

(3)   In subsection (1) and (2) above "dangerous" refers to danger either of injury to any person or of serious damage to property; and in determining for the purposes of those subsections what would be expected of, or obvious to, a competent and careful driver in a particular case, regard shall be had not only to the circumstances of which he could be expected to be aware but also to any circumstances shown to have been within the knowledge of the accused.

(4)   In determining for the purposes of subsection (2) above the state of a vehicle regard may be had to anything attached to or carried on or in it and to the manner in which it is attached or carried.'

1.6.13 Careless and inconsiderate driving

(1)   Classification – summary only.
(2)   This offence is not an arrestable offence within the meaning of the Police and Criminal Evidence Act 1984, s 24 (see Chapter 2).
(3)   Maximum penalties – £2,500 fine. Obligatory endorsement of driving licence, discretionary disqualification from driving or 3–9 penalty points.
(4)   Definition – Road Traffic Act 1988, s 3 (as amended by the Road Traffic Act 1991, s 2):

'If a person drives a mechanically propelled vehicle on a road or other public place without due care and attention, or without reasonable consideration for other persons using the road or place, he is guilty of an offence.'

1.6.14 Secondary participation

A person who aids, abets, counsels or procures the commission of an offence is a secondary party. Basically, a person who assists the principal offender at the scene of the crime is an aider or abettor and one who provides assistance before the crime is a counsellor or procurer of the offence.

An accomplice will often be jointly charged with a principal offender.

Example
John Smith steals goods while Alan Jones keeps a lookout.

Alan Jones' charge may read:

'Jointly with John Smith stole …' etc.

The charge reads as though Alan Jones is a principal offender. This is permissible by virtue of the Accessories and Abettors Act 1861, s 8.

1.7 PROFESSIONAL ETHICS

A solicitor involved in criminal litigation faces many ethical problems. Should a prosecutor reveal information to the defence which will assist the defence case? Can you act for a client who tells you that he is guilty but who wishes to plead not guilty? How should you react to a major change of story by your client? This section seeks to identify the major ethical problems which are likely to arise in a criminal case and suggests solutions to them.

1.7.1 Duty not to mislead the court

The general principle for a solicitor involved in criminal proceedings is that, while he owes a duty to his client to do his best for him, a solicitor must not mislead or deceive the court.

1.7.2 The prosecution

Prosecuting advocates are under a duty to ensure that all material evidence supporting the prosecution case is put before the court in a dispassionate and fair manner. In particular:

(1) all relevant facts known to the prosecution should be put before the court including, after conviction, facts relevant to mitigation;

(2) if a prosecution witness gives evidence in court which is inconsistent with any earlier statement made, there is a duty to disclose this fact to the defence.

When arguing a point of law, all relevant legal authorities should be cited, including those which are against the prosecution.

1.7.3 The defence

A number of ethical problems can arise when conducting a criminal defence. Always bear in mind the duty not to mislead the court (see **1.7.1**). In addition, the following guidelines may be of assistance.

(1) The client who admits his guilt. This may happen before or during the course of proceedings. If the client insists on giving evidence in the witness box denying his guilt, then a solicitor should decline to act. It is, however, proper to act on a not guilty plea if the defence merely intends to put the prosecution to proof of its case without calling defence evidence.

(2) Occasionally, a client will wish to plead guilty notwithstanding that his instructions indicate that he has a defence. Such a client should be advised of the defence available. If he insists on pleading guilty, the solicitor may continue to act but should advise the client that in mitigation it will not be possible to rely on facts that may constitute a defence.

(3) The client who gives inconsistent instructions. The mere fact that a client makes inconsistent statements to his solicitor does not make it improper for the solicitor to continue to act. If it becomes clear that the client is changing his instructions with a view to putting forward false evidence to the court, the solicitor should refuse to act.

(4) Disclosure of the defence case. A solicitor should not, without the express consent of his client, disclose details of his client's case to any other party. Requests for disclosure sometimes come, for example, from the solicitors acting for a co-defendant. Such requests should be treated with caution and the client's instructions taken.

(5) Arguing a point of law. All relevant authorities should be cited, including those which are against the advocate. This is a positive duty to assist the court in

contrast to matters of fact where the duty is a negative one – not to mislead the court.

(6)   **The client who gives a false name to the court.** A solicitor should not act for a client who, to the knowledge of the solicitor, gives a false name, address or date of birth to the court. If faced with this problem the solicitor should try to persuade the client to change his mind. If the client refuses to do so then the solicitor should cease to act.

(7)   **Knowledge of previous convictions.** On occasion, the list of previous convictions of a defendant produced to the court by the prosecution will be inaccurate. If asked to confirm the accuracy of the list, a solicitor should decline to comment. To confirm the list as accurate would amount to a positive deception of the court. A solicitor should not mislead the court. On the other hand, disclosing previous convictions without the client's express consent is a breach of the duty of confidentiality to the client. The solicitor should, wherever possible, obtain a list of previous convictions from the police or CPS sufficiently in advance of going to court so that he can discuss any problems with the client. The client should be warned of the dangers of misleading the court. If the client insists that, if asked, he will pretend the list is accurate, the solicitor must cease to act.

(8)   **Conflicts of interest.** A solicitor must not continue to act for two or more defendants where a conflict of interest arises between them. Within the context of criminal proceedings, a conflict can arise, for example, where one defendant decides to blame the other and changes his plea to not guilty. Even where pleas are consistent it may not be possible to act for the defendants if one is seeking to implicate the other or to allege that one played a larger role in the offence than the other. If a conflict arises while a solicitor is acting for both defendants then he should consider withdrawing from the case altogether. This would be appropriate where the solicitor has information in his possession about one defendant which could be used to assist the other defendant in the case.

(9)   **Interviewing prosecution witnesses.** Although there is no property in a witness, defence solicitors should proceed with caution when intending to interview a prosecution witness. The best course of action is to notify the prosecution of the fact that a witness is to be interviewed and to invite a representative to attend as an observer. This will avoid suspicion of an attempt to pervert the course of justice and allegations that a witness has been pressured in some way to change his evidence.

(10) If circumstances arise which require a solicitor to withdraw from a case (eg, see (6) and (7) above), the reason for withdrawal should not normally be given to the court. The solicitor should simply explain that a matter has arisen which makes it impossible for him to continue to act in the case.

1.8 EUROPEAN CONVENTION ON HUMAN RIGHTS

The Human Rights Act 1998, which came into force on 2 October 2000, is intended to give effect in domestic law to the rights and freedoms guaranteed by the European Convention for the Protection of Human Rights and Fundamental Freedoms (the Convention), to which the UK is a party.

(1) All legislation must, if possible, be interpreted so as to be compatible with the Convention (s 3(1)). Domestic courts must strive to find a construction consistent with the intentions of Parliament and the wording of legislation which is nearest to Convention rights. Courts should proceed on the basis that Parliament is deemed to have intended its statutes to be compatible with the Convention. The only basis for the courts concluding that Parliament has failed to carry that intention into effect is where it is impossible to construe a statute so as to be compatible with the Convention (Lord Chancellor, 18 November 1997, House of Lords Committee Stage, *Hansard* col 535).

(2) Where it is not possible to interpret primary legislation so as to be compatible with the Convention, the courts will have no power to strike it down. However, the House of Lords, the Judicial Committee of the Privy Council, the Court of Appeal and the High Court will have power to make a 'declaration of incompatibility' which (in theory) should prompt government action. Such a declaration does not affect the validity, continuing operation or enforcement of the provision in respect of which it is made (s 4(6)(a)). Nor does it bind the parties to the proceedings in which it is made (s 4(6)(b)). It is intended to operate as a clear signal to Parliament that an incompatibility has been found.

The Government envisages that a declaration of incompatibility will 'almost certainly' prompt legislative change (White Paper, 'Rights Brought Home: The Human Rights Bill' (Cmnd 3782), para 2.9). The Act provides a 'fast track' procedure for amending the law so as to bring it into conformity with the Convention (s 10).

(3) Where it simply is not possible to interpret subordinate legislation so as to be compatible with the Convention, the courts have power to disapply it. The only exception is where primary legislation prevents the removal of any incompatibility (s 4(4)(b)).

(4) All public authorities, including all courts and tribunals, must, if possible, act in a way which is compatible with the Convention. Public authorities include (but are not limited to) courts, tribunals and 'any person certain of whose functions are functions of a public nature' (s 6(3)). The definition is in wide terms and is intended to cover the police.

(5) Individuals who believe that their Convention rights have been infringed by a public authority can rely on their rights as a defence in civil and criminal proceedings or as the basis of an appeal, alternatively seek judicial review, or bring civil proceedings for damages (s 7 and s 8).

(6) Section 8(1) of the Act provides that:

'In relation to any act (or proposed act) of a public authority which the court finds is (or would be) unlawful, it may grant such relief or remedy, or make such order, within its powers as it considers just and appropriate.'

As a result, criminal courts will have the power to stay proceedings as an abuse of process, quash an indictment or charge, rule evidence inadmissible, quash convictions and even recognise new defences where Convention rights have been violated.

(7) In resolving Convention issues, all courts and tribunals must take into account the case-law of the European Court of Human Rights, Commission of Human Rights and the Committee of Ministers established under the Convention (s 2).

Since the Act came into force, practitioners have been able to rely on the Convention in criminal proceedings. Practitioners can test domestic law and practice for compliance with the Convention, particularly:

'Article 3

Prohibition of torture

No one shall be subjected to torture or to inhuman or degrading treatment or punishment. …

Article 5

Right to liberty and security

1.   Everyone has the right to liberty and security of person. No one shall be deprived of his liberty save in the following cases and in accordance with a procedure prescribed by law:

   (a)   the lawful detention of a person after conviction by a competent court;

   (b)   the lawful arrest or detention of a person for non-compliance with the lawful order of a court or in order to secure the fulfilment of any obligation prescribed by law;

   (c)   the lawful arrest or detention of a person effected for the purpose of bringing him before the competent legal authority on reasonable suspicion of having committed an offence or when it is reasonably considered necessary to prevent his committing an offence or fleeing after having done so;

   (d)   the detention of a minor by lawful order for the purpose of educational supervision or his lawful detention for the purpose of bringing him before the competent legal authority;

   (e)   the lawful detention of persons for the prevention of the spreading of infectious diseases, of persons of unsound mind, alcoholics or drug addicts or vagrants;

   (f)   the lawful arrest or detention of a person to prevent his effecting an unauthorised entry into the country or of a person against whom action is being taken with a view to deportation or extradition.

2.   Everyone who is arrested shall be informed promptly, in a language which he understands, of the reasons for his arrest and of any charge against him.

3.   Everyone arrested or detained in accordance with the provisions of paragraph 1(c) of this Article shall be brought promptly before a judge or other officer authorised by law to exercise judicial power and shall be entitled to trial within a reasonable time or to release pending trial. Release may be conditioned by guarantees to appear for trial.

4.   Everyone who is deprived of his liberty by arrest or detention shall be entitled to take proceedings by which the lawfulness of his detention shall be decided speedily by a court and his release ordered if the detention is not lawful.

5.   Everyone who has been the victim of arrest or detention in contravention of the provisions of this Article shall have an enforceable right to compensation.

Article 6

Right to a fair trial

1. In the determination of his civil rights and obligations or of any criminal charge against him, everyone is entitled to a fair and public hearing within a reasonable time by an independent and impartial tribunal established by law. Judgment shall be pronounced publicly but the press and public may be excluded from all or part of the trial in the interest of morals, public order or national security in a democratic society, where the interests of juveniles or the protection of the private life of the parties so require, or to the extent strictly necessary in the opinion of the court in special circumstances where publicity would prejudice the interests of justice.

2. Everyone charged with a criminal offence shall be presumed innocent until proved guilty according to the law.

3. Everyone charged with a criminal offence has the following minimum rights:

    (a) to be informed promptly, in a language which he understands and in detail, of the nature and cause of the accusation against him;

    (b) to have adequate time and facilities for the preparation of his defence;

    (c) to defend himself in person or through legal assistance of his own choosing or, if he has not sufficient means to pay for legal assistance, to be given it free when the interests of justice so require;

    (d) to examine or have examined witnesses against him and to obtain the attendance and examination of witnesses on his behalf under the same conditions as witnesses against him;

    (e) to have the free assistance of an interpreter if he cannot understand or speak the language used in court.

Article 7

No punishment without law

1. No one shall be held guilty of any criminal offence on account of any act or omission which did not constitute a criminal offence under national or international law at the time when it was committed. Nor shall a heavier penalty be imposed than the one that was applicable at the time the criminal offence was committed.

2. This Article shall not prejudice the trial and punishment of any person for any act or omission which, at the time when it was committed, was criminal according to the general principles of law recognised by civilised nations.'

There is no rule under the Act requiring a Convention point to be taken at any given stage in criminal proceedings. Convention points can be taken before the trial (eg by challenging the charge or indictment), at trial (by seeking to exclude evidence obtained in breach of the Convention or limiting the basis upon which adverse inferences can be drawn), or on appeal (eg by quashing a conviction on the basis that it was obtained in breach of the Convention). It is possible that courts may also examine Convention issues of their own volition since they are 'public authorities' under s 6 and, accordingly, are obliged to act in accordance with the Convention.

1.9 FURTHER READING

See, for example:

Archbold: Criminal Pleading, Evidence and Practice (Sweet & Maxwell, 2001);
Blackstone's Criminal Practice (Blackstone Press, 2001);
Pervasive and Core Topics (Jordans);
The Guide to the Professional Conduct of Solicitors (The Law Society, 1999);
Reid *A Practitioner's Guide to the European Convention on Human Rights* (Sweet & Maxwell, 1998);
Starmer *European Human Rights Law: The European Convention on Human Rights and the Human Rights Act 1998* (Legal Action Group, 1999);
Wadham and Mountfield *Human Rights Act 1998* (Blackstone Press, 1999).

Chapter 2

THE SUSPECT IN THE POLICE STATION

2.1 INTRODUCTION

The police have wide powers to arrest and detain a person, without charge, if that person is suspected of having committed a criminal offence. A suspect who is detained in a police station has the right to legal advice. A solicitor's role in the police station involves advising a suspect of his rights, 'sitting in' on police interviews with a suspect, ensuring 'fair play' in the police station and attending identification parades. This chapter examines the law governing the detention, treatment and questioning of a suspect and considers the role of a solicitor in the police station. The law is contained primarily in the Police and Criminal Evidence Act 1984, the Codes of Practice issued under that Act and the Criminal Justice and Public Order Act 1994. References to section numbers in this chapter are, unless otherwise stated, to the Police and Criminal Evidence Act 1984. References to 'Code C' are to the Code of Practice on the Detention, Treatment and Questioning of Suspects, and references to 'Code D' are to the Code of Practice on Identification Procedures. A diagram showing some of the ranks in the police appears as **Appendix 1(B)**.

2.2 THE SERIOUS ARRESTABLE OFFENCE (s 116 and Sch 5)

An important concept running through the Police and Criminal Evidence Act 1984 is the serious arrestable offence. It is relevant to the powers of the police to detain a suspect for more than 24 hours and to delay access to legal advice.

Of the offences covered in this book, the following are capable of being serious arrestable offences:

> Theft
> Burglary
> Robbery
> Taking a conveyance
> Aggravated vehicle-taking
> Assault occasioning actual bodily harm
> Wounding or inflicting grievous bodily harm.

An offence listed above will be a serious arrestable offence only if:

(1) it has led, inter alia, to the death of any person, serious injury of any person, substantial financial gain to any person, or serious financial loss to any person; or

(2) it is intended or is likely to lead to any of the consequences at (1) above.

Serious financial loss is assessed subjectively. Thus, theft of a relatively small amount of money from a poor person can legitimately be treated as a serious arrestable offence. Substantial financial gain is assessed objectively.

The initial decision as to whether an offence under investigation is a serious arrestable offence will be taken by a superintendent at the police station where a suspect is being held. If necessary, the defence can challenge the decision in court. This may be done, for example, as part of an argument that a confession should not be admitted in evidence (see Chapter 4).

In practice, the detailed provisions of the Act must be consulted if there is doubt as to whether an offence is a serious arrestable offence.

2.3 POLICE POWERS OF DETENTION

A flowchart showing procedure at the police station is included as **Appendix 1(C)**.

2.3.1 Volunteers

A person sometimes attends a police station on a voluntary basis to assist the police with their enquiries. Section 29 of the Act provides that:

> 'Where for the purposes of assisting with an investigation a person attends voluntarily at a police station … without having been arrested:
>
> (a)   he shall be entitled to leave at will unless he is placed under arrest;
> (b)   he shall be informed at once that he is under arrest if a decision is taken by a constable to prevent him from leaving at will.'

The status of a suspect is likely to change from volunteer to arrested suspect if answers given to police questions give rise to a reasonable suspicion that the detainee may have committed an offence.

2.3.2 Persons under arrest

Where a suspect is arrested at any place other than a police station, he must be taken to a police station by a police officer as soon as practicable after the arrest (s 30).

A person who is arrested and taken to a police station is taken before the custody officer. The custody officer is a police officer of at least the rank of sergeant. The custody officer:

> 'shall determine whether he has before him sufficient evidence to charge that person with the offence for which he was arrested and may detain him at the police station for such period as is necessary to enable him to do so' (s 37(1)).

To enable the custody officer to determine whether there is sufficient evidence to charge the arrested person, he will usually speak to the arresting officer. The test to be applied in determining whether there is sufficient evidence to charge is whether:

(1)   there is sufficient evidence for a prosecution to succeed; and
(2)   the officer is satisfied that the suspect has said all that he wishes to say about the offence under investigation (Code C, para 16.1).

In all but the most trivial of offences there is unlikely to be sufficient evidence to charge the suspect at this stage.

By s 37(2):

> 'If the custody officer determines that he does not have such evidence before him the person arrested shall be released either on bail or without bail unless the custody officer has reasonable grounds for believing that his detention without being charged is necessary to secure or preserve evidence relating to an offence for which he is under arrest or to obtain such evidence by questioning him.'

By s 37(3):

> 'If the custody officer has reasonable grounds for so believing he may authorise the person arrested to be kept in police detention.'

A suspect can, therefore, be detained for samples to be taken or while premises are searched. The most common ground for detention without charge is to question the suspect.

The custody officer is required to open and maintain a custody record for each suspect taken to the police station. The grounds for detention without charge must be recorded in the custody record and a chronological record of events occurring during the suspect's period of detention must be kept. An example of a custody record appears as **Appendix 2(A)**.

A legal representative attending the police station to advise a suspect is entitled to inspect the custody record (Code C, para 2.4). A copy of the custody record must be given to the suspect or his legal representative on request when the suspect is taken before a court or upon the suspect's release from police detention.

2.3.3 Periods of detention without charge

The basic detention process can conveniently be illustrated in chart form (see **Appendix 1(D)**).

The following points in particular should be noted.

(1) The basic maximum period of detention without charge is 24 hours. Normally, this runs from the time the arrested person arrives at the police station. If he went to the police station on a voluntary basis, then time runs from when he is arrested at the police station.

(2) If the offence under investigation is a serious arrestable offence further detention up to 36 hours on the detention clock can be authorised by a superintendent on certain specified grounds (s 42).

(3) Detention beyond 36 hours can only be authorised by a magistrates' court on the granting of a warrant of further detention. The grounds for granting a warrant of further detention are identical to the grounds for a superintendent authorising detention for up to 36 hours (s 43). A warrant may initially be granted for a period not exceeding 36 hours but can be extended for further periods until 96 hours have expired on the detention clock. This is the absolute maximum period of detention without charge.

(4) A review of detention must be carried out by an inspector within 6 hours of detention being first authorised and thereafter at 9-hourly intervals. This is to ensure that the initial grounds for detention still exist. Details of the reviews must be recorded in the custody record.

2.3.4 Bail following charge

When a person has been charged with an offence, the custody officer must decide whether to keep that person in custody until his court appearance. Section 38 provides that:

> 'Where a person arrested for an offence … is charged with an offence, the custody officer shall … order his release from police detention, either on bail or without bail, unless –
>
> (a)   …
>
> > (i)   his name or address cannot be ascertained or the custody officer has reasonable grounds for doubting whether a name or address furnished by him as his name or address is his real name or address;
> >
> > (ii)   the custody officer has reasonable grounds for believing that the person arrested will fail to appear in court to answer to bail;
> >
> > (iii) in the case of a person arrested for an imprisonable offence, the custody officer has reasonable grounds for believing that the detention of the person arrested is necessary to prevent him from committing an offence;
> >
> > (iv)   in the case of a person arrested for an offence which is not an imprisonable offence, the custody officer has reasonable grounds for believing that the detention of the person arrested is necessary to prevent him from causing physical injury to any other person or from causing loss of or damage to property;
> >
> > (v)   the custody officer has reasonable grounds for believing that the detention of the person arrested is necessary to prevent him from interfering with the administration of justice or with the investigation of offences or of a particular offence; or
> >
> > (vi)   the custody officer has reasonable grounds for believing that the detention of the person arrested is necessary for his own protection.'

The custody officer, in deciding whether a ground for refusal of bail applies, must have regard to the same factors as a court is required to consider when taking a bail decision (see **3.4.3**).

The custody officer has power, when granting bail, to impose the same conditions as a court (with the exception of residence at a bail hostel) (Bail Act 1976, s 3A). A full discussion of conditions of bail and when they may be appropriate can be found at **3.4.3**.

2.3.5 Release without charge on bail

The police may decide that there is insufficient evidence to charge a person with an offence but require him to return to the police station at a later date. This may happen for example, if the police have further enquires to make or where they are waiting for the results of forensic tests or they just need more time to decide whether or not to charge. In such a case, the person is released on bail. Where a person has been released on bail to return to the police station on a specified date, he may be arrested without a warrant if he fails to attend at the appointed time (Police and Criminal Evidence Act 1984, s 46A).

Section 34 of the Police and Criminal Evidence Act 1984 provides that where a person returns to the police station to answer bail (or is arrested for failing to do so) he is to be regarded as having been arrested for the original offence at that moment.

Therefore, the person is in the same position as a person who is being detained without charge and so the rules governing detention without charge set out in **2.3.3** apply.

2.4 THE RIGHT TO LEGAL ADVICE

2.4.1 Volunteers

A person who is attending a police station on a voluntary basis and who is not under arrest has an absolute right to legal advice in private or to communicate with anyone outside the police station at any time (Code C, note 1A). These rights are confirmed in a written notice given to the suspect (see **Appendix 2(B)**).

2.4.2 Persons under arrest

'Where a person has been arrested and is being held in custody in a police station, or other premises, he shall be entitled, if he requests, to have one friend or relative or other person who is known to him or is likely to take an interest in his welfare told, as soon as practicable … , that he has been arrested and is being detained there.' (s 56(1))

'A person arrested and held in custody in a police station or other premises shall be entitled, if he so requests, to consult a solicitor privately at any time.' (s 58)

On arrival at the police station, the suspect will be informed by the custody officer of the right to legal advice and that it is free of charge, the right to have someone informed of his arrest and the right to consult the Codes of Practice. These rights are confirmed in a written notice given to the suspect (see **Appendix 2(C)** and **(D)**). The suspect is then asked to sign the custody record to indicate whether or not he wishes to exercise his rights (see the custody record referred to at **2.3.2**). Even if the suspect indicates that he does not want to exercise his rights, he is entitled to change his mind at any time while he is in police detention.

The suspect is entitled to advice in person, in writing or by telephone (Code C, para 6.1) from his own solicitor, if available, or the duty solicitor. Duty solicitor schemes operate throughout most of the country to ensure that a solicitor is available on a 24-hour basis to attend police stations to advise suspects who are being detained. The advice and assistance given is free of charge, irrespective of the suspect's means, and the solicitor attending the police station is paid under contract on a fixed hourly rate by the Legal Services Commission.

2.4.3 Delaying access to legal advice

The right of access to legal advice can be delayed for a period not exceeding 36 hours from the time of the suspect's arrival at the police station if:

'(a) … a person is in police detention … for a serious arrestable offence; and
(b) if an officer of at least the rank of superintendent authorises it.' (s 58(6))

A superintendent can authorise the delaying of access to legal advice only if he has reasonable grounds for believing that the exercise of the right:

'(a)   will lead to interference with or harm to evidence connected with a serious arrestable offence or interference with or physical injury to other persons; or

(b)   will lead to the alerting of other persons suspected of having committed such an offence but not yet arrested for it; or

(c)   will hinder the recovery of any property obtained as a result of such an offence.' (s 58(8))

In effect, a superintendent may lawfully authorise delaying access to legal advice only if he has reasonable grounds to believe that the specific solicitor seeking access will, inadvertently or otherwise, pass on a message from the suspect which will lead to any of the consequences listed above coming about. Even if the superintendent has such grounds, he is required to offer the suspect access to a different solicitor on the duty solicitor scheme (see Code C, Annex B, para B4).

Access to legal advice cannot be delayed on grounds that:

(1)   the solicitor might advise the suspect not to answer questions (Code C, Annex B, para 3); or

(2)   the solicitor was initially instructed by a third party, provided the suspect wishes to see the solicitor. The suspect must be told that the solicitor has come to the police station and must be asked to sign the custody record to signify whether or not he wishes to see the solicitor (Code C, para 6.15 and Code C, Annex B, para 3).

The statutory right for a suspect to have a friend or relative notified of his arrest can be delayed on similar grounds to those for delayed access to legal advice.

2.5 INTERVIEWING THE SUSPECT

2.5.1 What is an interview?

'An interview is the questioning of a person regarding his involvement or suspected involvement in a criminal offence or offences which, by virtue of paragraph 10.1 of Code C, is required to be carried out under caution' (Code C, para 11.1A).

Example
A police officer notices a young man standing on a street corner with a large bag. He asks the man what he is doing. The replies are evasive. This will not be an interview. The officer then notices a broken window in the shop on the corner and that the man has fragments of glass on his clothing. Any further questioning will constitute an interview. The significance of this is that the rules on the conduct of interviews must be followed (see **2.5.2–2.8**).

Questioning solely to establish identity or ownership of a vehicle, or 'in furtherance of the proper and effective conduct of a search' is not an interview (Code C, para 10.1).

2.5.2 Interview following arrest

Following a decision to arrest a suspect, that suspect must not be interviewed about the relevant offence except at a police station (or other authorised place of detention) unless the consequent delay would be likely to:

(1) lead to interference with or harm to evidence connected with an offence or interference with or physical harm to other persons; or

(2) lead to the alerting of other persons suspected of having committed such an offence but not yet arrested for it; or

(3) hinder the recovery of property obtained in consequence of the commission of such an offence (Code C, para 11.1).

2.5.3 Interview after charge

Following charge, no further questions relating to the offence charged may be put unless further questioning is necessary to:

(1) prevent or minimise harm or loss to some other person or to the public; or

(2) clear up an ambiguity in a previous answer or statement; or

(3) give the suspect an opportunity to comment on information concerning the offence which has come to light since he was charged (Code C, para 16.5).

If any statement or interview record involving another person is to be put to the suspect, no reply or comment should be invited (Code C, para 16.4).

2.6 METHODS OF INTERVIEW

2.6.1 Tape-recording

All interviews at the police station except those concerning purely summary offences should be tape-recorded. The purpose of the tape-recording procedures is to provide an accurate and reliable account of police interviews with suspects in the police station.

Two tapes are used at an interview. When an interview comes to an end, the master tape should be sealed and signed by the suspect or by an interviewing officer. The other tape is the working copy from which a summary of the tape-recorded interview will be prepared by the police.

A summary of the tape-recorded interview will be sent to the defence. The defence has a right of access to a working copy of the tape and the defence solicitor will often listen to the tape to check the accuracy of the summary prepared by the prosecution.

If the defence agrees that the summary served by the prosecution is acceptable then it will be admissible in evidence at the trial (subject to any argument over the admissibility of any confession that may have been made (see **4.7**)). See the example of a record of a tape-recorded interview at **Appendix 2(E)**.

If the defence does not agree with the summary then the tape can be transcribed in full for use at the trial. If necessary, the tape can be played at the trial. The tape to be played in court will be the master copy and the seal will be broken in court. It may be necessary to play the tape in court where the manner in which something has been said is relevant; for example, if the admissibility of a confession is being challenged because of the conduct of the police during the interview, the way in which questions have been put may be relevant.

2.6.2 Non-taped interviews

Not all interviews will be tape-recorded. A suspect may, on occasions, be interviewed somewhere other than a police station. An interview concerning a purely summary offence may be conducted at a police station off-tape. Any conversation between a police officer and suspect which falls within the definition of an interview and which is not tape-recorded is subject to the following rules.

(1) An accurate record must be made of each interview whether or not the interview takes place at the police station (Code C, para 11.5).

(2) The record must be made during the course of the interview, unless in the investigating officer's view this would not be practicable or would interfere with the conduct of the interview, and must constitute either a verbatim record of what has been said, or failing this, an account of the interview which adequately and accurately summarises it (Code C, para 11.5(C)). Compiling such a record will usually involve writing down each question and answer during the interview.

(3) If an interview record is not made during the course of the interview, it must be made as soon as practicable after completion of the interview (Code C, para 11.7).

(4) Unless it is impracticable, the person interviewed must be given the opportunity to read the interview record and to sign it as correct, or to indicate the respects in which he considers it inaccurate (Code C, para 11.10).

(5) A record of an interview which has not been taped will be served on the defence. If the interview record has been signed by the defendant or his solicitor then it will be admissible in evidence (subject to the admissibility of any confession that may have been made being challenged (see **4.6.2**)). If the record is not signed by the defence then it is not admissible in evidence. Instead, the interviewing officer will give oral evidence of what happened at the interview, using any contemporaneous notes made to refresh his memory (see **4.3.2**).

(6) Rather than be interviewed, a suspect may offer to make a 'written statement under caution'. This is simply a prepared statement setting out the suspect's version of events or a confession. See the example of a statement at **Appendix 2(F)**. Note the caution at the top of the page. There is nothing to prevent the police from asking further questions on the written statement made by the suspect.

2.6.3 Comments outside interview

A written record should also be made of any comments made by a suspected person, including unsolicited comments, which are outside the context of an interview but which might be relevant to the offence. Any such record must be timed and signed by the maker. Where practicable, the person shall be given the opportunity to read that record and to sign it as correct or to indicate the respects in which he considers it inaccurate. Any refusal to sign should be recorded (Code C, para 11.13).

Example

A police officer arrests a suspect on suspicion of an assault occasioning actual bodily harm. On the way to the police station, the suspect says, 'I hit him but I was provoked'. The suspect volunteered this information; it was not in response to any question put by the police officer. Such a statement by the suspect does not constitute an interview. The police officer, on arrival at the police station, should make a record of what the suspect said and the time he said it. He should then sign the record and give the suspect the opportunity to read it and to sign it as correct or to indicate the respects in which he considers it inaccurate.

At the beginning of an interview carried out in a police station, the interviewing officer, after cautioning the suspect, should put to the suspect any significant statement or significant silence which has occurred before the suspect's arrival at the police station. The interviewing officer should ask the suspect whether he confirms or denies that earlier statement or silence, and whether he wishes to add anything. A 'significant' statement or silence is one which appears capable of being used against a suspect (Code C, para 11.2A).

2.7 THE RIGHT TO HAVE A SOLICITOR PRESENT AT INTERVIEWS

A person who has asked for legal advice may not be interviewed or continue to be interviewed until he has received such legal advice (Code C, para 6.6).

Exceptions to this rule are where:

(1) the right to legal advice can lawfully be delayed (see **2.4.3**); or
(2) a superintendent has reasonable grounds to believe that:

    (a) delay will involve immediate risk of harm to persons or serious loss of damage to property; or
    (b) a solicitor has agreed to attend but waiting for his arrival would cause unreasonable delay to the process of investigation; or

(3) a nominated solicitor cannot or will not attend and the suspect has declined the duty solicitor or the duty solicitor is unavailable and an inspector has authorised the interview; or
(4) the suspect has changed his mind and agrees in writing or on tape to the commencement of the interview and an inspector has authorised the interview.

2.8 SAFEGUARDS FOR THE SUSPECT

2.8.1 Reminders of the right to legal advice (Code C, para 6.5)

A suspect must be reminded of the right to free legal advice:

(1) immediately prior to the commencement or recommencement of any interview at a police station;
(2) before a review of detention takes place;
(3) after charge, if a police officer wishes to draw the attention of the suspect to any written or oral statement made by another person;
(4) after charge, if further questions are to be put to a suspect about the offence (see **2.5.3** as to when this is possible);
(5) before an identification parade, group identification or video identification takes place;
(6) before an intimate body sample is requested.

If, on being informed or reminded of the right to legal advice, the suspect declines to speak to a solicitor in person, the suspect should be informed of the right to communicate with a solicitor by telephone.

If a suspect continues to waive his right to legal advice, he should be asked his reasons for doing so. Any reasons should be recorded on the custody record or interview record, as appropriate.

2.8.2 The caution

A caution must be given by a police officer to a suspect in the following terms:

> 'You do not have to say anything. But it may harm your defence if you do not mention when questioned something which you later rely on in court. Anything you do say may be given in evidence.'

A caution is required:

(1) on or immediately before arrest;
(2) before an interview;
(3) following a break in questioning (if there is any doubt as to whether the suspect appreciates that he is still under caution) (Code C, paras 10.1 and 10.5).

2.8.3 Detention conditions

In any period of 24 hours, a detained person must be allowed a continuous period of at least 8 hours' rest. This period should normally be at night (Code C, para 12.2).

No person who is unfit through drink or drugs, to the extent that he is unable to appreciate the significance both of questions put to him and his answers, may be questioned about an alleged offence unless a superintendent considers that delay will involve an immediate risk of harm to persons or serious loss of or serious damage to property (Code C, para 12.3 and Code C, Annex C).

Interview rooms should be adequately heated, lit and ventilated (Code C, para 12.4).

Persons being questioned or making statements must not be required to stand (Code C, para 12.5).

Breaks in interviewing should be made at recognised meal-times (Code C, para 12.7).

Short breaks for refreshments shall be provided at intervals of approximately 2 hours.

2.8.4 Suspects at risk

Juveniles (under 17) (Code C, paras 1.5–1.7)

An 'appropriate adult' must be informed that the juvenile has been arrested and should be asked to attend the police station.

An 'appropriate adult' should be the parent or guardian of the juvenile. If the parent or guardian is unsuitable (eg because he or she is also involved in the offence), a social worker should be called. If a social worker is unavailable, another responsible adult aged 18 or over (who is not a police officer or employed by the police) should be called. A solicitor who is present at the police station in his professional capacity may not act as 'appropriate adult'.

The purpose of the 'appropriate adult' attending 'is to ensure the presence of an impartial adult to safeguard the rights of the juvenile'.

Mentally disordered/handicapped suspects (Code C, paras 1.4–1.8)

'If an officer has any suspicion or is told in good faith that a person … may be mentally disordered or mentally handicapped or mentally incapable of understanding the significance of questions put to him … that person shall be treated as a mentally disordered or mentally handicapped person.'

An 'appropriate adult' must be informed that the suspect has been arrested and should be asked to attend the police station.

An 'appropriate adult' should be a relative, guardian or other person responsible for the custody of the suspect. Failing this, a specialist social worker should be called. If a social worker is unavailable, another responsible adult aged 18 or over (who is not a police officer or employed by the police) should be called.

The purpose of the 'appropriate adult' is as for juveniles.

2.9 TACTICAL CONSIDERATIONS

2.9.1 Purpose of solicitor's attendance

'The solicitor's only role in the police station is to protect and advance the legal rights of his client' (Code C, para 6D).

2.9.2 Record of attendance

A solicitor's presence in the police station makes him a potential witness in the case. It is essential, therefore, that the solicitor makes a contemporaneous record of everything that happens at the police station. This record should include details of initial contact with the custody officer, information given by the investigating officer, advice given to the client and any other matter that seems to be of significance. (See sample form at **Appendix 2(G)**.)

2.9.3 Custody record

On arrival at the police station, a solicitor should speak to the custody officer and ask to inspect the custody record. A solicitor has a right to inspect the custody record as soon as practicable after arrival at the police station (Code C, para 2.4). Matters such as reasons for detention, periods of detention, review periods and details of any interviews should be noted by the solicitor from the custody record.

2.9.4 The investigating officer

After speaking to the custody officer, a solicitor should, wherever possible, speak to the investigating officer about the offence. The investigating officer should be asked what evidence the police have against the suspect. A careful record should be made of information given. If the investigating officer is not forthcoming about the evidence available this is something that should be borne in mind when formulating advice to the client (see **2.9.5**).

2.9.5 Advising the suspect

A suspect held in the police station may be frightened, disorientated and suspicious of anyone who comes to see him. The solicitor should explain to the suspect the role of the solicitor who has been called to see him and, as far as possible, attempt to put him at ease.

The solicitor should take instructions from the suspect. A pro forma for this purpose appears at **Appendix 2(G)**. The solicitor should then consider the information given to him by the police and his instructions from his client and formulate advice to the client.

2.9.6 Criminal Justice and Public Order Act 1994 – the right to remain silent

Section 34 – failure to mention facts when questioned or charged

'(1)   Where in any proceedings against a person for an offence, evidence is given that the accused:

   (a)   at any time before he was charged with the offence, on being questioned under caution by a constable trying to discover whether or by whom the offence had been committed, failed to mention any fact relied on in his defence in those proceedings; or

   (b)   on being charged with the offence or officially informed that he might be prosecuted for it, failed to mention any such fact,

   being a fact which in the circumstances existing at the time the accused could reasonably have been expected to mention when so questioned, charged or informed, as the case may be ... the court or jury ... may draw such inferences from the failure as appear proper.'

Example 1

Joe is being questioned about a suspected assault. He refuses to answer the questions put by the police. At his trial, Joe raises self-defence. Under s 34, a court may draw inferences from Joe's failure to mention self-defence when being interviewed or when charged.

Example 2

Joanne is being questioned about a suspected theft. She does not answer questions put by the police at interview. At her trial, Joanne raises an alibi defence: she was at home at the time of the theft. Under s 34, a court may draw inferences from Joanne's failure to mention the alibi when being interviewed or when charged.

The following points should be noted about s 34.

(1)   The section does not take away the right of a suspect to remain silent. It simply enables a court to draw inferences from silence if facts are raised in court in the defence of the suspect. If a suspect remains silent and does not raise facts in his defence then s 34 has no effect.

(2)   The section states that a court may draw inferences from silence. Such inferences are not mandatory and may only be drawn if the magistrates or jury are satisfied that in the circumstances existing at the time of the interview it

would have been reasonable to expect the suspect to mention the relevant facts (see 'The right to remain silent – advising the client' below for examples of when a court may decide not to draw adverse inferences).

(3) In *R v Argent (Brian)* [1997] 2 Cr App R 27, the Court of Appeal said that before a jury could draw such inferences as appear proper under s 34(1)(a), the following six formal conditions had to be met.

    (a) There had to be proceedings against a person for an offence.

    (b) The alleged failure had to occur before a defendant was charged.

    (c) The alleged failure had to occur during questioning under caution by a constable or other person authorised under s 34(4).

    (d) The questioning had to be directed to trying to discover whether or by whom the alleged offence had been committed.

    (e) The alleged failure by the defendant had to be to mention any fact relied on in his defence in those proceedings.

    (f) The fact which the defendant failed to mention was a fact which, in the circumstances existing at the time, he could reasonably have been expected to mention when so questioned.

(4) It was generally thought that the inference which the prosecution seeks to draw from failure to mention facts in interview is that they have been subsequently fabricated. In *R v Randall* [1998] 6 *Archbold News* 1, the Court of Appeal held that s 34 could apply where a defendant had an account to give but did not want it subject to scrutiny. A similar approach was taken in *R v Daniel (Anthony Junior)* [1998] 2 Cr App R 373, CA, where the court held that s 34 was not confined to cases of recent fabrication but was apt to cover 'a reluctance to be subject to questioning and further enquiry' (at 383). The same approach was followed by the Court of Appeal in *R v Beckles and Montague* [1999] Crim LR 148, *R v McGuiness (Cyril)* [1999] Crim LR 318 and *R v Taylor* [1999] Crim LR 75.

(5) In *Condron and Another v United Kingdom* (2000) *The Times*, May 9, the European Court of Human Rights held that a trial judge had not properly directed the jury on the issue of the defendants' silence during police interview. As a consequence, the applicants had not received a fair trial within the meaning of Article 6 of the European Convention on Human Rights. In the court's opinion, as a matter of fairness, the jury should have been directed that if it was satisfied that the applicants' silence at the police interview could not sensibly be attributed to their having no answer to the police's allegations or none that could stand up to cross-examination, it should not draw an inference. The court considered that a direction to that effect was more than merely 'desirable' as found by the Court of Appeal.

The court noted that the responsibility for deciding whether or not to draw an inference rested with the jury. It was impossible to ascertain what weight, if any, was given to the applicants' silence since a jury did not provide reasons for its decisions.

The court did not accept the Government's submission that the fairness of the applicants' trial was secured by the appeal process. The Court of Appeal had no means of ascertaining whether or not the defendants' silence played a significant role in the jury's decision to convict. The Court of Appeal was concerned with the safety of the defendants' conviction, not whether they had received a fair trial. Since the jury was not properly directed, the imperfection in the direction could not be remedied on appeal.

Section 36 – failure to account for objects, substances or marks

'(1)   Where:

   (a)   a person is arrested by a constable, and there is:

      (i)   on his person; or
      (ii)   in or on his clothing or footwear; or
      (iii) otherwise in his possession; or
      (iv)   in any place in which he is at the time of his arrest,

   any object, substance or mark, or there is any mark on any such object; and

   (b)   that or another constable investigating the case reasonably believes that the presence of the object, substance or mark may be attributed to the participation of the person arrested in the commission of an offence specified by the constable; and

   (c)   the constable informs the person arrested that he so believes, and requests him to account for the presence of the object, substance or mark; and

   (d)   the person fails or refuses to do so, then … the court or jury … may draw such inferences from the failure or refusal as appear proper.'

Example

Fred is arrested on suspicion of assaulting John. On being interviewed, he is asked to account for the fact that on arrest his shirt was covered in blood and he had cut knuckles. Fred does not reply. Under s 36, a court may draw inferences from Fred's failure to account for the bloodstains and cuts.

The following points should be noted about s 36:

(1)   There is a degree of overlap between ss 34 and 36. However, whilst s 34 can only apply if a suspect later raises facts in his defence, s 36 will operate irrespective of any defence put forward. It can apply even if no defence is raised at the trial.

Example

Following a street fight, Joe is arrested nearby. His shirt is badly torn. The police inform Joe that he is suspected of assault at the street fight and ask him to account for his torn shirt. Joe refuses to answer any questions.

If Joe gives evidence at his trial that he was walking home from a night club and tripped up, tearing his shirt, s 34 will apply. Joe did not mention the facts at the interview.

As Joe failed to account for his torn shirt, s 36 will apply irrespective of any defence put forward by Joe.

(2)   As with s 34, the court may draw inferences but there is no obligation to do so (see further 'Advising the client' below).

(3)   The section can apply only if the accused has been told, in ordinary language, by the officer requesting the explanation, the effect of failure to comply with the

request (s 36(4)). The following points must be brought to the attention of the suspect:

- the offence under investigation;
- the fact that the suspect is being asked to account for;
- that the officer believes this fact may be due to the suspect's taking part in the commission of the offence in question;
- that a court may draw an inference from failure to comply with the request;
- that a record is being made of the interview and that it may be given in evidence if the suspect is brought to trial (Code C, para 10.5B).

Section 37 – failure to account for presence at a particular place

'(1)   Where:

    (a)   a person arrested by a constable was found by him at a place at or about the time the offence for which he was arrested is alleged to have been committed; and

    (b)   that or another constable investigating the offence reasonably believes that the presence of the person at that place and at that time may be attributed to his participation in the commission of the offence; and

    (c)   the constable informs the person that he so believes, and requests him to account for that presence; and

    (d)   the person fails or refuses to do so,

    then … the court or jury … may draw such inferences from the failure or refusal as appear proper.'

Example

Denis is arrested on suspicion of theft. He is found by a police officer standing close to a shop which has a window broken. Goods are missing from the shop. When questioned about the alleged offence, Denis is asked to account for his presence by the shop window. Denis does not reply. A court may draw inferences from Denis's refusal to account for his presence outside the shop.

The following points should be noted about s 37.

(1)   There is a degree of overlap between ss 34 and 37. However, whilst s 34 can apply only if a suspect later raises facts in his defence, s 37 will operate irrespective of any defence put forward. It can apply even if no defence is raised at the trial.

Example

Following a burglary, Joan is arrested walking down a passageway close to the scene of the crime. Joan is interviewed by the police who tell her that she is suspected of committing the burglary. Joan is asked to account for her presence in the passageway. She remains silent at the interview.

If, at her trial, Joan explains that she was in the passageway as she was taking a short cut home, s 34 will apply. Joan did not mention the facts at the interview.

As Joan failed to account for her presence in the passageway, s 37 will apply irrespective of any defence put forward by Joan.

(2)   As with s 34, the court may draw inferences but there is no obligation to do so (see further 'The right to remain silent – advising the client' below).

(3)   As with s 36, this section can apply only if the accused has been told in ordinary language by the officer requesting the explanation, the effect of failure to comply with the request (see further Code C, para 10.5B above).

Points common to ss 34, 36 and 37

The following points apply to ss 34, 36 and 37.

(1)   The sections will normally apply only to interviews at a police station (it is important to remember the general prohibition on interviewing outside a police station (see **2.5.1**)). The suspect will have been cautioned and given the opportunity of taking legal advice.

(2)   By s 38(3), 'a person shall not have the proceedings against him committed to the Crown Court for trial, have a case to answer or be convicted of any offence solely on an inference' drawn under s 34, s 36 or s 37. In other words, the prosecution must always have some other evidence. A defendant cannot be convicted solely because he refused to answer questions.

(3)   No inferences can be drawn from silence when a suspect is questioned at a police station while denied access to legal advice (Youth Justice and Criminal Evidence Act 1999, s 58).

This provision brings the law into compliance with the judgment of the European Court of Human Rights in the case of *Murray v United Kingdom (Right to Silence)* (1996) 22 EHRR 29. In this case, the court held that there was a breach of Article 6 of the European Convention on Human Rights as a result of denying the applicant access to legal advice in circumstances where inferences could be drawn from his silence during police questioning.

Advising the client

In formulating advice to a client on whether to remain silent, a legal adviser must balance the potential effects of the law against good reasons for not answering questions. If a court finds that there were good reasons for remaining silent then inferences should not be drawn from the exercise of that right. In *R v Roble (Ali Hersi)* [1997] Crim LR 449, the Court of Appeal indicated that good reasons for advising silence might be that the interviewing officer had disclosed little or nothing of the nature of the case against the defendant, so that the legal adviser cannot usefully advise his client, or where the nature of the offence, or the material in the hands of the police is so complex, or relates to matters so long ago, that no immediate response is feasible. In *R v Argent (Brian)* [1997] 2 Cr App R 27, the Court of Appeal stated that a court should not interpret the expression 'in the circumstances' in s 34(1) restrictively. Matters such as the time of day, the suspect's age, experience, mental capacity, state of health, sobriety, tiredness, personality and legal advice were all relevant circumstances.

In particular, a legal adviser at the police station should consider:

(1)   the extent of the evidence disclosed by the police. If there is little or no evidence then silence is likely to remain the best advice. All that the suspect is likely to achieve by answering questions is to incriminate himself.

If the police refuse to disclose the evidence available then, normally, a suspect should be advised to remain silent. This is because it is not possible to assess the strength of the case against the suspect and provide proper advice;

(2) the ability of the suspect to deal with an interview. If a suspect is highly emotional, inarticulate or otherwise unfit to deal with an interview then silence is likely to be the best course of action;

(3) whether there is any other good explanation for remaining silent. For example, a suspect may be afraid of associates or may wish to protect another person.

If a suspect decides to remain silent on legal advice, then:

(1) the legal adviser should explain the potential effect of ss 34, 36 and 37 but state that there appears to be a good reason for a court not drawing inferences should the matter proceed to trial. The client should be warned that the final decision on inferences will be one to be taken by the court;

(2) the legal adviser, with permission from the suspect, should make it clear to the police the reasons for remaining silent. This is best done on tape at the start of the interview. It is possible that the legal adviser will be called to give evidence at the trial to confirm the reasons for the advice given.

Legal professional privilege

Communications between a defendant and his solicitor prior to interview by the police are subject to legal professional privilege. The privilege can be waived by the defendant, though not by the solicitor.

The prosecution may allege that the defendant's failure to mention facts in interview is because they have been subsequently fabricated. There is no waiver of professional privilege where a solicitor gives evidence that the defendant informed him of the material facts at the time of the police interview (*R v Wilmot (Alan)* (1989) 89 Cr App R 341).

If a defendant at trial gives as a reason for not answering police questions that he has been advised by his solicitor not to do so, that advice does not amount to a waiver of privilege. But that bare assertion is unlikely by itself to be regarded as a sufficient reason for not mentioning matters relevant to the defence. So, it will be necessary, if the defendant wishes to invite the court not to draw an inference under s 34, to go further and state the basis or reason for the advice. This may amount to a waiver of privilege, so that the defendant, or, if his solicitor is also called to give evidence, his solicitor, can be asked whether there were any other reasons for the advice, and the nature of the advice given, so as to explore whether the advice may also have been given for tactical reasons. (*R v Condron (Karen); R v Condron (William)* [1997] 1 Cr App R 185, CA; see also *R v Roble (Ali Hersi)* [1997] Crim LR 449, CA and *R v Bowden (Brian Thomas)* (1999) 2 Cr App R 176, CA.)

Selective silence

This is not a good idea. The suspect is answering some questions and not others. Apart from the possibility of ss 34, 36 and 37 applying, such an interview will not impress a jury or magistrates. Clients should be advised to make a decision either to remain silent or to answer questions and to stick by that decision.

Answering questions (explanations or denials)

Reasons for advising a suspect to answer questions in order to put forward explanations or denials include:

(1) to avoid inferences under ss 34, 36 and 37 where there does not appear to be any good reason for remaining silent;
(2) where a client has a convincing story, an early explanation may avoid charge, particularly where there is little or no evidence against him.

Always remember that suspects are often under immense pressure at a police station and may be inclined to say anything in an attempt to get out as quickly as possible. Before advising a suspect to answer questions, it is important to go through his story carefully and to warn him that if he tells lies now it could damage his defence at trial.

Making a written statement

It may be advisable for a suspect to make a written statement rather than answer police questions. A written statement will enable the suspect to refer to relevant facts without the pressure of police questioning. Such a written statement may be taken by the legal adviser before the suspect is interviewed by the police. The suspect should sign and date the written statement, which should be as full as possible and also anticipate whether the suspect is likely to be asked questions under s 36 or s 37.

The legal adviser will have to consider carefully whether to hand the written statement to the police. If the statement is handed in to the police it may be produced as part of the prosecution case.

Not handing the statement to the police may be an appropriate strategy where the legal advisor has doubts about the instructions received or about information that has been disclosed by the police. Such a strategy will prevent an inference that the defence had been fabricated but it will not prevent all inferences being drawn. These could include an inference that the defendant has made up his defence prior to interview but was not sufficiently confident to expose it to police questioning, or that he had not thought up all the details of the defence at the time of the police interview.

Handing in the statement during interview is a strategy designed to prevent inferences being drawn. This may fail, however, if the defence at trial goes beyond the facts set out in the statement. In such circumstances, while not preventing inferences, such a statement may minimise the inferences in the same way as a statement that is not handed to the police.

Alternatively, the statement may be handed in on charge. Handing in the statement on charge may be useful if the legal adviser believes that the police will not have enough evidence to charge. A statement given to the police during the interview may give the police sufficient evidence to charge. Thus, the legal adviser may consider advising a no comment interview and submitting the statement only if the police decide to charge the suspect. Assuming that the defence put forward at trial is consistent with the statement, no inferences could be drawn under s 34(1)(b). An inference could still be drawn under s 34(1)(a), however, that the defendant was not sufficiently confident of his defence to expose it to police questioning.

Making a confession

If the police evidence appears to be strong and the suspect admits his guilt then there may be advantages in making a confession at the police interview. This can be good mitigation when the suspect is being sentenced, particularly if he implicates others or gives information that leads to the recovery of stolen property.

The Criminal Law Committee of The Law Society has issued guidance to help solicitors decide whether it is in the best interests of their client to answer police questions (see **Appendix 4**).

Whatever advice is given to a client, the final decision as to whether or not to answer police questions is that of the client.

2.9.7 Preparing the suspect for the interview

It is important to explain to a suspect the procedure to be followed at a tape-recorded interview and to warn him about likely police tactics. The following points should be covered:

(1) that the interview will be tape-recorded and all parties will be asked to identify themselves on tape;

(2) that the interview can be stopped at any time if the suspect wants further advice;

(3) if the suspect is to remain silent he should be advised to use a stock phrase such as 'No comment'. Most suspects find this easier than remaining in total silence;

(4) police tactics – a suspect who wishes to remain silent should be warned:

- that the police may try to get him to talk by asking apparently innocuous questions;
- that the police may try to alienate him from his solicitor by suggesting that poor advice has been given;
- that the police may make threats such as of arresting members of his family unless he speaks.

The suspect should be advised to ignore any of these tactics and remain silent;

(5) that the legal adviser is present to protect the suspect's interests and will intervene in the interview as and when necessary.

2.9.8 The solicitor's role at an interview

It is important to understand that a solicitor is not at an interview simply as an observer. It may be necessary for the solicitor to intervene to object to improper questioning or to give the client further advice in private. The following points should be noted.

(1) At the start of a tape-recorded interview, a legal adviser should make an opening statement explaining the role he intends to play in the interview. This will leave the police in no doubt about the reason for the adviser's presence. It also gives an opportunity to state the advice given to the client and the reasons for that advice. The suggested form of statement is:

I am … a solicitor/authorised representative with [firm name]. I am now required to explain my role. My role is to protect my client's rights. I shall continue to advise my client throughout the interview.

I shall intervene in the interview if:

- **my client asks for, or needs legal advice; or**
- **your questioning is inappropriate; or**
- **you raise matters which are not based on matters that have been made known to me.**

After receiving legal advice my client has decided:

[either]

- **to exercise the right to silence [if you consider it appropriate to give a reason] because [reason]. Please respect that decision.**

[or]

- **to answer questions which you may raise which are relevant to my client's arrest/voluntary attendance.**

(Shepherd, *Police Station Skills for Legal Advisers; a Pocket Reference* (The Law Society, 1997))

(2) A client may need further advice if, for example, matters that the legal adviser was not aware of are raised in the interview. It may also be necessary to give further advice if a client is becoming agitated or uncertain about the conduct of the interview.

(3) Examples of improper questioning include:

- where questions are put in a confusing manner, for example two or three questions rolled into one;
- where questions are put in an aggressive or bullying fashion;
- where questions are put which are not based on evidence of which the solicitor is aware. Advice given to the client will have been on the basis of the evidence disclosed to the solicitor. If evidence has been held back it may be necessary to take further instructions.

(4) The police sometimes threaten to exclude legal advisers who have intervened in an interview. It is therefore important to be familiar with the provisions of the Code of Practice in this area:

'The solicitor may intervene in order to seek clarification or to challenge an improper question to his client or the manner in which it is put, or to advise his client not to reply to particular questions, or if he wishes to give his client further legal advice.' (Code C, para 6D)

The Code further provides that an adviser may be excluded only:

'… if the solicitor's approach or conduct prevents or unreasonably obstructs proper questions being put to the suspect or his response being recorded. Examples of unacceptable conduct include answering questions on a suspect's behalf or providing written replies for him to quote.' (Code C, para 6D)

An investigating officer has no power to exclude a legal adviser from an interview. The investigating officer must:

'… stop the interview and consult an officer not below the rank of superintendent … After speaking to the solicitor, the officer who has been consulted will decide whether or not the interview should continue in the presence of that solicitor.'

(5) If a suspect, against advice, breaks his silence during the interview and begins to answer questions, it is permissible for a legal adviser to remind the suspect of his earlier advice to remain silent. It is also possible to stop the interview to remind the client of the earlier advice. However, continuous interruptions for this purpose would constitute misconduct which could lead to the adviser being excluded from the interview.

(6) The police may seek to dictate the seating positions of parties at an interview:

'The solicitor should be positioned in such a way that there can be no natural eye contact between him and the suspect, nor should he be in a position where he can easily catch the eye of the main interviewer. This makes it much more difficult for him to support the suspect non-verbally and, because he cannot have eye contact with the main interviewer, it is more difficult for him to interject and interrupt the interview verbally.' John Walkley *Police Interrogation* (Police Review Publishing Co Ltd, 1987)

Needless to say, any attempt to do this should be resisted. It is important for a legal adviser to be seated in a position whereby he has eye contact with his client and is properly able to advise him.

2.10 IDENTIFICATION

2.10.1 Finding a suspect

Where a witness has seen an offence being committed, that witness may be able to give a description of the culprit to the police. The Code of Practice on Identification Procedures prescribes two possible courses of action:

(1) a police officer may take a witness to a particular neighbourhood or place to see whether he can identify the person whom he said he saw on the relevant occasion. Any identification made will be admissible in evidence (Code D, para 2.17);

(2) a witness may be shown photographs, photofit, identikit or similar pictures. Any identification from photographs will not normally be admissible in evidence (Code D, para 2.18). One of the reasons for this is that it indicates that the defendant has a criminal record.

2.10.2 Methods of identification where there is a suspect

Once an arrest has been made, the Code of Practice on Identification Procedures prescribes four methods of identification:

(1) identification parades;
(2) group identifications;
(3) video identifications;
(4) confrontations.

All four identification methods must be organised by a uniformed officer of at least inspector rank. No officer involved with the investigation of the case may take part (Code D, para 2.2).

The purpose of any method of identification is to test the reliability of an eye-witness who saw someone committing an offence and to obtain admissible evidence of identification for use in court.

2.10.3 Identification parades

In a case that involves disputed identification evidence, a parade must be held if the suspect consents and it is practicable to hold one. It may be impracticable to hold a parade in some circumstances; for example, if the suspect has an unusual appearance.

A parade may also be held if the investigating officer considers that it would be useful and the suspect consents (Code D, para 2.3). In *R v Forbes* [2001] 1 AC 473, the House of Lords held that an identification parade should be held if the suspect consented and, unless the exceptions applied, whenever a suspect disputed identification. The requirements of para 2.3 of Code C imposed a mandatory obligation on the police. The House of Lords recognised that it might be futile to hold an identification parade in some cases. For example if an eyewitness to a crime had made it plain to the police that he could not identify the culprit, or if the case was one of pure recognition of someone well known to the eyewitness. However, notwithstanding that there had been a breach of para 2.3, the trial judge was right in not excluding the identification evidence under Police and Criminal Evidence Act 1984, s 78.

Before an identification parade, the identification officer must explain a number of things to the suspect, including:

(1) that he is entitled to free legal advice and is entitled to have a solicitor or friend present;
(2) that he does not have to consent to take part and that a consequence of refusing to do so may be the holding of a confrontation and that evidence of refusal may be given at any subsequent trial (see **2.10.6**);
(3) whether the witnesses have been shown photographs or other pictures.

The identification officer must make a record of the parade on forms provided. An example of an identification parade record appears at **Appendix 2(H)**.

The parade must consist of at least eight persons in addition to the suspect who so far as possible, resemble the suspect in age, height, general appearance and position in life (Code D, Annex A, para 8).

Witnesses must be properly segregated both before and after the parade and the officer conducting a witness to a parade must not discuss with him the composition of the parade and, in particular, must not disclose whether a previous witness has made any identification (Code D, Annex A, para 13).

2.10.4 Group identifications

If the suspect refuses a parade, or the holding of a parade is impracticable, arrangements must, if practicable, be made to allow the witness an opportunity to see the suspect in a group of people (Code D, para 2.6).

The suspect should be asked for his consent to a group identification. However, where consent is refused, the identification officer has a discretion to proceed with a group identification if it is practicable to do so (Code D, para 2.8).

Before a group identification, the officer in charge of the identification must explain to the suspect his rights, as for an identification parade (Code D, para 2.15).

There is no set format for a group identification. A group identification may be arranged, for example, in a room of people, a railway station, a bus station, or a shopping parade. The suspect may be asked to stand anywhere in a group or to walk through a busy shopping area. The witness will be asked whether or not he saw the person he thinks committed the offence.

2.10.5 Video identifications

The identification officer may show a witness a video film of a suspect if the investigating officer considers that, because of the refusal of the suspect to take part in an identification parade or group identification, or other reason, this would be the most satisfactory course of action (Code D, para 2.10).

The suspect should be asked for his consent to a video identification. However, where such consent is refused, the identification officer has a discretion to proceed with a video identification if it is practicable to do so (Code D, para 2.11).

If a video film identification is to be used, a video should be made of the suspect and at least eight other persons of similar age, height, general appearance and position in life (Code D, Annex B, para B3).

The participants should all be filmed in the same positions and carrying out the same activity under identical conditions (Code D, Annex B, para B4).

Only one witness may see the film at a time. The film may be frozen and there is no limit on the number of times that a witness may see the film (Code D, Annex B, para B10).

2.10.6 Confrontations

If no parade, group identification or video identification procedure is possible, the suspect may be confronted by the witness. The consent of the suspect is not required.

A confrontation involves taking the witness to the suspect and asking whether the suspect is the person in question.

Confrontation is only to take place if none of the other procedures are practicable (Code D, para 2.13). A confrontation should be a last resort.

2.10.7 Tactical considerations

A suspect may wish to be advised as to whether or not it is in his best interests to agree to stand on an identification parade. It will normally be in his best interests to do so. A refusal can lead to one of the other methods of identification being used. If the police decide that a group identification or a video identification is not practicable then a confrontation may take place. A confrontation is the least satisfactory method of identification as it involves a witness being asked whether the suspect is the person who was seen at the relevant time. Also, a refusal to take part in a parade (or to co-operate in a group or video identification) may be given in evidence.

A legal adviser attending the police station is entitled to be given details of the description of a suspect as first given by a potential witness. The police are obliged to keep a record of this description (Code D, para 2.10).

A solicitor attending an identification parade can object to the composition of the parade. Relevant considerations will include whether the participants in the parade satisfy the requirements as to age, height, appearance, etc. Bear in mind that too many objections may force the police into using an alternative method of identification.

All relevant matters should be recorded and the solicitor and suspect will be given an opportunity to comment on any relevant matter which occurred during the course of the parade. Any comments made will be recorded by the officer in charge of the case.

2.11 EVIDENTIAL CONSIDERATIONS

2.11.1 Challenging inferences from silence

In the Crown Court, any arguments over the admissibility of the defendant's silence when being interviewed will take place in the absence of the jury.

The defence may seek to argue that evidence of the defendant's silence should not go before the jury because of a breach of the Code of Practice such as a failure to caution the defendant. Such a breach will not automatically render the evidence inadmissible but will be a relevant factor for the court to consider.

If a judge rules that evidence of the silence is inadmissible the jury will not hear the evidence. If the evidence is ruled admissible then the judge will direct the jury on the inferences that they are entitled to draw. It will be for the jury to decide whether or not actually to draw the inferences.

In a magistrates' court, it will be for the magistrates to rule on the admissibility of a defendant's silence and to decide whether or not to draw inferences.

2.11.2 Confessions and identification evidence

Evidence of a confession and the outcome of an identification parade, group identification, video identification or confrontation will usually be admissible in evidence.

A breach of the Codes of Practice will not automatically render any evidence obtained inadmissible. However, a breach may be relevant to a challenge by the defence at the trial to the admissibility of evidence such as an identification parade or a confession (see **4.2.4** and **4.6.2**).

2.12 SAMPLES

2.12.1 Intimate samples (s 62)

Intimate body samples are samples of blood, semen or any tissue, fluid, urine or pubic hair, a dental impression, or a swab taken from a person's body orifice other than the mouth.

An intimate sample may be taken:

- if the suspect consents; and
- if a superintendent authorises the taking of the sample on the basis that the offence under investigation is a recordable offence and that samples will tend to confirm or disprove the suspect's involvement in the offence.

A recordable offence includes an offence punishable by imprisonment.

If a suspect refuses to consent to the taking of an intimate sample then inferences can be drawn from that refusal. A refusal of consent is also capable of amounting to corroboration of any evidence against the person in relation to which the refusal is material.

Example
X is being questioned about a rape. He denies having intercourse with the victim and refuses to give a sample of semen. This refusal is capable of corroborating the evidence of the victim that intercourse did take place.

2.12.2 Non-intimate samples (s 63)

Non-intimate body samples include samples of hair, saliva and samples taken from fingernails or toenails.

The consent of a suspect is not required provided a superintendent's authority is given (the grounds are the same as for intimate samples).

A non-intimate sample can also be taken from a person without consent if he has been convicted of a recordable offence.

2.13 FURTHER READING

See, for example:

Eric Shepherd, *Police Station Skills for Legal Advisers; a Pocket Reference* (The Law Society, 1997);
Ed Cape with Jawaid Luqmani *Defending Suspects at Police Stations* (Legal Action Group, 1999).

Chapter 3

COMMENCEMENT OF CRIMINAL PROCEEDINGS

3.1 PRELIMINARY CONSIDERATIONS

3.1.1 Time-limits

In this chapter, section numbers refer to the Magistrates' Courts Act 1980 unless otherwise indicated.

If the offence to be prosecuted is a summary offence, a magistrates' court cannot deal with the prosecution if the information is laid more than 6 months after the alleged offence was committed (s 127). An information is laid when it is received at the court office by an authorised officer (see **3.2.2**).

For most indictable offences (including offences triable either way) there are no statutory time-limits for commencing criminal proceedings. It should be noted, however, that a defendant has a common law right to be protected from undue delay. Courts have a discretion to dismiss proceedings which constitute an abuse of process of the court. The defendant would have to show either substantial delay in bringing the prosecution which cannot be justified, or bad faith on the part of the prosecution. In practice, both are very difficult to establish.

3.1.2 The Road Traffic Offenders Act 1988 (as amended by the Road Traffic Act 1991)

'Subject to section 2 of this Act a person shall not be convicted of an offence to which this section applies unless –

(a) he was warned at the time the offence was committed that the question of prosecuting him for some one or other of the offences to which this section applies would be taken into consideration, or

(b) within 14 days of the commission of the offence a summons for the offence was served on him, or

(c) within 14 days of the commission of the offence a notice of the intended prosecution specifying the nature of the alleged offence and time and place where it is alleged to have been committed was … served on him or on the person, if any, registered as the keeper of the vehicle at the time of the commission of the offence.' (s 1)

'The requirement of section 1 of this Act does not apply in relation to an offence if, at the time of the offence or immediately after it, an accident occurs owing to the presence on a road of the vehicle in respect of which the offence was committed.' (s 2)

The offences to which these sections apply include dangerous driving and careless driving.

3.2 COMMENCING THE PROSECUTION

The prosecution usually begins in one of two ways: by charge or by summons. A flowchart summarising the two ways in which criminal proceedings may be commenced is included at **Appendix 1(E)**.

3.2.1 Charge

Having been arrested, the defendant will be taken to a police station, charged and either released on bail to appear before the next available court sitting (Police and Criminal Evidence Act 1984, s 47(3A)) or kept in police custody and taken before a magistrates' court 'as soon as practicable' (Police and Criminal Evidence Act 1984, s 46(2)). An example of a charge sheet appears at **Appendix 2(I)**.

Following charge, the CPS lawyer in the police station will review the police file and determine which of the following hearings will be necessary.

Defendant charged and bailed

EARLY FIRST HEARING (EFH)

This hearing is where the defendant is likely to enter a 'simple guilty plea'. A 'simple guilty plea' is where the defendant admits all the elements of the offence, or the offence is witnessed by the police and there is no indication that the defendant intends to deny it. In addition, the offence must involve no complex issues, meaning that there must be no more that two defendants or three key witnesses.

The CPS lawyer will prepare an abbreviated file which will be disclosed to the solicitor representing the defendant at court. The file must contain the charge sheet and key witness statements.

If the court is informed that a case is likely to be a 'simple guilty plea' it will list it before a full bench so that the defendant can be sentenced that day or the case can be adjourned for the court to obtain a pre-sentence report. The prosecution will usually be represented by a designated case worker, a non-legally qualified CPS representative.

EARLY ADMINISTRATIVE HEARING (EAH)

If the case is not likely to be a 'simple guilty plea' the defendant's first appearance before a magistrates' court may take the form of an early administrative hearing (EAH) (Crime and Disorder Act 1998, s 50). An EAH may occur when the plea is not known, a not guilty plea is expected, or guilty pleas are expected but the case is not one that can be classified as a 'simple guilty plea'. The prosecution will usually be represented by a CPS lawyer.

The main purpose of the EAH is to enable arrangements to be made for the defendant to obtain representation and to consult a solicitor. Sometimes it may be possible at the EAH for the pleas to be entered and if the defendant enters a not guilty plea a date will be set for a pre-trial review (PTR).

At the EAH, the case will be adjourned. A single justice may remand the defendant on bail or in custody. A justices' clerk cannot remand the defendant in custody.

Defendant charged and detained

REMAND COURT

The defendant will be kept in custody and taken before a magistrates' court 'as soon as practicable'. The magistrates will decide how the case is to proceed.

Defendant charged with an indictable only offence

The first hearing for an indictable only offence will take the form of a preliminary hearing (see **7.7.2**).

3.2.2 Summons

For less serious offences (which may not involve an arrest at all), the prosecution will lay an information. This involves informing a magistrate or magistrates' clerk of the alleged offence with a request for a summons to be issued. Normally an information will be in writing and must specify one offence only. An information which alleges more than one offence is bad for duplicity. An example would be an information alleging that D assaulted A on 15 October and B on 15 October. Assuming that the assaults were two separate acts, two informations are required. This is an important rule as once the trial has commenced there is no power to amend the information to cure the defect. In practice, arguments over duplicity on informations are often complex and the detail involved is beyond the scope of this book.

Following the laying of an information, the magistrate or the magistrates' clerk will issue a summons. A single summons may cover more than one information. The summons will usually be served by posting it to the defendant's last-known or usual address. An example of a summons and certificate of service appears at **Appendix 2(J)**.

3.3 FINANCING THE DEFENCE – CRIMINAL DEFENCE SERVICE

Only contracted firms (or public defenders) are able to undertake Criminal Defence Service work funded by the Legal Services Commission.

Criminal Defence Service work falls into two categories:

- advice and assistance; and
- representation orders.

3.3.1 Advice and assistance

The law relating to advice and assistance is to be found in the Access to Justice Act 1999, s 13 and the Criminal Defence Service (General) (No 2) Regulations 2001, SI 2001/1437, regs 5 and 6.

A solicitor will claim under this scheme if he is advising a suspect at the police station, appearing as a duty solicitor at court or representing a suspect in an application for a warrant of further detention or for an extension of such a warrant. It is also available to a defendant who is being represented in court by his own solicitor at an early hearing (and if a guilty plea is entered and the case is adjourned for sentence, at one sentencing hearing). Such advice and assistance (including advocacy assistance) is non-means tested.

In all other cases advice and assistance (including advocacy assistance) is subject to a means test. If the applicant's capital is above a prescribed figure, he does not qualify for advice and assistance. If the applicant's weekly disposable income is above a prescribed figure, again he will not qualify. Applicants automatically satisfy the means test if they receive income support, income based job seekers allowance, working families tax credit or disabled persons tax credit (only if any abatement from the maximum allowance is not more than £70).

Solicitors are remunerated under contract by a fixed hourly rate paid by the Legal Services Commission. There is an upper financial limit on the amount that can be claimed. The upper financial limit can be extended on application to the Legal Services Commission. In general authority to extend the upper limit may only be granted where the work carried out to date and the further work proposed is reasonable. If an extension is refused there is a right of review to the Funding Review Committee of the Legal Services Commission Regional Office.

A claim for payment should be made on the prescribed form and submitted to the Legal Services Commission Regional Office.

3.3.2 Representation orders

Representation in court in a criminal case is normally financed by a representation order.

The law relating to representation orders is largely to be found in the Access to Justice 1999, s 14 and the Criminal Defence Service (General) (No 2) Regulations 2001, SI 2001/1437.

A representation order is available to cover representation in a magistrates' court, the Crown Court, the High Court, the Court of Appeal and the House of Lords.

> 'Any question as to whether a right to representation should be granted shall be determined according to the interests of justice.' (Access to Justice Act 1999, Sch 3, para 5(1))

The interests of justice test

The factors to be taken into account in determining whether it is in the interests of justice for representation to be granted are contained in the Access to Justice Act 1999, Sch 3, para 5(2). They are:

> 'Whether the individual would, if any matter arising in the proceedings is decided against him, be likely to lose his liberty or suffer serious damage to his reputation.'

Loss of liberty may, for example, be apparent from the nature and seriousness of the offence. Loss of livelihood will be relevant, for example, where on conviction the applicant will lose his job. Serious damage to reputation will include a person of previous good character who is charged with a criminal offence involving something like dishonesty or violence.

> 'Whether the determination of any matter in the proceedings may involve consideration of a substantial question of law.'

A substantial question of law will include difficult points of substantive criminal law connected with the offence charged. It may also include points of evidence such as the admissibility of a confession or consideration of the rules relating to cases involving disputed identification evidence.

> 'Whether the individual may be unable to understand the proceedings or to state his own case.'

> 'Whether the proceedings may involve the tracing, interviewing or expert cross-examination of witnesses on behalf of the individual.'

Expert cross-examination of a prosecution witness will include cross-examination of identification witnesses, cross-examination of police officers as to what happened at a police station and generally any cross-examination that requires an element of legal knowledge.

> 'Whether it is in the interests of another person that the individual be represented.'

An accused is prohibited from personally cross-examining certain witnesses (see **4.3.2**). In such cases, it is likely that the court will determine that it is in the interests of justice for representation to be granted.

Guidelines

In May 1994, joint guidelines were issued by the Lord Chancellor's Department, the Legal Aid Board (now abolished and replaced by the Legal Services Commission) and the Justices' Clerks' Society with the intention of effecting greater consistency of approach when considering the interests of justice test. The guidelines do not replace the statutory criteria set out above but should be used as an aid to their application.

The guidelines include the following.

(1) THE SCHEDULE 3 CRITERIA

The Sch 3 criteria are not exhaustive. For example, the fact that a community punishment order is a possibility may be a relevant factor.

(2) DEPRIVATION OF LIBERTY

- Reference should be made to the Magistrates' Association Sentencing Guidelines (see **Appendix 3**) which provide examples of aggravating factors and mitigating factors for various types of offence. These will assist in deciding whether there is a real and practical risk of loss of liberty.
- Conviction should be assumed.
- Representation should normally be granted upon a committal to the Crown Court for sentence.

(3) LOSS OF LIVELIHOOD

- This should be a direct consequence of the conviction or sentence.
- This will normally refer to current livelihood.
- 'Assertions that disqualification from driving will result in a loss of livelihood should be examined critically … Though a grant could be justified in exceptional circumstances (eg if the applicant could show that the disqualification would result in a real risk of dismissal), representation would not usually be justified where the accused sought to avoid a "totting up" disqualification, having acquired twelve or more penalty points.'

(4) SERIOUS DAMAGE TO REPUTATION

- 'This would relate to those cases in which the offence, or the offender's circumstances, are such that the disgrace of conviction, or consequent damage to the applicant's standing, would greatly exceed the direct effect of the penalty which might be imposed.'
- 'Reputation, for these purposes, is a question of good character, including honesty and trustworthiness.'
- 'The loss of reputation on a conviction for dishonesty is absolute and not relevant to the amount.'
- 'Consideration should be given to whether an accused who is undertaking vocational or professional training might suffer damage to reputation so serious that there is a risk that future livelihood might be lost.'

(5) SUBSTANTIAL QUESTION OF LAW

- 'Representation should only be granted under this criterion if a question of law is raised which the applicant cannot be expected to deal with unaided and is a substantial question and is relevant to the applicant's case.'

(6) TRACING AND INTERVIEWING WITNESSES

- 'Details of the witnesses and why there is a necessity for representation to trace and/or interview them, should be included in the application. If details of witnesses are not included, consideration of the application for representation should be deferred until the applicant has provided the court with sufficient information to make a determination.'

(7) EXPERT CROSS-EXAMINATION OF A PROSECUTION WITNESS

- This 'refers to expert cross-examination of a witness and *not* only to cross-examination of an expert witness'.
- 'Representation should be granted … when there is a need for professional cross-examination of a witness. This may very likely be the case where the evidence is provided by an expert since an accused person would rarely be capable, for example, of cross-examining a medical or handwriting expert. It may also apply in other cases, such as those where shades of emphasis in the evidence can make an action appear more sinister than it was in fact.'

Where to apply for representation

If a case is before a magistrates' court, any application for a representation order should be made to that court.

A magistrates' court which sends a person to the Crown Court for trial or commits a person to the Crown Court for trial or sentence or from which a person appeals to the Crown Court against his conviction or sentence may grant a representation order for the proceedings before the Crown Court (Criminal Defence Service (General) (No 2) Regulations 2001, reg 9).

The Crown Court may grant a representation order for any case that has been sent for trial or has been committed or appealed to it.

'Through representation orders'

If the case is going to be sent to the Crown Court for trial under s 51 of the Crime and Disorder Act 1998 (see **7.7**), a solicitor should apply for a 'through representation order' which will enable the solicitor to claim for work done that is relevant to proceedings before a magistrates' court and the Crown Court.

How to apply for representation

An application for a representation order in respect of proceedings in a magistrates' court may be made orally or in writing to the justice's clerk (Criminal Defence Service (General) (No 2) Regulations 2001, reg 8).

The more common method of application is in writing using Form A (**Appendix 2(K)**).Particular care should be taken in completing the section of the application form dealing with the 'interests of justice test'. As much information as possible should be given to convince the court that a representation order should be granted to the applicant.

The scope of a representation order

If a representation order is granted, a certificate will be issued to the solicitor. An example of a representation order appears at **Appendix 2(L)**.

The following points should be noted in relation to the scope of the certificate.

(1) Representation orders covering proceedings in a magistrates' court or the Crown Court extend not merely to preparation and representation but also to advice on, and assistance in, preparing a notice of appeal. A separate representation order is necessary, however, for the conduct of the appeal itself.

(2) A representation order in the magistrates' court will normally consist of representation by solicitor only. Where there is more than one defendant, the same solicitor will act for all defendants unless there is a conflict of interest. If there is a conflict, separate representation is permitted.

(3) In a magistrates' court, representation by both solicitor and advocate (barrister or solicitor with higher rights of audience) is permitted if the offence is an indictable offence which is unusually grave or difficult and, in the opinion of the court it is desirable to have representation by solicitor and advocate.

(4) In a magistrates' court, where the order does not provide for representation by an advocate, the solicitor can still instruct an advocate to conduct the proceedings in court. However, the solicitor will not be paid for dictating and delivering the brief to an advocate and no payment will be made for accompanying an advocate in court.

(5) Representation in the Crown Court normally consists of representation by a solicitor and advocate. For guidance on when an advocate need be attended by a solicitor's representative at the Crown Court, see Solicitor's Professional Conduct Rule 20.04 (*Law Society's Gazette*, 17 March 1999). The principles contained in Rule 20.04 match provisions restricting the circumstances in which remuneration can be paid for attendance at the Crown Court.

(6) Representation orders are not generally retrospective. However, pre-order work may be claimed under a representation order (once granted) from the date on which a properly completed application form was received by the court. Pre-order work may be undertaken using advice and assistance.

Refusal of representation

An applicant who is refused representation can always make another application to the court (Criminal Defence Service (Representation Order Appeals) Regulations 2001, SI 2001/1168).

Payment of fees under a representation order

Work carried out in a magistrates' court under a representation order is remunerated by a standard fee in most cases. At the conclusion of the case, a claim for payment should be made on the prescribed form and submitted to the Legal Services Commission Regional Office.

Certain complex cases are outside the standard fee scheme and are remunerated at fixed hourly rates on a 'work done basis'.

Work done in the Crown Court is in some cases remunerated by the payment of standard fees. In other cases, payment is on a 'work done basis' although fixed hourly rates are prescribed. A claim for payment should be made to the Crown Court Taxing Office.

3.3.3 Court duty solicitors

The duty solicitor schemes aim to provide an emergency service to those appearing in a magistrates' court who would otherwise be unrepresented. Representation is available on that day only and is free of charge. A duty solicitor will make bail applications, apply for adjournments and present pleas in mitigation. The regulations do not permit a duty solicitor to conduct the trial of a not guilty plea or committal proceedings.

Duty solicitor schemes are staffed by contracted solicitors on a rota basis. Remuneration is provided from the Legal Services Commission at fixed hourly rates for advice and assistance (including advocacy assistance). Subject to checking that the client does not want any other solicitor to handle the case and explaining that the client may choose any solicitor to act or a public defender, it is permissible, and indeed usual, for the duty solicitor to agree to take over the conduct of cases that will proceed further. Further work must be financed privately or under a representation order.

3.3.4 Further reading

The *Legal Services Commission Manual* (Sweet & Maxwell) is the standard reference work for publicly funded criminal work. See also Ede and Edwards *Criminal Defence* (The Law Society, 2000).

3.4 ADJOURNMENTS, REMANDS AND BAIL

3.4.1 Adjournments

Magistrates may adjourn a case at any time.

Common reasons for adjournments include:

(1) to enable the prosecution or defence to prepare their case. Examples include enabling the prosecution to receive a full file from the police or for the defence to be provided with advance disclosure of the prosecution case;
(2) to fix a date for committal proceedings or trial;
(3) to obtain reports to assist the court in sentencing.

3.4.2 Remands

When a court adjourns a case, it will also consider whether or not to remand the defendant. If the case is adjourned without a remand, the court has not taken any steps to ensure that the defendant attends the next hearing. A remand is an adjournment upon which the court decides to attempt to ensure the defendant's attendance at the next hearing.

A remand may be in custody until the adjourned hearing date or on bail. Magistrates may remand the defendant in any case. Unless the offence is very trivial (eg careless driving), the defendant is likely to be remanded on an adjournment.

Individual duration of remands

BEFORE CONVICTION OR COMMITTAL FOR TRIAL

The general rule is that a defendant may not be remanded in custody for more than 8 clear days at a time. Where the defendant is remanded on bail, subject to his consent, there is no time-limit (Magistrates' Courts Act 1980, s 128).

Where there are successive remands in custody, a defendant need only be brought before the court on every fourth remand, provided he has consented (and such consent has not been withdrawn) and has a solicitor acting for him (whether present in court or not) (Magistrates' Courts Act 1980, s 128(3A)).

Further, a court has power under s 128A to remand a defendant in custody for up to 28 days if it has previously remanded him in custody for the same offence, he is before the court, and it can set a date to remand him to on which it expects the next stage of the proceedings to take place (this may be within the 28-day remand period).

AFTER CONVICTION

After conviction by magistrates, adjournments may be for successive periods of 4 weeks unless the defendant is remanded in custody, in which case the maximum period is 3 weeks (s 10(3)).

FOLLOWING COMMITTAL TO THE CROWN COURT

If a defendant is committed to the Crown Court for trial or sentence, he is remanded on bail or in custody until the case is due to be heard.

Time-limits

Under the Prosecution of Offences Act 1985, s 22(1), the Home Secretary has the power to make regulations which lay down time-limits for the prosecution to complete any stage in criminal proceedings and the maximum overall period that a defendant may be remanded in custody.

The Prosecution of Offences (Custody Time Limits) Regulations 1987, SI 1987/229 lay down maximum overall periods for which a defendant charged with an either way offence can be remanded in custody awaiting completion of a particular stage in the proceedings.

The maximum overall periods of remand in custody at the magistrates' court are:

* 70 days before summary trial unless the decision for summary trial is taken within 56 days, in which case the limit is reduced to 56 days;
* 70 days before committal proceedings. (Regulations 4.2 and 4.4.)

When the time-limits have expired, the defendant must be released on bail unless the court considers it reasonable to extend the period.

Example

Joe appears before the magistrates, for the first time, on a charge of assault occasioning actual bodily harm. He is remanded in custody for 7 days. At the next hearing, Joe is remanded in custody for a further 28 days, after which committal proceedings are to take place. Twenty-eight days later, Joe is back before the court. The prosecution asks for a further 28-day remand as it is not ready to proceed to committal. The magistrates agree, on the basis that the committal will take place at the next hearing. By the time of the next hearing, Joe will have been in custody for 63 days (7 + 28 + 28). If the prosecution is not ready to proceed with committal on that date, then Joe can only be remanded in custody for a further 7 days (and then must be released on bail) unless the magistrates agree that it is reasonable to extend the custody time-limit.

The maximum overall periods for remands in custody at the Crown Court (for indictable only or either way offences) are:

- 182 days from sending the case for trial and the start of the trial less any period (or the aggregate of any periods) during which the defendant has been in the custody of the magistrates' court since that first appearance for the offence (reg 5(6)(B), as amended by the Prosecution of Offences (Custody Time Limits) (Modification) Regulations 1998, SI 1998/3037);
- 112 days from committing the case for trial and the start of the trial (reg 5(3)(a)).

3.4.3 Bail

The nature of bail

Whenever magistrates adjourn a case and decide to remand the defendant, they must also decide whether the remand should be in custody or on bail.

A defendant who is granted bail is under a duty to surrender to custody at the time and place appointed (Bail Act 1976, s 3(1)).

A defendant who fails, without reasonable cause, to surrender to custody is guilty of the offence of absconding. The burden of proving reasonable cause lies on the defendant (Bail Act 1976, s 6).

The offence of absconding is punishable on summary conviction in a magistrates' court with up to 3 months' imprisonment and/or a £5,000 fine. In the Crown Court, the matter is dealt with as a criminal contempt and is punishable with up to 12 months' imprisonment and/or an unlimited fine.

If a defendant fails to surrender to bail, the court may issue a warrant for his arrest (Bail Act 1976, s 7(1), (2)).

Limitations on bail (Criminal Justice and Public Order Act 1994, s 25)

A court may, only in exceptional circumstances, grant bail to a person charged with:

- murder;
- attempted murder;
- manslaughter;
- rape; or

- attempted rape,

if that person has been previously convicted of any one of these offences. There is no requirement that the previous conviction be for the same offence as the current charge before the court.

The right to bail (Bail Act 1976, s 4)

A court has an obligation to grant bail (except in the 'limited bail' cases above, and as provided in Sch 1 (see below)):

(1) prior to conviction, to all defendants;
(2) after conviction, to a defendant whose case is then adjourned for reports or enquiries;
(3) to offenders brought before a magistrates' court for breach of a community rehabilitation order or community punishment order.

The basic right to bail does not apply:

(1) where magistrates having convicted a defendant commit him to the Crown Court for sentence (see **9.2.16**);
(2) when a person is appealing against conviction or sentence.

Exceptions to the right to bail for a defendant charged with an imprisonable offence (Bail Act 1976, Sch 1, Part I)

A defendant need not be granted bail if:

(1) the court is satisfied that there are substantial grounds for believing that the defendant, if released on bail, would:

    (a) fail to surrender to custody, or
    (b) commit an offence while on bail, or
    (c) interfere with witnesses or otherwise obstruct the course of justice, whether in relation to himself or any other person (para 2);

(2) the offence is an indictable or either way offence and it appears to the court that the defendant was on bail in criminal proceedings at the date of the offence (para 2A);
(3) the court is satisfied that the defendant should be kept in custody for his own protection or, if he is a child or young person, for his own welfare (para 3);
(4) the defendant is in custody in pursuance of the sentence of a court (para 4);
(5) the court is satisfied that it has not been practicable to obtain sufficient information for the purpose of taking the decisions required … for want of time since the institution of the proceedings against him (para 5);
(6) having been released on bail in or in connection with proceedings for the offence, he has been arrested for absconding or breaking conditions of bail (para 6);
(7) the case is adjourned for enquiries or a report, and it appears to the court that it would be impracticable to complete the enquiries or make the report without keeping the defendant in custody (para 7).

Factors

In considering whether the para 2 or para 2A grounds set out above apply, a court should take into account the following factors:

'(a) the nature and seriousness of the offence or default (and the probable method of dealing with the defendant for it),

(b) the character, antecedents, associations and community ties of the defendant,

(c) the defendant's record as respects the fulfilment of his obligations under previous grants of bail in criminal proceedings,

(d) except in the case of a defendant whose case is adjourned for inquiries or a report, the strength of the evidence of his having committed the offence or having defaulted.' (Bail Act 1976, Sch 1, Pt I, para 9)

These factors are not exceptions to the defendant's right to bail. They are factors that the court takes into account when deciding whether to grant bail. Such factors can be used by the prosecution to explain why a particular exception to the defendant's right to bail applies or by the defence in support of the defendant's bail application.

These factors are considered below.

THE NATURE AND SERIOUSNESS OF THE OFFENCE AND THE PROBABLE METHOD OF DEALING WITH IT

This factor is particularly relevant to an argument that, if released on bail, the defendant will fail to surrender to custody. If the offence is a serious one the prosecution may say that a custodial sentence is likely to follow conviction and if released on bail the defendant will not wish to face that possibility. The defence will sometimes argue that the very fact that an offence is serious will mean that the defendant is likely to answer bail as he will not wish to make matters any worse for himself than they are already. Furthermore, the defence may acknowledge that the offence is serious, state that the defendant is pleading not guilty and is anxious to attend court to clear his name.

THE DEFENDANT'S CHARACTER AND ANTECEDENTS

The defendant's criminal record is admissible on an application for bail. A history of offending may be relevant to an argument that the defendant would commit an offence while on bail. If he has a history of committing the particular type of offence with which he is charged then, if released on bail, he may offend again. A defendant's previous good character will also be relevant.

THE DEFENDANT'S ASSOCIATIONS

This factor may be relevant to arguments that the defendant will commit an offence while on bail or interfere with witnesses. If it is alleged that the defendant associates with known criminals or is perhaps a member of an organised gang this could indicate that he will commit further offences. If a prosecution witness is known to the defendant or is perhaps a relative then an argument may be put forward that he will attempt to interfere with that witness by persuading him to change his evidence.

THE DEFENDANT'S COMMUNITY TIES

This is likely to be relevant in relation to an argument that the defendant will fail to surrender to custody. If the defendant is of no fixed abode, has no relatives in the area, or has no job then it can be argued that if released on bail there is little to keep him in the area. Conversely, if he has a fixed residence, family ties or secure employment this may indicate that he will stay in the area and surrender to custody.

THE DEFENDANT'S RECORD IN RELATION TO PREVIOUS GRANTS OF BAIL

Any history of failing to surrender to custody or committing offences while on bail will be relevant. Conversely, a defendant with a criminal record who has no history of failure to surrender or of committing offences while on bail is entitled to have this taken into account when a court decides whether there are substantial grounds for believing that he would fail to surrender to custody or would commit an offence while on bail.

STRENGTH OF EVIDENCE

Except where the case has been adjourned for enquiries or report, the strength of the evidence against the defendant will be a consideration.

If the prosecution alleges that the evidence against the defendant is strong, this will support an argument of probable failure to surrender to custody. This factor is unlikely to be used in isolation but, if combined with a serious offence which indicates a custodial sentence on conviction, it can be very persuasive. Equally, the defence can argue that the evidence against the defendant is not strong (eg it may consist of disputed identification evidence) and that as a result the defendant is anxious to attend the trial to clear his name.

The arguments cited above are illustrative only and the factors can be used in any way by the prosecution or defence to support or oppose an application for a remand in custody.

The other grounds for refusing bail are largely self-explanatory. The ground that it has not been practicable to obtain sufficient information for the purpose of taking the decisions required is likely to be used where a defendant is taken before a court following an overnight arrest and charge.

Exceptions to the right to bail for a defendant charged with a non-imprisonable offence (Bail Act 1976, Sch 1, Part II)

If the defendant is charged with a non-imprisonable offence, the prosecution will not normally oppose bail. Grounds for refusing bail are:

(1) it appears to the court that, having been previously granted bail in criminal proceedings, the defendant has failed to surrender to custody in accordance with his obligations under the grant of bail and the court believes, in view of that failure, that the defendant, if released on bail (whether subject to conditions or not), would fail to surrender to custody (para 2);

(2) the defendant ought to be kept in custody for his own protection or, if he is a child or young person, for his own welfare (para 3);

(3) the defendant is in custody in pursuance of the sentence of a court (para 4);

(4) the defendant, having been released on bail in the proceedings, has been arrested for absconding or breaking conditions of bail (para 5).

These grounds are largely self-explanatory.

Conditions of bail (Bail Act 1976, s 3)

A defendant may be required by a court:

'... to comply, before release on bail or later, with such requirements as appear to the court to be necessary to secure that –

(a) he surrenders to custody,

(b)   he does not commit an offence while on bail,

(c)   he does not interfere with witnesses or otherwise obstruct the course of justice whether in relation to himself or any other person,

(d)   he makes himself available for the purpose of enabling enquiries or a report to be made to assist the court in dealing with him for the offence,

(e)   before the time appointed for him to surrender to custody, he attends an interview with an authorised advocate or authorised litigator, as defined by s 119(1) of the Courts and Legal Services Act 1990.' (s 3(6))

'Authorised advocate' includes a barrister or solicitor and 'authorised litigator' includes a solicitor.

Conditions may be suggested by the defence when attempting to persuade a court to grant bail or they may be imposed by the court of its own volition. Such conditions include sureties, security, reporting regularly to a police station, a curfew and a condition of non-communication with named prosecution witnesses. This list is not exhaustive, and any condition may be imposed which appears to be realistic.

SURETIES

A surety is a person who enters into a recognisance of money (eg X stands surety for Y in the sum of £10,000) and is under an obligation to use every reasonable effort to ensure the defendant's appearance at court. The surety is not required to pay over any money at this stage.

If the defendant fails to appear, the court is required to declare the immediate and automatic forfeiture of the recognisance (Magistrates' Courts Act 1980, s 120(1A)). After declaring the recognisance forfeited, the court must issue a summons to the surety to appear before the court to explain why he should not pay the sum. The court will then decide whether all, part or none of the sum should be paid.

In considering the suitability of a proposed surety the Bail Act 1976, s 8(2) states that:

'regard may be had (amongst other things) to –

(a)   the surety's financial resources;

(b)   his character and any previous convictions of his; and

(c)   his proximity (whether in point of kinship, place of residence or otherwise) to the person for whom he is to be surety.'

Thus a person without any assets or with a substantial criminal record or who lives a long way from the defendant is unlikely to be acceptable. As a matter of professional conduct, a solicitor should not stand surety for his client.

A court may indicate that it is prepared to grant bail subject to a suitable surety being found. In such a case, the amount of the recognisance should be fixed by the court and the suitability of any surety who is found can be determined by a magistrate, a magistrates' clerk or an inspector at a police station. If a surety is rejected in these circumstances, it is possible to apply to the court for a final decision (see Bail Act 1976, s 8(4), (5)).

Sureties may be put forward to overcome a prosecution objection that the defendant will fail to surrender to custody.

SECURITY

The defendant may be required to give security for his surrender in the form of money or chattels.

This condition is again relevant to a prosecution objection to bail on the basis that the defendant will fail to surrender to custody. Deposit of a sum of money is an example of security.

REPORTING TO A POLICE STATION

This condition can again be used to overcome a prosecution objection that the defendant will fail to surrender to custody. Reporting to a police station can be daily or even twice daily, where appropriate.

CURFEW

An example of the imposition of a curfew is that the defendant shall not leave his place of residence between the hours of 6 pm and 7 am. The condition is frequently used to overcome an objection to bail that the defendant will commit further offences while on bail. It may be particularly relevant where the defendant is charged with or has a history of night-time offending.

NON-COMMUNICATION WITH PROSECUTION WITNESSES

This condition can be used to overcome a prosecution objection to bail that the defendant will interfere with witnesses. If the named witness is a relative with whom the defendant resides it will, of course, be necessary to find the defendant alternative accommodation.

RESIDENCE

A condition of residence, frequently expressed as a condition to live and sleep at a specified address, can be used to overcome a prosecution objection to bail that the defendant will fail to surrender to custody. It can be used where the defendant has a known address or where he is allegedly of no fixed abode. If the defendant is of no fixed abode, it may be possible to find a place for him at a bail hostel. These are institutions (often run by the Probation Service) which can provide accommodation for people who would otherwise be refused bail on the basis of no fixed abode. Strict conditions, for example as to hours kept, have to be complied with.

Variation and breach of conditions

The court may vary conditions or, subsequent to the granting of bail, impose them on application by either party.

The police have power to arrest without warrant for breach of bail conditions (Bail Act 1976, s 7). Breach of condition is not, of itself, an offence but will create a ground for a court to refuse bail in the present proceedings.

Bail procedure

If the prosecution is objecting to bail, the following procedure will apply.

(1) The prosecutor will make an application for a remand in custody and will hand in to the court a list of the defendant's previous convictions. The prosecutor will state the statutory objections to bail being granted and will cite relevant facts of the case in support.

(2)   The defence advocate will make an application for bail. A good application for bail will deal with each of the prosecution objections in turn, offering conditions of bail where appropriate.

(3)   Evidence may be called at a bail hearing. The court may wish to hear from a prospective employer or someone who is prepared to offer a home to the defendant. However, the usual rules of evidence do not apply and the court may accept hearsay from witnesses and mere assertions of fact from the advocates.

(4)   The court decides whether to remand in custody or on bail. If bail is granted subject to a surety, the court will hear evidence on oath from the surety in order to be satisfied as to the suitability of the surety.

A court which grants or withholds bail or which imposes or varies conditions must make a record of the decision in the prescribed form. A copy will then be given to the defendant.

Further, a magistrates' court or Crown Court must give reasons (and include a note of them in the record) for withholding bail or for imposing or varying conditions and it must normally give the defendant a copy of the note (Bail Act 1976, s 5).

An example of the prescribed form appears as **Appendix 2(M)**. A chart summarising the above procedure is included as **Appendix 1(F)**.

In preparing for a bail application, it is useful for the defence solicitor to discuss the grounds for objection with the prosecutor and to see whether or not the objections can be overcome by the imposition of suitable conditions.

Further applications when bail is refused

TO THE MAGISTRATES' COURT

If a court refuses bail, it is under a duty at each subsequent hearing to consider the question of bail, provided that:

(1)   the defendant is still in custody; and
(2)   the right to bail still applies.

This does not necessarily mean that the court must hear another full bail application. Part IIA of Sch 1 to the Bail Act 1976 provides:

> 'At the first hearing after that at which the court decided not to grant the defendant bail he may support an application for bail with any argument as to fact or law that he desires (whether or not he has advanced that argument previously).' (para 2)

> 'At subsequent hearings the court need not hear arguments as to fact or law which it has heard previously.' (para 3)

Example
D is remanded in custody for seven days on 7 June following a bail application by his solicitor. The solicitor may make a further application on 14 June using the same arguments. If D is remanded in custody again, new arguments will be necessary before the court will hear a further application. New arguments could include matters such as the availability of a job or a surety.

In applying this rule, the court should ignore a hearing at which bail was refused on the basis that it has not been practicable to obtain sufficient information about the defendant (*R v Calder Justices ex parte Kennedy* [1992] Crim LR 496). In the example above, if D was remanded in custody on 7 June on the insufficient information ground, he would still be entitled to bail applications at his next two hearings.

If a magistrates' court remands a person in custody after a fully argued bail application, it must issue a certificate confirming that it has heard full argument. An example of a full argument certificate appears at **Appendix 2(M)** (bottom right-hand corner).

TO THE CROWN COURT (SUPREME COURT ACT 1981, s 81, AS AMENDED BY THE CRIMINAL JUSTICE ACT 1982, s 60)

A person who has been remanded in custody by a magistrates' court may apply to the Crown Court for bail provided that the magistrates have issued a full argument certificate on the bail application which has been refused.

A person who has been committed in custody to the Crown Court for trial or sentence or who has appealed to the Crown Court can apply to the Crown Court for bail. No full argument certificate is required as the magistrates no longer have jurisdiction to hear applications in the case.

The rights to apply to the Crown Court above are entirely separate. The test is whether or not the case has yet been sent to the Crown Court for trial, sentence or appeal. If it has not, then a full argument certificate is required. If it has been sent to the Crown Court, a full argument certificate is not required.

TO A HIGH COURT JUDGE IN CHAMBERS (CRIMINAL JUSTICE ACT 1967, s 22(1))

In any case where a magistrates' court or the Crown Court has refused bail or granted bail subject to conditions, an application may be made to a High Court judge in chambers who may admit that person to bail.

REPRESENTATION

A grant of representation in criminal proceedings will cover representation in related bail proceedings (Access to Justice Act 1999, Sch 3, para 2(2)). This means that representation in Crown Court or High Court bail proceedings falls within the scope of the original grant of representation in the magistrates' court.

Challenging grants of bail

By s 1 of the Bail (Amendment) Act 1993:

> 'Where a magistrates' court grants bail to a person who is charged with or convicted of:
>
> (a)   an offence punishable by a term of imprisonment of five years or more; or
>
> (b)   an offence under s 12 (taking a conveyance without authority) or s 12A (aggravated vehicle taking) of the Theft Act 1968,
>
> the prosecution may appeal to a judge of the Crown Court against the granting of bail.'

Such an appeal can be made only if the prosecution objected to the magistrates granting bail to the defendant.

Prosecution request for reconsideration of bail (Bail Act 1976, s 5B)

If a defendant is charged with an indictable or either way offence and a magistrates' court has granted him bail, the prosecution can ask the magistrates to reconsider their decision. This power can be exercised only if information has come to light which was not available to the court when the decision to grant bail was taken.

A magistrates' court which reconsiders a bail decision may:

- vary conditions of bail;
- impose new conditions of bail; or
- withhold bail.

3.5 FURTHER READING

Further details on the law of bail can be found in numerous publications including:

Archbold: Criminal Pleading, Evidence and Practice (Sweet & Maxwell, 2001);
Blackstone's Criminal Practice (Blackstone Press, 2001);
John Sprack *Emmins on Criminal Procedure* (Blackstone Press, 2000).

Practical guidance can be found in:

Ede and Edwards *Criminal Defence* (The Law Society, 2000).

Chapter 4

CRIMINAL EVIDENCE

4.1 INTRODUCTION

The law of evidence regulates the way in which a criminal case may be presented to a jury or to magistrates. The rules of evidence determine whether the prosecution must prove the guilt of the defendant or whether it is for the defendant to establish his innocence, the standard of proof required and the methods of proving a case.

It is not possible to understand evidence in isolation. The first step is to appreciate how the rules of evidence to be examined in this chapter fit into the procedural progress of a trial. A summary of the general principles appears below. Each of the principles referred to is dealt with later in some detail, but an initial overview is essential.

Presentation of evidence – An overview

Stage A

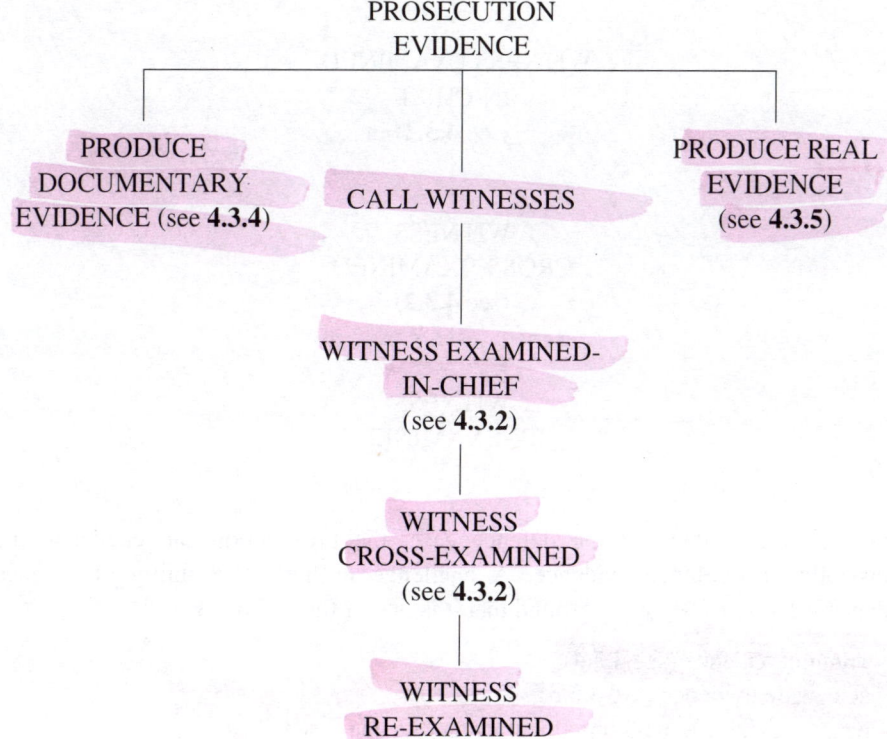

Note that at any stage of the prosecution case, the defence can challenge the admissibility of prosecution evidence. A challenge to the admissibility of prosecution evidence is likely to be on the grounds that the evidence infringes one of the following rules:

(1) opinion evidence (see **4.5.4**);

(2) self-made evidence (see **4.5.3**);

(3) the bad character and previous criminal convictions of the defendant (see **4.7.2**);

(4) hearsay evidence including confessions made by the defendant and documentary hearsay (see **4.6**).

The court also has a general discretion to exclude prosecution evidence where its admission would have an adverse effect on the fairness of the proceedings (see **4.2.4**).

Stage B: Defence submission of no case to answer

In certain circumstances, the defence may, at the close of the prosecution case, make a submission of no case to answer. If this succeeds then the prosecution case will have failed (see further **4.2.2**).

Stage C

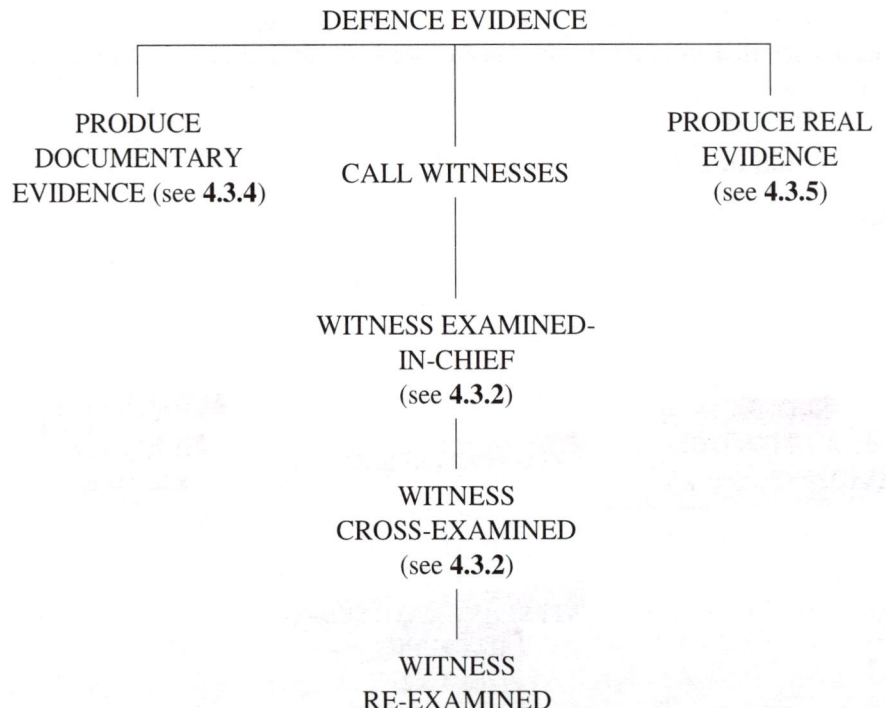

DEFENCE EVIDENCE

PRODUCE DOCUMENTARY EVIDENCE (see **4.3.4**)

CALL WITNESSES

PRODUCE REAL EVIDENCE (see **4.3.5**)

WITNESS EXAMINED-IN-CHIEF (see **4.3.2**)

WITNESS CROSS-EXAMINED (see **4.3.2**)

WITNESS RE-EXAMINED

Note that at any stage of the defence case, the prosecution can challenge the admissibility of defence evidence. A challenge to the admissibility of defence evidence is likely to be on the ground that it is one of the following:

(1) opinion evidence (see **4.5.4**);

(2) self-made evidence (see **4.5.3**);

(3) hearsay evidence including documentary hearsay (see **4.6**).

If the defendant gives evidence, there are restrictions on the type of question that may be put to him in cross-examination (see **4.7.5**).

Stage D: Closing speeches (and, in the Crown Court, judge's summing up)

Relevant evidential considerations include:

(1) burdens and standards of proof (see **4.2.1**);
(2) evidential burdens (see **4.2.2**);
(3) corroboration (see **4.4**);
(4) identification evidence (see **4.4.2**).

Stage E: Verdict

When studying the rules of evidence which follow, the overall framework of a criminal trial should be borne in mind and, when necessary, reference back to the above summary should be made.

4.2 PRELIMINARY POINTS OF EVIDENCE

This section will consider:

(1) who must prove what;
(2) to what standard;
(3) whether there are any matters that a court can take into account without hearing evidence;
(4) whether the law imposes any requirements as to the amount of evidence required.

4.2.1 Burdens and standards of proof

As a general rule, the prosecution is required to prove the guilt of the defendant beyond reasonable doubt. This means that at the end of a case the magistrates or jury should be told to consider all of the evidence in the case (both prosecution and defence) and to convict only if they are *sure* of the defendant's guilt (*Woolmington v DPP* [1935] AC 462; *Walters (Henry) v The Queen* [1969] 2 AC 26).

In exceptional cases, the burden of proof falls on the defence. For example, if a defendant wishes to plead insanity he is required to prove that fact.

If the burden of proof rests with the defence, the standard of proof required is proof on a balance of probabilities. This is a lower standard of proof than proof beyond reasonable doubt. It was explained in *Miller v Ministry of Pensions* [1947] 2 All ER 372 as simply meaning 'more probable than not'.

Subject to *Woolmington* and *Walters*, a defendant who wishes to introduce a defence to a case (eg alibi, self-defence, mechanical defect in a vehicle) does not have the burden of proving that defence. It is for the prosecution, as part of the requirement to prove the case beyond reasonable doubt, to satisfy the magistrates or jury that the defence is not true.

4.2.2 The evidential burden

The evidential burden arises in the following ways in a criminal case.

The burden on the prosecution

It has been seen at **4.2.1** that the prosecution will present its case first. At the end of the prosecution case, the defence should consider whether the prosecution has presented sufficient evidence to justify a finding of guilt (remember that the defence will not have adduced any evidence at this stage). A submission of no case to answer can be made at this stage. Such a submission will succeed if the prosecution has failed to adduce evidence in support of a material part of the offence. For example, on a charge of theft, if no evidence has been presented to prove that the goods taken 'belonged to another', a submission should succeed.

A submission of no case to answer is made to the judge in the Crown Court and to the magistrates at summary trial.

If no submission is made, or if it fails, then the prosecution has satisfied 'the evidential burden'. This does not mean that the prosecution is entitled to a conviction at this stage. It means that the case can proceed to the next stage where the defence has an opportunity to present evidence to the court.

The burden on the defence

The defence does not have to adduce any evidence. It can simply hope that the jury or magistrates will not accept that the prosecution evidence is sufficient to prove the case beyond reasonable doubt. However, if the defendant wishes to rely on a specific defence to a charge (eg self-defence, alibi, mechanical defect as an explanation for a motor accident on a charge of careless driving) then some evidence of that defence must be put before the magistrates or jury. To this extent there is an evidential burden on the defence. It is important to remember that the defendant is not required to prove his defence. All that is necessary is to put some evidence before the court and the evidential burden is satisfied. The prosecution must satisfy the magistrates or jury that the defence is not true.

In certain circumstances, courts are entitled to infer a fact against the defendant. Such cases again place an evidential burden on the defendant. See further **4.2.3**.

> *Example*
>
> D is charged with theft. Evidence is adduced to show that D was found in possession of recently stolen property. There is now an evidential burden on D to give an explanation for possession of the goods. In the absence of a credible explanation, the jury or magistrates are entitled to infer that D is the thief.

4.2.3 Proof by evidence

In deciding whether the prosecution has proved its case beyond reasonable doubt, a jury or magistrates can only take into account a fact which has been proved by evidence.

> *Example*
>
> D is charged with assault. No admissible evidence is put forward in support of a defence of self-defence. During his closing speech at the end of the trial, D's advocate raises the issue of self-defence. This cannot be taken into account as no evidence has been adduced in support of the fact.

This rule is subject to a number of exceptions.

Facts formally admitted

In order to narrow the issues to be decided at a criminal trial, it is possible for the prosecution or defence formally to admit certain facts. For example, on a charge of theft, the sole issue to be decided may be whether the defendant was acting dishonestly. The defence can make a formal admission to the effect that the defendant appropriated goods belonging to another with the intention to permanently deprive. This relieves the prosecution of the burden of adducing evidence of these facts and the trial can proceed solely on the issue of dishonesty.

A formal admission can be made either before or at the trial. If an admission is made out of court by the defendant, it must be made in writing and made by, or be approved by, the defendant's counsel or solicitor (Criminal Justice Act 1967, s 10).

A formal admission is not to be confused with admissions made to the police by a suspect when being questioned about suspected involvement in an offence.

Judicial notice

If a court takes judicial notice of a fact then evidence of that fact will not be required.

A court is obliged by law to take judicial notice of matters of law. Thus, there is no requirement to prove the content of a public Act of Parliament.

A court may take judicial notice of matters of common knowledge, including local knowledge. An example would be the rules of the road. On a driving charge, the prosecution would not be required to prove that, in Britain, motorists should drive on the left-hand side of the road. This would be a matter of common knowledge. The distance between towns and the time taken to travel between them are matters of local knowledge and may not have to be proved by evidence.

Inferences of fact

In many criminal cases, there will be no available direct evidence from eye witnesses to support the prosecution or defence case. A court, in reaching a verdict, will be entitled to draw inferences from the existence of other proven facts. The fact that the fingerprints of the defendant were found on burgled premises and that he was seen in the vicinity of the property around the time of the crime may lead to an inference that he committed the crime.

Two common examples of inferences arising in criminal cases are as follows.

(1) THE DOCTRINE OF RECENT POSSESSION

A court is entitled to infer that a person found in possession of recently stolen goods is the thief or a handler. Such an inference may only be drawn in the absence of a credible explanation from the defendant. If the prosecution gives evidence of possession of recently stolen property there is an evidential burden on the defendant to put forward an explanation (see **4.2.2**).

(2) THE DOCTRINE OF CONTINUANCE

If evidence is adduced to prove that a certain state of affairs existed at a particular time, a court is entitled to infer that it continued to exist at another reasonably proximate time. For example, on a charge of dangerous driving, evidence may be given that the defendant was driving at great speed 500 yards from the scene of the accident, giving rise to the charge. The court may infer that this speed continued to the scene of the accident. Again, there may be an evidential burden on the defendant if he wishes to rebut the inference that may be drawn.

4.2.4 Improperly obtained evidence

At common law, evidence illegally or unfairly obtained was admissible. Courts would not exclude evidence which was relevant simply because it had been obtained by the police as a result of an illegal search (*Kuruma v The Queen* [1955] AC 197).

In relation to evidence obtained from the defendant which was tantamount to a self-incriminatory admission (eg a confession or evidence from an identification parade), the court has a general discretion to exclude such evidence if it had been improperly obtained (*R v Sang* [1980] AC 402).

4.2.5 Court's discretion to exclude evidence

The Police and Criminal Evidence Act 1984, s 78 gives criminal courts a statutory discretion to exclude prosecution evidence:

> 'In any proceedings the court may refuse to allow evidence on which the prosecution proposes to rely to be given if it appears to the court that, having regard to all of the circumstances, including the circumstances in which the evidence was obtained, the admission of the evidence would have such an adverse effect on the fairness of the proceedings that the court ought not to admit it.'

The section has been interpreted broadly in line with the existing common law. Thus the fact that evidence has been obtained as a result of an illegal search is unlikely to be a ground for exclusion under s 78.

In *Khan v United Kingdom* [2000] Crim LR 684, the European Court of Human Rights considered the relationship between s 78 and Article 6 of the European Convention on Human Rights.

The court held that since domestic law did not regulate the use of covert listening devices at the time of the applicant's conviction, the applicant's right to respect for private and family life, as guaranteed by Article 8 of the Convention, had been violated.

The applicant also alleged a breach of Article 6(1) of the Convention. He argued that the use, as the sole evidence in his case, of the material which had been obtained in breach of Article 8 was not compatible with the 'fair hearing' requirements of Article 6.

The court noted that it was not its role to determine, as a matter of principle, whether particular types of evidence, for example, unlawfully obtained evidence, might be admissible or, indeed, whether the applicant was guilty or not.

In examining whether, in all the circumstances, including the way in which the evidence was obtained, the proceedings as a whole were unfair, the court observed that the recording of the applicant's conversation had not been unlawful in the sense of being contrary to domestic criminal law, even though it had been obtained in breach of Article 8.

At each level of jurisdiction the domestic courts assessed the effect of admission of the evidence on the fairness of the trial and discussed, among other matters, the non-statutory basis for the surveillance. In the court's view it was clear that, had the domestic courts been of the view that the admission of the evidence would have given rise to substantive unfairness, they would have exercised their discretion under s 78 to exclude it. As a result, the court found that the use at the applicant's trial of the secretly taped material did not conflict with the requirements of a fair trial guaranteed by Article 6(1).

There are two major areas of operation of s 78:

(1) identification evidence; and
(2) confessions.

Section 78 has no application to committal proceedings.

Confessions are examined at **4.6.2**; identification evidence and s 78 are discussed below.

IDENTIFICATION EVIDENCE

A breach of the identification code does not automatically render evidence inadmissible. It is something that a court will take into account in determining an application to exclude such evidence under s 78. Examples include: *R v Gaynor* [1988] Crim LR 242, where evidence of a group identification was excluded because insufficient effort had been made to arrange an identification parade; *R v Gall* (1990) 90 Cr App R 64, breach of the rule that an investigating officer should take no part in the parade procedure; *R v Nagah (Jasant Singh)* (1991) 92 Cr App R 334, where a confrontation identification was disallowed because the defendant had requested an identification parade and it was practicable to hold one.

If evidence is to be excluded under s 78 because of a breach of the identification code, the defence will have to show why it would be unfair to admit it. The mere fact that there has been a technical breach which does not lead to unfairness will be insufficient to exclude evidence (*R v Grannell (Robert James Lawson)* (1990) 90 Cr App R 149).

4.3 METHODS OF PROOF

Evidence may be presented by:

(1) calling witnesses;
(2) adducing documentary evidence;
(3) adducing real evidence.

A number of technical rules must be borne in mind when presenting certain types of evidence.

4.3.1 Witnesses – competence and compellability

Competence

Competence means that the witness will be permitted to testify. The general rule is that all witnesses are competent to give evidence. Only if a witness cannot understand questions asked of him in court, or cannot answer them in a way that can be understood (with, if necessary, the assistance of special measures – see **4.3.2**), will the witness not be able to testify (Youth Justice and Criminal Evidence Act 1999, s 54).

The only exception to the general rule relates to the defendant. The defendant is not competent to give evidence for the prosecution in his own trial, nor is any co-defendant in the proceedings (see **4.7.1**).

Determining whether a witness is competent

A witness's competence to give evidence may be challenged by the prosecution, the defence or the court itself.

In assessing the witness's competence to give evidence, the court is required to take into account any special measures it has granted, or is planning to grant, to the witness (see **4.3.2**).

If the witness's competence is challenged, the court will ask questions of the witness (not the party that is calling or cross-examining the witness). Any such questioning will be done in the presence of both the prosecution and the defence. The court will be allowed to ask for expert advice about the witness's competence. It will be the responsibility of the party calling the witness to satisfy the court that the witness is competent.

Determining whether witnesses are to be sworn

References to swearing an oath include making an affirmation. The question of whether a witness is eligible to swear an oath may be raised by either the prosecution or the defence or by the court itself. The procedure used to determine this question will be the same as the procedure outlined above for determining competence (Youth Justice and Criminal Evidence Act 1999, s 55).

No witness under the age of 14 is to be sworn. A witness of 14 or over is eligible to give sworn evidence only if he understands the solemnity of a criminal trial and that taking an oath places a particular responsibility on him to tell the truth. If no evidence is offered suggesting that the witness does not understand those two matters there is a presumption that the witness is to give sworn evidence.

As with considerations of competence, the question of whether a witness should be sworn is to be considered in the absence of any jury (but in the presence of both the prosecution and the defence). Expert evidence can be received on this subject.

Unsworn evidence

Any witness who is competent to be a witness but is not allowed to give evidence on oath may give unsworn evidence (Youth Justice and Criminal Evidence Act 1999, ss 56 and 57).

Compellability

The general rule is that all witnesses can be compelled to attend court to give evidence by the service of a witness summons. The only exceptions relate to the defendant and the defendant's spouse (see **4.7.1**).

4.3.2 Oral evidence from witnesses

Special measures

There are a number of special measures available to help witnesses (other than the defendant) who might otherwise have difficulty giving evidence in criminal proceedings or who might be reluctant to do so (Youth Justice and Criminal Evidence Act 1999, ss 16–33).

The following can apply to the court for special measures to help them give evidence in court:

(1) children under the age of 17;

(2) those who suffer from a mental or physical disorder, or have a disability or impairment that is likely to affect their evidence; and

(3) those whose evidence is likely to be affected by their fear or distress at giving evidence in the proceedings.

Witnesses who are alleged to be victims of a sexual offence will be considered to be eligible for help with giving evidence unless they tell the court that they do not want to be considered eligible. Otherwise, it is for the court to determine whether a witness falls into any of these categories. The court must also determine whether making particular special measures available to an eligible witness will be likely to improve the quality of the evidence given by the witness.

Both the prosecution and defence will be able to apply, normally before the trial, for the court to make a direction authorising the use of special measures for a witness they are calling. A court may also decide to make a direction even if no such application has been made.

The special measures that are available are:

(1) screens, to ensure that the witness does not see the defendant;

(2) allowing an interview with the witness, which has been video-recorded before the trial, to be shown as the witness's evidence-in-chief at trial;

(3) allowing a witness to give evidence from outside the court by live television link;

(4) clearing people from the court so that evidence can be given in private;

(5) not wearing the court dress of wigs and gowns;

(6) allowing a witness to be cross-examined before the trial about their evidence and a video recording of that cross-examination to be shown at trial instead of the witness being cross-examined live at trial;

(7) allowing an approved intermediary to help a witness communicate with legal representatives and the court;

(8) allowing a witness to use communication aids.

Examination-in-chief

LEADING QUESTIONS

A witness is examined-in-chief by the party calling that witness. As a general rule, leading questions should not be asked on matters which are in dispute. It is, however, permissible to ask a leading question where the object is to elicit a denial of an opponent's case. For example, it would be permissible to ask a defendant, 'were you in the pub at the time of the assault?'.

A leading question is one which suggests the answer expected or assumes the existence of a fact which has not been proved.

Example
X is called as a prosecution witness. He is to testify to the fact that he saw D, at 11 am on 6 October, steal some goods from Tescos.

The prosecutor cannot say to X, 'Did you see D steal goods from Tescos at 11 am on 6 October?' This is a leading question.

Instead, the evidence should be elicited in this way:

Q   Where were you on 6 October at about 11 am?
A   In Tescos.
Q   Did you see anything unusual in the shop?
A   Yes, I saw D put some chocolate into his pocket.
Q   What happened then?
A   D walked out of the shop without paying for the chocolate.

MEMORY REFRESHING

A witness who is called to give evidence may refresh his memory in the witness-box from a document which was made or verified by him substantially contemporaneously with the events in question. This means that the witness wrote down what he saw or dictated what he saw to someone else and checked the accuracy of the document. This must have been done while the facts were fresh in the witness's memory. This is a question of fact in every case.

A document which is used to refresh the witness's memory does not become evidence in the case in its own right. However, the other party has the right to request and inspect a document used for this purpose.

UNFAVOURABLE WITNESSES

A witness who is called to give evidence may not give the evidence expected of him. He may be nervous, forgetful or stupid. However, if the failure to testify as expected is not deliberate, the party calling the witness is not allowed to contradict or to try to discredit that witness.

HOSTILE WITNESSES

If a witness appears to be unwilling to tell the truth on behalf of the party calling him then the party may apply to the judge or magistrates to declare that witness 'hostile'. If declared hostile, the witness may:

(1) be cross-examined by the party calling him. Leading questions may now be asked of the witness to show that he is being untruthful; and, with leave of the court,
(2) have any previous inconsistent statement put to him by the party calling him (Criminal Procedure Act 1865, s 3).

In practice, witnesses are commonly shown to be hostile by proving that they have made an earlier out-of-court statement from which they appear to be deliberately and dishonestly departing.

A previous inconsistent statement is not admissible to prove the truth of anything contained in the statement. Thus, it is not open to the judge or magistrates to accept the statement as true (unless the witness admits that it is true when cross-examined).

The statement can be used to undermine the credibility of the witness.

Cross-examination

Following examination-in-chief, a witness may be cross-examined by the other party (or all other parties). Leading questions may be asked.

The purposes of cross-examination include:

(1) to put the case of the cross-examiner to the witness. A failure to challenge a witness's evidence implies acceptance of it;
(2) to challenge the credibility of the witness;
(3) to elicit information helpful to the cross-examiner.

Restrictions on the defendant's right to cross-examination

A defendant is prohibited from personally cross-examining witnesses in the following circumstances:

(1) when the witness is the alleged victim of a sexual offence;
(2) when the witness is a child who is either the alleged victim, or a witness to the commission of the alleged offence, in a case involving sexual offences, kidnapping or abduction, cruelty or physical assault. This includes child witnesses who are co-defendants;
(3) in any other case, when the court is satisfied, upon an application or on its own initiative, that the circumstances of the case merit it.

In such circumstances, the defendant must appoint a legal representative to conduct the cross-examination on his behalf. Where the defendant refuses or fails to do so, the court must consider whether to appoint a legal representative to test the witness's evidence in the defendant's interests (Youth Justice and Criminal Evidence Act 1999, ss 34–40).

Cross-examination as to credit – general rule

A witness called by another party may be cross-examined as to credit where it is relevant as to whether the witness's evidence should be believed. Questions as to credit may include questions as to the witness's character, criminal convictions, previous inconsistent statements and whether a witness is biased in relation to the proceedings because of, for example, a grudge or relationship with a party to the proceedings.

As a general rule, the answer given to a credit question is final. This means that the cross-examiner cannot pursue the matter raised any further by calling independent evidence to prove the fact, but there are exceptions.

Cross-examination as to credit – exceptions

With certain credit questions the answer given is not final. The cross-examining party is allowed to call other evidence to prove the matter denied by the witness in cross-examination. These exceptional cases include:

(1) when it is alleged that a witness is biased;
(2) when it is alleged that the witness has made a previous inconsistent statement (Criminal Procedure Act 1865, ss 4, 5). If a previous inconsistent statement is proved (either by the witness admitting that he made it or by independent evidence), it is not admissible to prove the truth of anything stated in it. Thus the trial judge or magistrates cannot accept the previous inconsistent statement as true (unless the witness admits that it is true). It is relevant only to the credibility of the witness;
(3) when the question is to show that the witness has been convicted of a criminal offence (Criminal Procedure Act 1865, s 6). If a witness denies a conviction then it may be proved by producing a certificate signed by the clerk to the

convicting court and proving that the person named in the certificate is the witness being cross-examined (Police and Criminal Evidence Act 1984, s 73).

4.3.3 Written statements from witnesses

As an alternative to a witness giving oral evidence, a written statement may be admissible in evidence. The major provisions enabling a witness statement to be admitted in evidence include:

(1) Criminal Justice Act 1967, s 9;
(2) Criminal Justice Act 1988, ss 23, 24, 30;
(3) Criminal Procedure and Investigations Act 1996, s 68 and Sch 2, paras 1 and 2.

These provisions require an appreciation of the rule against hearsay and are discussed at **4.6**.

4.3.4 Documentary evidence

A document must be authenticated by a witness if it is to be admitted in evidence. This will usually involve calling a witness to explain to the court how the document came into existence.

By the Criminal Justice Act 1988, s 27, a copy document is admissible even though the original is still in existence.

The content of a document may be hearsay evidence. The principal provisions governing the admissibility of documentary hearsay are discussed at **4.6**.

4.3.5 Real evidence

Items such as objects produced in court (exhibits) and places viewed by the court, are classified as real evidence. Items produced in court may include photographs, tape recordings and video recordings. Real evidence will normally require the additional testimony of a witness to explain the relevance of the evidence to the prosecution or defence case.

4.4 CORROBORATION AND IDENTIFICATION EVIDENCE

4.4.1 Corroboration

In determining the guilt or innocence of the defendant, the jury or magistrates will have regard to the cogency (or weight) of evidence before them. As a general rule, the law does not give specific weight to particular types of evidence, but in certain cases there are rules relating to corroboration of a witness's evidence.

The meaning of corroboration

Corroboration is other independent evidence which supports the evidence to be corroborated in a material particular and which implicates the defendant in the crime charged (*R v Baskerville* [1916] 2 KB 658).

Examples of corroboration

(1) The evidence of another witness.

(2)   A confession by the defendant (see **4.6.2**).

(3)   Lies told by the defendant. These are capable of amounting to corroboration provided the jury or magistrates are satisfied that:

    (a)   the lie is deliberate and relates to a material issue in the case; and

    (b)   the lie is told because of realisation of guilt; and

    (c)   the lie is proved by evidence independent of the witness to be corroborated. An admission by the defendant would suffice (see *R v Lucas (Ruth)* [1981] QB 720).

(4)   Circumstantial evidence, for example possession of stolen property or forensic evidence linking the defendant to the crime, is capable of amounting to corroboration.

(5)   The refusal of a defendant, without good cause, to give an intimate body sample to the police is capable of amounting to corroboration of any other evidence in the case to which the refusal is material. In a rape case, for example, the refusal of a semen sample could corroborate the prosecution case on an issue of whether intercourse took place between the victim and the defendant. It would not provide corroboration on an issue of consent (Police and Criminal Evidence Act 1984, s 62).

(6)   The refusal of a defendant, without good cause, to stand on an identification parade is capable of amounting to corroboration of any other evidence in the case to which the refusal is material.

In the Crown Court, the judge directs the jury as to evidence which is capable, as a matter of law, of amounting to corroboration. It is for the jury to decide whether to accept or reject the evidence. In a magistrates' court, the magistrates, taking advice from their clerk if necessary, decide what is capable of amounting to corroboration. They also decide whether or not to accept the evidence.

Special rules

CASES WHERE CORROBORATION IS ESSENTIAL

In a limited number of cases there cannot be a conviction on the evidence of a single witness. Corroboration is required. These include treason, perjury and the offence of speeding (unless the evidence is from a roadside camera).

If, at the close of the prosecution case, no evidence has been adduced which is capable of amounting to corroboration, a submission of no case to answer will succeed (see **4.2.2**). If there is evidence capable of amounting to corroboration then it is left to the jury or magistrates to decide, when considering their verdict, whether or not to accept the evidence as corroboration.

It is important to remember that a defendant cannot be convicted of any offence if the only evidence against him is an inference under ss 34, 36 or 37 of the Criminal Justice and Public Order Act 1994 (Criminal Justice and Public Order Act 1994, s 38(3)).

OTHER CASES

If a judge feels that the evidence of any type of witness is suspect, for whatever reason, he may direct a jury on the special need for caution and the dangers of convicting on that evidence alone (*R v Makanjuola; R v E* [1995] 1 WLR 1348).

Examples of such cases include:

(1) witnesses with a purpose of their own to serve in giving false evidence. Such witnesses may be:

- other parties to the crime charged. They may be giving evidence for the prosecution (having pleaded guilty) or evidence in their own defence. In either case they may be trying to put the blame on a co-defendant or minimising their role to get a lighter sentence;
- witnesses with a grudge against the defendant;
- witnesses whom a defendant alleges committed the offence;

(2) where a prosecution witness is a mental patient (*R v Spencer (Alan Widdison); R v Smails (George Glenville)* [1986] 3 WLR 348).

In a magistrates' court, it is always open to an advocate, when making a closing speech, to address the bench on the dangers of convicting on the evidence of a 'suspect' witness alone.

4.4.2 Disputed identification evidence

Special guidelines apply when a prosecution witness's evidence visually identifies the defendant and the identification is disputed (*R v Turnbull* [1977] QB 224).

When the rules apply

The *Turnbull* guidelines apply where there is evidence that a witness visually identified the defendant. This will usually come:

(1) from evidence that the person who committed the crime was picked out at an identification parade, group identification, video identification or confrontation; or

(2) from evidence that the witness recognised the person who committed the crime as someone previously known to him, for example 'It was Fred Smith'.

If the witness has simply given a description to the court of the person who committed the crime and there is no direct evidence that it was the defendant other than the fact that his physical appearance matches the description then the *Turnbull* guidelines do not apply.

> *Example 1*
> Joe is on trial for theft. A prosecution witness tells the court that he saw a man commit the crime and later identified Joe as that man at an identification parade.
>
> (1) If Joe denies being at the scene of the theft, the *Turnbull* guidelines apply.
> (2) If Joe admits to being at the scene of the theft but denies that he was the person who committed the crime, the *Turnbull* guidelines apply 'if there is a possibility of the witness being mistaken' (*R v Thornton* [1995] 1 Cr App R 598). This will depend on the facts of the case. If the defendant was the only person present then the *Turnbull* direction would seem to be inappropriate. If, however, there were a number of people present, the guidelines will apply (*R v Slater (Robert David)* [1995] 1 Cr App R 584).
> (3) If Joe admits taking the goods and pleads absence of mens rea, the *Turnbull* guidelines do not apply. The identification is not disputed.

Example 2

Jane is on trial for assault. A witness tells the court that he saw Jane commit the offence. He says that he knows Jane by sight and name as they live on the same road.

(1) If Jane denies being at the scene of the assault, the *Turnbull* guidelines apply.

(2) If Jane admits to being at the scene of the assault but claims that it was someone else who hit the victim, the *Turnbull* guidelines may apply (*R v Thornton* (above)).

(3) If Jane admits hitting the victim but pleads self-defence, *Turnbull* does not apply as the identification is not in dispute.

Example 3

Peter is on trial for taking a conveyance. The victim of the crime tells the court that he saw a man 'about 6ft tall, with brown spiky hair and a moustache'. Peter matches this description but he was not picked out at an identification parade.

The *Turnbull* guidelines cannot apply as there is no direct evidence identifying Peter as the man who committed the offence.

The **Turnbull** *guidelines – Crown Court cases*

In Crown Court cases, the trial judge should assess the quality of the identification evidence, that is to say, he should look at the circumstances of the original sighting of the offender by the witness. Factors to be taken into account will include:

(1) the length of observation;
(2) distance;
(3) lighting;
(4) conditions;
(5) whether the person identified was someone already known to the witness?
(6) how closely the description given to the police matches the appearance of the defendant?

IDENTIFICATION POOR AND WITHOUT SUPPORT

If the evidence is assessed as being of poor quality and without support then the judge should stop the trial at the end of the prosecution case and direct an acquittal.

IDENTIFICATION GOOD

If the judge considers the quality of the initial sighting to be good, he should, when summing up the case to the jury, point out the dangers of relying on identification evidence (including the fact that it is easy for an honest witness to be mistaken) and direct the jury to take into account the factors listed above when considering the quality of the evidence.

IDENTIFICATION POOR BUT SUPPORTED

If the judge considers the quality of the initial sighting to be poor, but supported by other evidence, then a similar warning should be given.

Supporting evidence is some independent evidence that suggests that the identification of the defendant may be correct. It may, for example, come via a confession, possession of stolen property, or lies told by the defendant. There is no requirement that supporting evidence should fulfil all the legal criteria of corroboration. In particular, it need not be independent of the identifying witness.

The Turnbull *guidelines – magistrates' court cases*

In magistrates' court cases, the same principles apply as in Crown Court cases (above). Therefore:

(1) if the case is one which appears to consist of poor quality identification evidence without support, a submission of no case to answer should be made (see **4.2.2**). This will be on the basis that the evidence is manifestly unreliable;

(2) in any other type of case, the defence advocate is likely to deal with *Turnbull* in his closing speech by pointing out the unreliability of identification evidence.

4.5 PARTICULAR RULES OF ADMISSIBILITY OF EVIDENCE

This paragraph is concerned with the content of evidence to be given by witnesses or which is contained in a document. Even though a witness may be competent to give evidence or a document can be authenticated, it is open to the prosecution or defence to challenge the evidence on the basis that it infringes one of the general principles of admissibility. Evidence may be inadmissible due to its being:

(1) irrelevant;
(2) self-made;
(3) opinion;
(4) privileged.

4.5.1 Challenging the admissibility of evidence

By agreement

It may be possible to agree with an opposing advocate that evidence is inadmissible. If so, such evidence will not be given at the trial and the jury or magistrates will not know about it.

By application to the court

CROWN COURT CASES

A challenge to the admissibility of evidence is made to the judge in the absence of the jury. If the challenge is on agreed facts then the advocates present legal argument to the judge who will make a ruling. If the evidence is ruled inadmissible, the jury will never hear it. If the evidence is admissible, the witness will testify in front of the jury. If there is a factual dispute involved (eg whether the police pressured the defendant into confessing) then the judge will hear evidence from relevant witnesses for the prosecution and defence in the absence of the jury before ruling on admissibility. This procedure is known as a trial within a trial. It is commonly used to challenge the admissibility of a confession and is examined in more detail at **4.6.2**.

MAGISTRATES' COURT CASES

As magistrates are arbiters of both fact and law they must rule on the admissibility of evidence. This will often mean that the magistrates will have heard details of evidence which they find inadmissible. Such evidence should be ignored when a verdict is being considered. The special problems involved in challenging the admissibility of a confession are discussed at **4.6.2**.

4.5.2 Relevance

Evidence of a fact is not admissible unless that fact is relevant to an issue to be decided by the court. Relevant evidence will include direct evidence from a witness who perceived an event. It will also include circumstantial evidence from which a fact can be inferred. Even though a fact may be relevant, it can still be ruled inadmissible because it offends one of the other principles of admissibility of evidence which follow.

4.5.3 Self-made evidence

General rule

As a general rule, a witness is not allowed to support the evidence given at a trial by introducing a statement which he has made on a previous occasion. For example, if the defendant is charged with assault and gives evidence of self-defence, he will not be allowed to tell the court that, 'I told my wife the day after the incident that I was acting in self-defence'. Similarly, the wife could not testify as to what her husband told her. In either case, the evidence adds nothing to the testimony given in court. The rule against self-made evidence is subject to a number of exceptions. These include:

(1) rebutting a suggestion of recent fabrication;
(2) statements forming part of the res gestae;
(3) exculpatory statements made to the police.

Rebutting a suggestion of recent fabrication

If, during cross-examination of a witness, it is put to a witness that he has recently concocted his testimony, evidence of previous statements can be admitted to rebut the assertion. In the example given in relation to the general rule, the defendant could call his wife to prove that he raised the issue of self-defence the day after the incident. The evidence would be admissible solely to show that the suggestion of recent fabrication was incorrect.

Statements forming part of the res gestae

If a statement is made 'in circumstances of spontaneity or involvement in the event so that the possibility of concoction can be disregarded' (see *Ratten (Leith McDonald) v The Queen* [1972] AC 378), it will be admissible in evidence under the res gestae principle. This is on the basis that a statement which is made at the time of a relevant act should be put before the court to help explain the event. The res gestae principle is well known in the United States by the graphic name 'the excited utterance rule'. In *R v Roberts* [1942] 1 All ER 187, the defendant testified to the fact that a gun had gone off accidentally, killing his girlfriend. He was not allowed to testify that while he was in police custody he had told his father that it was an accident. This was too far removed from the event to fall within the res gestae principle. The Court of Appeal held, however, that the defendant should have been allowed to call witnesses to recount the defendant's explanation which had been made contemporaneously with or within a few minutes of the shooting. Such evidence formed part of the res gestae. The res gestae principle is also an exception to the rule against hearsay.

Exculpatory statements made to the police

When being questioned by the police about an offence the defendant may put forward an explanation which, if accepted by a court, would exonerate him. Such statements are generally admissible in evidence but only to show consistency with testimony given at the trial. See *R v Pearce (David Anthony)* (1979) 69 Cr App R 365.

> #### Example
> D is charged with assault. When interviewed by the police he claims that he was elsewhere at the time of the commission of the offence. If D gives evidence at his trial in support of his alibi evidence, his statement made to the police is admissible to show consistency. If, however, D fails to testify, his statement made to the police is of no evidential value. It is not open to D to say to the court, 'my defence is in my statement to the police, please take it into account'.

Although the statement will not assist the prosecution case, as a matter of practice the interviewing officer will give evidence of the interview during the prosecution evidence and the statement will be received by the court as an exception to the rule against self-made evidence.

4.5.4 Opinion evidence

Ordinary witnesses

A witness may relate to the court any fact that he has personally perceived. Inevitably, parts of his evidence will include opinions such as the fact that a car was travelling at about 60 mph, or that a person appeared to be drunk. This is acceptable as the witness is simply relating to the court the facts as he saw them. However, the witness is not allowed to give an opinion on matters which it is the function of the court to decide. In particular, therefore, the witness cannot give his opinion on the ultimate issue to be determined, ie the guilt or innocence of the defendant.

Expert witnesses

Expert opinion evidence is admissible in relation to matters which are outside the competence of a jury or magistrates. Examples include matters of science, medicine and technology.

It is for the judge or magistrates to decide who is an expert. There is no fixed test and the presence or absence of formal qualifications is not conclusive.

Any party to criminal proceedings in the Crown Court who proposes to adduce expert evidence at the trial is required to give advance disclosure to all other parties of the substance of the evidence as soon as practicable following committal to the Crown Court for trial or being sent to the Crown Court for trial. If advance disclosure is not given then expert evidence cannot be adduced without leave of the court (Crown Court (Advance Notice of Expert Evidence) Rules 1987, SI 1987/716).

The rules requiring advance notice of expert evidence have been extended to trials in the magistrates' court by the Criminal Procedure and Investigations Act 1996, s 20 and the Magistrates' Courts (Advance Notice of Expert Evidence) Rules 1997, SI 1997/705.

Expert evidence can be difficult for a lay person to understand. To assist magistrates and juries, s 30 of the Criminal Justice Act 1988 provides that:

> 'an expert report shall be admissible as evidence in criminal proceedings, whether or not the person making it attends to give oral evidence in those proceedings.'

This provision enables the jury or magistrates to have a copy of the written report by the expert in front of them as they listen to his oral evidence.

The provision is drawn widely enough to enable a written report to be admissible in the absence of the expert. Section 30(2) states that:

> 'if it is proposed that the person making the report shall not give oral evidence, the report shall only be admissible with the leave of the court.'

Even if such leave were given, the amount of weight attached to the report is likely to be less than if the author of the report testified in person.

The written report of a prosecution expert witness is admissible at committal proceedings. No leave is required to admit it (Criminal Justice Act 1988, s 4A).

4.5.5 Privilege

Public policy privilege

As a matter of public policy, evidence which discloses the identity of a police informant is normally inadmissible. The rule extends to prevent the identification of premises used for police surveillance (*R v Rankine* [1986] 2 All ER 566). The reason for this protection is that it is in the public interest for the identity of those who help the police to be kept secret. The protection can be overridden if disclosure is necessary to show the innocence of the defendant. Thus, if the defendant alleges that he has been 'set up' by a particular person, X, the prosecution could be forced to reveal whether or not its informant was X.

Legal professional privilege

Communications between a client and his solicitor are privileged if the purpose of the communication is the giving or receiving of legal advice. In a criminal case, the practical effect of this is that letters, telephone calls, statements, etc are privileged. The defence cannot be compelled to reveal the content of such communications to any other party.

Communications between the defendant or his solicitor and a third party are also privileged, provided they are made in contemplation of pending or anticipated proceedings and the purpose, or dominant purpose, was to prepare for the litigation. Witness statements are obvious examples. The defence cannot be compelled to reveal the content of such communications to any other party.

Privilege against self-incrimination

A witness is not bound to answer a question if, in the opinion of the court, the answer would tend to expose him to proceedings for a criminal offence. This privilege is limited in the case of a defendant who elects to go into the witness box to give evidence. He will be obliged to answer questions even though the answer may tend to incriminate him as to the offence for which he is charged (Criminal Evidence Act 1898, s 1(e)).

4.6 HEARSAY EVIDENCE

4.6.1 The rule against hearsay

Hearsay is:

(1)   an oral or written statement
(2)   made out of court
(3)   which is now being repeated to the court
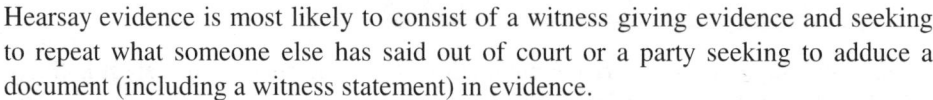(4)   to try to prove the truth of the matter stated out of court.

Hearsay evidence is most likely to consist of a witness giving evidence and seeking to repeat what someone else has said out of court or a party seeking to adduce a document (including a witness statement) in evidence.

Not all such evidence will be hearsay. It is necessary to consider why the party is seeking to adduce the evidence. If the purpose is to prove that anything in the statement or document is true then it will be hearsay. If it is being adduced for some other purpose, for example to show the state of mind of the maker or hearer of the statement, irrespective of its truth, then it is not hearsay (*Subramaniam v Public Prosecutor* [1956] 1 WLR 965).

Example 1
PC Smith wants to say to the court:

'I arrived at Tescos. I was met by a store detective who told me that the defendant had left the store without paying for goods.'

If the prosecution in a criminal trial for theft is asking the court to accept the truth of the store detective's statement (ie that D left the store without paying for goods) then it will be hearsay.

If, on the other hand, where the defendant is bringing a civil action for wrongful arrest against PC Smith, PC Smith is simply asking the court to accept that the statement was made to him by the store detective (thereby giving him reasonable grounds to suspect that the defendant had committed an arrestable offence) then it will not be hearsay. The court is not being asked to accept the truth of the store detective's statement.

Example 2
D is charged with burglary by entering a dwellinghouse as a trespasser with intent to steal. His defence is that he was simply trying to recover some of his own property in the house. The prosecution wants to call a witness to say:

'The day before the offence D told me that there was some valuable jewellery in the house and that he was going to steal it.'

This will not be hearsay. The court is not being asked to accept the truth of anything said by D (ie that there was some valuable jewellery in the house), merely that he intended to steal. It is relevant only to his state of mind when entering the house.

Example 3

X makes a written statement in D's defence confirming an alibi. X is not available to give evidence. X's written statement will be hearsay as the court is being asked to accept the truth of the statement.

Example 4

D is charged with stealing £300 in cash from the safe at his place of work. The prosecution wishes to put in evidence a ledger compiled by a clerk showing that on the day of the offence £300 was deposited in the safe. The ledger will be hearsay as the court is being asked to accept the truth of the statement made in it, ie that £300 was deposited.

The general rule is that hearsay evidence is not admissible. This exclusionary rule is subject to a number of exceptions. These include:

(1) confessions;
(2) Criminal Justice Act 1988, ss 23, 24 and 30 (see **4.5.4** for s 30);
(3) Criminal Justice Act 1967, s 9;
(4) statements forming part of the res gestae;
(5) Criminal Procedure and Investigations Act 1996, s 68, and Sch 2, paras 1 and 2.

4.6.2 Confessions

A confession includes:

'any statement wholly or partly adverse to the person who made it, whether made to a person in authority or not and whether made in words or otherwise.' (Police and Criminal Evidence Act 1984, s 82(1))

Confessions can be made only by the defendant.

The most common examples of confessions will be admissions of guilt made by a defendant, orally or in writing, when being interviewed by the police. However, a confession can be made to anyone. If a defendant says to a friend, 'I did the burglary at number 10 last night', that would constitute a confession.

As a general rule, confessions are admissible in evidence (but only against the maker – they are inadmissible against anyone else implicated in the confession) as an exception to the rule excluding hearsay evidence. If a defendant says to the police, 'I stole the goods', the interviewing officer will give evidence of the defendant's statement. The court will be asked to accept the truth of that statement. It will be hearsay but admissible as an exception to the general exclusionary rule. Sometimes a confession statement will include statements which are favourable to the defendant.

Example

'I hit the victim in the face' (confession) '… but in self-defence' (favourable to the defence).

These are often referred to as 'mixed statements'. The whole statement is admissible as an exception to the rule excluding hearsay (*R v Sharp (Colin)* (1988) 86 Cr App R 274).

Challenging the admissibility of confessions

Although, as a general principle, confessions are admissible in evidence, by the Police and Criminal Evidence Act 1984, s 76(2)(a), (b):

> 'If in any proceedings where the prosecution proposes to give in evidence a confession made by an accused person, it is represented to the court that the confession was or may have been obtained –
>
> (a) by oppression of the person who made it; or
>
> (b) in consequence of anything said or done which was likely, in the circumstances existing at the time, to render unreliable any confession which might be made by him in consequence thereof,
>
> the court shall not allow the confession to be given in evidence against him except insofar as the prosecution proves to the court beyond reasonable doubt that the confession (notwithstanding that it may be true) was not obtained as aforesaid.'

The magistrates at committal proceedings have no power to exclude confession evidence (Police and Criminal Evidence Act 1984, s 76(9)).

OPPRESSION

Oppression includes 'torture, inhuman or degrading treatment, and the use or threat of violence (whether or not amounting to torture)' (s 76(8)). In *R v Fulling* [1987] 2 WLR 923, the Court of Appeal considered the meaning of oppression (the statutory definition not being intended to be a complete definition). It was held that the word 'oppression' was to be given its ordinary dictionary meaning, ie 'exercise of authority or power in a burdensome, harsh or wrongful manner; unjust or cruel treatment of subjects, inferiors, etc; the imposition of unreasonable or unjust burdens'. Deliberate police misconduct in the form of a serious breach of the Code of Practice or a course of misconduct may constitute oppression.

> *Example*
> D was unlawfully held at the police station, unlawfully denied access to legal advice and questioned about an offence for which he had not been arrested. His confession was excluded on the oppression ground: *R v Davison* [1988] Crim LR 442.

THE 'UNRELIABILITY' GROUND

Under s 76(2)(b) it is necessary to consider:

(1) the thing said or done which is the subject of the application to exclude the confession;

(2) whether that thing said or done is likely to render any confession which might have been made by the defendant unreliable.

The thing said or done will usually involve a breach of the Code of Practice on the Detention, Treatment and Questioning of Suspects. Such breaches may include denial of access to legal advice, inducements to confess and failure to summon an independent adult in cases involving juveniles or mental disorder. However, a breach of the Code will not of itself lead to exclusion of the confession. There must be a causal link between the breach and the unreliability of any confession that might have been made. Thus, if denial of access to legal advice is relied upon, it will be difficult to establish a causal link if the defendant is an experienced criminal who says that he was fully aware of his rights. On the other hand, a young, inexperienced defendant may find it easier to establish the unreliability principle in such circumstances.

It should be noted that, in contrast to oppression, the unreliability ground need not necessarily involve any misconduct on the part of the police.

Example 1

R v Harvey [1988] Crim LR 241: H and her lesbian lover were questioned about a murder. H had a low IQ and was an alcoholic. H's lover, in the presence of H, confessed. H then made a confession exonerating her lover. The lover subsequently died and H was tried for murder, the prosecution relying on her confession. The confession was excluded on the unreliability ground, the court finding that H may well have been trying to protect her lover who had initially confessed in H's presence.

Example 2

R v Trussler (Barry) [1988] Crim LR 446: T, a drug addict, was kept in custody for 18 hours. He was interviewed several times without being given any rest and was denied access to legal advice. His confession was excluded on the unreliability ground.

Example 3

R v Alladice (Colin Carlton) (1988) 87 Cr App R 380: A was denied access to legal advice and confessed to a robbery. When giving evidence, A stated that he knew of his rights and that he understood the caution. A's application to exclude his confession was correctly rejected by the trial judge. Although there had been a serious breach of the Code of Practice, there was nothing to suggest that this might render any confession made by A unreliable.

THE DISCRETION TO EXCLUDE A CONFESSION

If the prosecution fails to discharge the burden of proof imposed by the Police and Criminal Evidence Act 1984, s 76, exclusion of a confession is mandatory. The court also has a general discretion to exclude prosecution evidence under s 78 on the basis that the admission of the evidence will have an adverse effect on the fairness of the proceedings (see **4.2.4**). Again, breaches of the Code of Practice may be the basis of an application under s 78.

In *R v Canale (Ramon Michael)* [1990] 2 All ER 187, the defendant denied making certain statements attributed to him by the police. The interviewing officers had failed to make a contemporaneous note of two of the interviews and had therefore failed to give the defendant a chance to comment on the accuracy of the record of these interviews. The evidence was excluded under s 78 on the basis that its admission would be unfair to the defendant. The court had been deprived of the assistance of contemporaneous notes and had thereby lost the most cogent evidence which would have been available to resolve the conflict of evidence between the parties. As with s 76, a breach of the Code will not lead to automatic exclusion of the confession. If *Canale* had not challenged the accuracy of the officer's evidence, it is difficult to see how the absence of contemporaneous notes could have led to a successful application to exclude under s 78.

The discretion to exclude a confession has also been used where the police have misrepresented the strength of the evidence available to them and have thereby effectively tricked the defendant into confession (*R v Mason* [1988] 1 WLR 139).

THE PROCEDURE FOR CHALLENGING THE ADMISSIBILITY OF A CONFESSION

In the Crown Court, the admissibility of a confession will be determined by the judge, in the absence of the jury, at a 'trial within a trial'. The interviewing officer will give evidence as to how the confession was obtained and the defendant will be given the opportunity of relating his version of events. The judge will then rule on admissibility. If it is ruled to be inadmissible, the confession will not be put to the jury. If it is ruled to be admissible, the interviewing officer will give evidence of it to the jury. It is open to the defence to attack the cogency of the confession in order to persuade the jury to attach no weight to it.

When challenging the admissibility of a confession, the defendant will often allege police misconduct. Since the jury will not be present at the trial within a trial, such allegations will not expose the defendant to cross-examination on any previous convictions under s 1(3)(ii) of the Criminal Evidence Act 1898 (see **4.7.5**) if he later gives evidence to the jury. If, however, the allegations are repeated in front of the jury s 1(3)(ii) will apply.

In the magistrates' court, a ruling as to the admissibility of the confession can be sought when the interviewing officer gives evidence (*R v Liverpool Juvenile Court ex parte R* [1988] QB 1). If the application is made under s 76, the magistrates must hold a 'trial within a trial'. There is no such obligation if the application is made under s 78. If submissions are made under both s 76 and s 78, then both applications should be examined at the same 'trial within a trial' (*Halawa v Federation Against Copyright Theft* [1995] 1 Cr App R 21). Alternatively, the question of admissibility can be left to the end of the trial. Whatever the procedure adopted, it is inevitable that the magistrates will know that a confession has been made. Furthermore, if the defendant makes allegations of police misconduct in challenging the confession, this may expose him to cross-examination on his previous convictions.

The fact that a confession is excluded under s 76 shall not affect the admissibility in evidence of any facts discovered as a result of the confession. However, the prosecution may not call evidence that such facts were discovered as a result of a statement made by the defendant.

> *Example*
> Martin is charged with murder. As a result of statements made by him, the police are able to recover both the murder weapon and the body. If the confession is ruled inadmissible, the jury will hear evidence as to where and when these items were discovered. If his confession is ruled admissible, the jury will, in addition, hear that the defendant was able to say exactly where these items could be found.

If a confession is relevant as showing that the accused speaks, writes or expresses himself in a particular way, so much of the confession as is necessary to show that he does so will be admissible (s 76(4)–(6)).

4.6.3 Criminal Justice Act 1988

First-hand hearsay (s 23)

'(1) ... a statement made by a person in a document shall be admissible in criminal proceedings as evidence of any fact of which direct oral evidence by him would be admissible if –

(i) the requirements of one of the paragraphs of subsection (2) below are satisfied; or

(ii) the requirements of subsection (3) below are satisfied.

(2) The requirements mentioned in subsection (1)(i) above are –

(a) that the person who made the statement is dead or by reason of his bodily or mental condition is unfit to attend as a witness;

(b) that –

(i) the person who made the statement is outside the United Kingdom; and

(ii) it is not reasonably practicable to secure his attendance; or

(c) that all reasonable steps have been taken to find the person who made the statement, but that he cannot be found.

(3) The requirements mentioned in subsection (1)(ii) above are –

(a) that the statement was made to a police officer or some other person charged with the duty of investigating offences or charging offenders; and

(b) that the person who made it does not give oral evidence through fear or because he is kept out of the way.'

The practical effect of this provision is to make first-hand documentary hearsay admissible in evidence (subject to the conditions cited below).

Example 1

Joe witnesses a crime. He makes a statement in writing, relating what he saw.

Joe's statement is first-hand hearsay. Joe is the witness as to fact and he has reduced what he said into writing.

Example 2

Joe witnesses a crime. He tells Jenny what he saw. Jenny makes a statement in writing, relating what Joe told her.

Jenny's statement is multiple hearsay. Joe's evidence has now gone through two stages of reporting.

Multiple hearsay is not covered by s 23.

Example 3

Ann deposits £300 in a safe. She records the deposit in a ledger.

Assuming that the ledger is to be adduced in evidence to prove the truth of the statement in it, ie the deposit of £300, this would be first-hand hearsay. Ann is the witness with first-hand knowledge. The record in the ledger has gone through one stage of reporting.

Under the provisions of s 23, the evidence will be admissible only if there is a prescribed reason for not calling the maker of the statement (Joe in Example 1, Ann in Example 3) to give evidence. The prescribed reason must be established by evidence to the appropriate standard of proof and such evidence must be admissible (*R v Acton Justices ex parte McCullen; R v Tower Bridge Magistrates Court ex parte Lawlor* (1991) 92 Cr App R 98; *R v Mattey (Jimmy Cyril); R v Queeley (Juanita Amelia)* [1995] 2 Cr App R 409).

A statement prepared for use in pending or contemplated criminal proceedings or a criminal investigation will only be admissible with leave of the court. The court should admit the statement if it is in the interests of justice to do so (s 26). Therefore, in Example 1, leave of the court will be required; in Example 3, it will not as the ledger is produced for business purposes rather than for use in criminal proceedings.

The court has a general discretion to exclude a statement otherwise admissible under s 23 (s 25).

A flowchart summarising the admissibility of evidence under s 23 is included as **Appendix 1(G)**.

Hearsay in 'business documents' (s 24)

'(1)   ... a statement in a document shall be admissible in criminal proceedings as evidence of any fact of which direct oral evidence would be admissible, if the following conditions are satisfied –

(i)   the document was created or received by a person in the course of a trade, business, profession or other occupation, or as the holder of a paid or unpaid office; and

(ii)   the information contained in the document was supplied by a person (whether or not the maker of the statement) who had, or may reasonably be supposed to have had, personal knowledge of the matters dealt with.

(2)   Subsection (1) above applies whether the information contained in the document was supplied directly or indirectly but, if it was supplied indirectly, only if each person through whom it was supplied received it –

(a)   in the course of a trade, business, profession or other occupation; or

(b)   as the holder of a paid or unpaid office.'

The practical effect of this provision is to make first-hand and multiple hearsay in certain documents admissible subject to the conditions cited below.

Example 1
Ann deposits £300 in a safe. She tells William, a clerk, who records the deposit in a ledger.

 Ann .... William .... William's statement in ledger

The ledger, if adduced to prove the deposit of £300, will be multiple hearsay. As it is created by William in the course of a business, it is admissible under s 24.

Example 2
Ann deposits £300 in a safe. She tells William, a clerk. William passes on the information to Julian, who records the deposit in a ledger.

 Ann ....William .... Julian .... Julian's statement in ledger

The ledger, if adduced to prove the deposit of £300, will be multiple hearsay. As the information was passed on by William in the course of a business to Julian who, also acting in the course of a business, recorded the deposit in a ledger, it is admissible under s 24.

Example 3

Sarah witnesses a crime. She tells PC Smith what she saw. PC Smith makes a statement setting out what Sarah told him but does not get her to sign it.

Sarah ………………….. PC Smith ………………….. PC Smith's statement

The written statement of PC Smith, if adduced to prove the truth of anything contained in it will be multiple hearsay. As PC Smith made the statement as the holder of a paid office, it is admissible under s 24.

Where the statement has been prepared for use in pending or contemplated criminal proceedings or a criminal investigation, it will be admissible only if:

(1) there is a prescribed reason as stated in s 23 (see above) for not calling the maker of the statement; or

(2) the person who made the statement cannot reasonably be expected (having regard to the time which has elapsed since he made the statement and to all the circumstances) to have any recollection of the matters dealt with in the statement (s 24(4)).

Therefore, in Examples 1 and 2 above, the ledgers will be admissible without a prescribed reason as they were not prepared for use in criminal proceedings or a criminal investigation. In Example 3, a prescribed reason is required for Sarah as the police officer's statement will have been prepared for such purpose.

Where the supplier of the information and the creator of the document are different persons, the maker of the statement is to be taken to be the person who supplied the information (*R v Derodra* [2000] 1 Cr App R 49, CA).

Leave of the court is required to admit a statement prepared for use in pending or contemplated criminal proceedings or a criminal investigation. The court should admit the statement only if it is in the interests of justice to do so (s 26).

The court has a discretion to exclude a statement otherwise admissible under s 24 (s 25).

Leave of the court (s 26)

'26. Where a statement which is admissible in criminal proceedings by virtue of section 23 or 24 above appears to the court to have been prepared … for the purposes –

(a) of pending or contemplated criminal proceedings; or

(b) of a criminal investigation,

the statement shall not be given in evidence in any criminal proceedings without the leave of the court, and the court shall not give leave unless it is of the opinion that the statement ought to be admitted in the interests of justice; and in considering whether its admission would be in the interests of justice, it shall be the duty of the court to have regard –

(i) to the contents of the statement;

(ii)   to any risk, having regard in particular to whether it is likely to be possible to controvert the statement if the person making it does not attend to give oral evidence in the proceedings, that its admission or exclusion will result in unfairness to the accused or, if there is more than one, to any of them; and

(iii) to any other circumstances that appear to the court to be relevant.

This section shall not apply to proceedings before a magistrates' court inquiring into an offence as examining justices.'

The court must consider the risk of unfairness to the accused (s 25(2)(d) and s 26) and also any unfairness to the prosecution if the evidence is admitted (ie in terms of the result of the trial rather than the prosecution as a party to the proceedings) (*R v W* [1997] Crim LR 678).

In *R v Cole* [1990] 1 WLR 865, the Court of Appeal held that the court shall take into account:

(a)   the availability for cross-examination of prosecution witnesses;

(b)   the availability of witnesses for the defence; and

(c)   the availability of the defendant himself to give evidence in support of any defence raised,

in deciding whether it is likely to be possible to controvert the statement.

Discretion to exclude (s 25)

'25. (1)   If, having regard to all the circumstances [the court] is of the opinion that in the interests of justice a statement which is admissible by virtue of section 23 or 24 above never the less ought not to be admitted, it may direct that the statement shall not be admitted.

(2)   … it shall be the duty of the court to have regard –

(a)   to the nature and source of the document containing the statement and to whether or not, having regard to its nature and source and to any other circumstances that appear to the court to be relevant, it is likely that the document is authentic;

(b)   to the extent to which the statement appears to supply evidence which would otherwise not be readily available;

(c)   to the relevance of the evidence that it appears to supply to any issue which is likely to have to be determined in the proceedings; and

(d)   to any risk, having regard in particular to whether it is likely to be possible to controvert the statement if the person making it does not attend to give oral evidence in the proceedings, that its admission or exclusion will result in unfairness to the accused or, if there is more than one, to any of them.'

A flowchart summarising the admissibility under s 24 is included as **Appendix 1(H)**.

Summary

The two main types of evidence likely to be adduced under the provisions of ss 23 and 24 are:

• witness statements; and
• 'business documents'.

WITNESS STATEMENTS

If a statement is first-hand hearsay, it is admissible under s 23. A prescribed reason will be required for not calling the maker of the statement and leave of the court will be required.

If a statement is multiple hearsay it can only be admitted under s 24. It will be necessary:

- to show that it was created or received by a person in the course of a trade, business, profession, etc;
- to identify the witness with personal knowledge of the matters dealt with in the statement;
- to show a prescribed reason for not calling the maker of the statement;
- to obtain leave of the court.

'BUSINESS DOCUMENTS'

These will not usually have been made in anticipation of litigation. They will have been created for use in a business.

Business documents are best admitted under s 24 (whether first-hand or multiple hearsay) as:

- no prescribed reason is required for not calling the maker of the statement in the document; and
- leave of the court will not be required.

4.6.4 Criminal Justice Act 1967, s 9(1), (2)

'(1) In any criminal proceedings, other than committal proceedings, a written statement by any person shall, if such of the conditions mentioned in the next following subsection as are applicable are satisfied, be admissible as evidence to the like extent as oral evidence to the like effect by that person.

(2) The said conditions are –

(a) the statement purports to be signed by the person who made it;

(b) the statement contains a declaration by that person to the effect that it is true to the best of his knowledge and belief and that he made the statement knowing that if it were tendered in evidence, he would be liable to prosecution if he wilfully stated in it anything which he knew to be false or did not believe to be true;

(c) before the hearing at which the statement is tendered in evidence, a copy of the statement is served, by or on behalf of the party proposing to tender it, on each of the parties to the proceedings; and

(d) none of the other parties or their solicitors, within seven days from the service of the copy of the statement, serves a notice on the party so proposing objecting to the statement being tendered in evidence under this section.'

An example of the correct form of a s 9 statement is included as **Appendix 2(N)**.

In practice, the use of s 9 statements should largely be confined to evidence which is not in dispute.

4.6.5 Criminal Procedure and Investigations Act 1996, s 68 and Sch 2, paras 1 and 2

'68 Use of written statements and depositions at trial

Schedule 2 to this Act (which relates to the use at the trial of written statements and depositions admitted in evidence in committal proceedings) shall have effect.'

'SCHEDULE 2

STATEMENTS AND DEPOSITIONS

Statements

1. (1) Sub-paragraph (2) applies if –

    (a)   a written statement has been admitted in evidence in proceedings before a magistrates' court inquiring into an offence as examining justices,

    (b)   in those proceedings a person has been committed for trial,

    (c)   for the purposes of section 5A of the Magistrates' Courts Act 1980 the statement complied with section 5B of that Act prior to the committal for trial,

    (d)   the statement purports to be signed by a justice of the peace, and

    (e)   sub-paragraph (3) does not prevent sub-paragraph (2) applying.

(2)   Where this sub-paragraph applies the statement may without further proof be read as evidence on the trial of the accused, whether for the offence for which he was committed for trial or for any other offence arising out of the same transaction or set of circumstances.

(3)   Sub-paragraph (2) does not apply if –

    (a)   it is proved that the statement was not signed by the justice by whom it purports to have been signed,

    (b)   the court of trial at its discretion orders that sub-paragraph (2) shall not apply, or

    (c)   a party to the proceedings objects to sub-paragraph (2) applying.

(4)   If a party to the proceedings objects to sub-paragraph (2) applying the court of trial may order that the objection shall have no effect if the court considers it to be in the interests of justice so to order.

Depositions

2. (1) Sub-paragraph (2) applies if –

    (a)   in pursuance of section 97A of the Magistrates' Courts Act 1980 (summons or warrant to have evidence taken as a deposition etc) a person has had his evidence taken as a deposition for the purposes of proceedings before a magistrates' court inquiring into an offence as examining justices,

    (b)   the deposition has been admitted in evidence in those proceedings,

    (c)   in those proceedings a person has been committed for trial,

    (d)   for the purposes of section 5A of the Magistrates' Courts Act 1980 the deposition complied with section 5C of that Act prior to the committal for trial,

    (e)   the deposition purports to be signed by the justice before whom it purports to have been taken, and

    (f)   sub-paragraph (3) does not prevent sub-paragraph (2) applying.

(2) Where this sub-paragraph applies the deposition may without further proof be read as evidence on the trial of the accused, whether for the offence for which he was committed for trial or for any other offence arising out of the same transaction or set of circumstances.

(3) Sub-paragraph (2) does not apply if –

    (a) it is proved that the deposition was not signed by the justice by whom it purports to have been signed,

    (b) the court of trial at its discretion orders that sub-paragraph (2) shall not apply, or

    (c) a party to the proceedings objects to sub-paragraph (2) applying.

(4) If a party to the proceedings objects to sub-paragraph (2) applying the court of trial may order that the objection shall have no effect if the court considers it to be in the interests of justice so to order.'

Written statements and depositions which have been admitted as evidence in committal proceedings (see Chapter 7) can be read at the trial in the Crown Court. These written statements and depositions will have been tendered by the prosecution only. This provision allows for written statements or depositions to be admitted at the Crown Court trial where all parties agree.

It is not, however, limited to cases where the parties agree. If the court considers it to be in the interests of justice, the court may order that the written statement or deposition be read at the trial.

4.6.6 Res gestae

The principles of admissibility of a statement under the res gestae principle are discussed at **4.5.3**. Such statements are admissible as an exception to the rule against hearsay evidence.

4.7 THE DEFENDANT

This paragraph deals with rules of evidence which are of particular application to the defendant.

4.7.1 Competence and compellability

The defendant as a prosecution witness

A defendant is not competent as a prosecution witness. Thus, if two defendants are jointly charged the prosecution cannot call one as a witness against the other unless he has pleaded guilty or is tried separately from the other defendant (*R v Richardson* (1967) 51 Cr App R 381). This means that at Stage A of the trial (see **4.1**) a defendant cannot be called to give evidence unless he pleads guilty or is tried separately.

The defendant as a defence witness

A defendant is a competent defence witness but is not compellable (Criminal Evidence Act 1898, s 1(1)).

If a defendant does give evidence then he must be called before any other witnesses for the defence, unless the court 'otherwise directs' (Police and Criminal Evidence Act 1984, s 79).

If a defendant gives evidence in his own defence and in so doing implicates a co-defendant then this is admissible evidence against that co-defendant.

If the defendant does not give evidence he is likely to be subject to the provisions of s 35 of the Criminal Justice and Public Order Act 1994.

Section 35 – failure of defendant to give evidence

'(1) At the trial of any person for an offence, subsections (2) and (3) below apply unless –

    (a) the accused's guilt is not in issue; or

    (b) it appears to the court that the physical or mental condition of the accused makes it undesirable for him to give evidence.

(2) … the court shall at the conclusion of the evidence for the prosecution, satisfy itself (in the case of proceedings on indictment, in the presence of the jury) that the accused is aware that the stage has been reached at which evidence can be given for the defence and that he can, if he wishes, give evidence and that, if he chooses not to give evidence, or having been sworn, without good cause refuses to answer any question, it will be permissible for the court or jury to draw such inferences as appear proper from his failure to give evidence or his refusal, without good cause, to answer any question.

(3) … the court or jury, in determining whether the accused is guilty of the offence charged, may draw such inferences as appear proper from the failure of the accused to give evidence or his refusal, without good cause, to answer any question.'

Thus, if the prosecution evidence has raised issues which call for an explanation from the defendant and he fails to give evidence, a court will be entitled to infer guilt from that failure.

In *R v Cowan (Donald); R v Gayle (Ricky); R v Ricciardi (Carmine)* [1995] 4 All ER 939, the Court of Appeal considered how the judge should direct the jury. It was essential that it should be made clear to the jury that:

(1) the burden of proof remained on the prosecution throughout;

(2) the defendant was entitled to remain silent;

(3) before drawing an adverse inference from the defendant's silence, they had to be satisfied that there was a case to answer on the prosecution evidence;

(4) an adverse inference from failure to give evidence cannot on its own prove guilt;

(5) no adverse inference could be drawn unless the only sensible explanation for the defendant's silence was that he had no answer to the case against him, or none that could have stood up to cross-examination.

The procedure to be adopted in relation to s 35 is found in the *Practice Direction (Crown Court: Defendant's Evidence)* [1995] 2 All ER 499.

The defendant's spouse as a prosecution witness

A spouse is competent to give evidence for the prosecution. The spouse is not compellable except in certain specified cases (eg where the offence involved an assault on that spouse or it was an assault or sexual offence on a person under 16) (Police and Criminal Evidence Act 1984, s 80).

This rule does not apply to a witness who has been, but is no longer, married to the defendant (s 80(5)).

The defendant's spouse as a defence witness

The defendant's spouse is always competent to give evidence on behalf of the defendant and a co-defendant.

The defendant's spouse is compellable to give evidence for the defendant.

4.7.2 Evidence of the character of the defendant

A defendant can adduce evidence of his own good character. This may be done by asking questions of a prosecution witness to establish the defendant's good character, or by the defendant's own oral evidence, or by calling character witnesses. If a defendant is of good character, this is relevant to his credibility as a witness and it may be relevant to show an absence of propensity to commit the type of offence charged.

As a general rule, the prosecution cannot adduce evidence of a defendant's bad character and convictions. This common law prohibition prevents evidence of bad character from being adduced as part of the prosecution evidence. It is not to be confused with the separate statutory provisions (which are dealt with later) governing the cross-examination of a defendant on his convictions.

There are a number of exceptions to this rule. They include:

(1) rebutting an assertion of good character;
(2) similar fact evidence.

4.7.3 Rebutting an assertion of good character

If the defence has adduced evidence of the defendant's good character (by asking questions of a prosecution witness to establish the defendant's good character, or by the defendant's own oral evidence, or by calling character witnesses), the prosecution may adduce evidence in rebuttal. The prosecution may, with leave of the court, reopen its case at the conclusion of the defence case and adduce its own evidence of the defendant's convictions.

4.7.4 Similar fact evidence

This topic is dealt with in outline only.

As a general rule, the prosecution cannot adduce evidence of the previous behaviour of the defendant if the purpose in so doing is simply to show a disposition to commit offences similar to the offence being tried. For example, if the defendant is on trial for theft by way of shoplifting, evidence cannot usually be adduced of the fact that the defendant has committed this kind of offence before.

Problems can arise when the prosecution seeks to adduce evidence of the defendant's behaviour on other occasions for some reason other than to show a general disposition to commit the offence in question. It should be noted that it is the conduct behind the offence which is relevant, not the fact of a criminal conviction.

In *R v Lunt* (1987) 85 Cr App R 241, the Court of Appeal laid down guidelines for the correct approach to 'similar fact' evidence as follows.

(1) 'Similar fact' evidence will be admissible only if it goes beyond showing a 'tendency to commit the crime charged' and is 'positively probative' of an issue in the case.

(2) In determining the admissibility of 'similar fact' evidence, it is first necessary to identify the issue in the case to which the evidence is directed and then to decide whether or not it is positively probative of that issue and does more than simply reveal the defendant's bad character.

In *R v Lunt*, it was stressed that examples of properly admitted similar fact evidence will be rare.

The essential feature is that the probative force of the evidence 'is sufficiently great to make it just to admit the evidence, notwithstanding that it is prejudicial to the accused in tending to show that he was guilty of another crime' (*Director of Public Prosecutions v P (A Father)* [1991] 3 All ER 337, HL).

Examples of issues to which similar fact evidence may be relevant include the following.

Identification

In *R v Straffen* [1952] 2 QB 911, the defendant, who had escaped from Broadmoor, was accused of strangling a girl. Evidence was admitted of the fact that the defendant had strangled two other girls and that the features of the two previous crimes were very similar to the offence charged. Because of this, the 'similar fact' evidence was admitted, not to show that the defendant had a disposition to commit murder but because the features of the cases provided a very strong indication that the defendant was guilty of the offence charged.

Plausibility of the defendant's explanation

In *R v Smith* (1915) 11 Cr App R 229, the defendant was charged with murdering his wife who was found drowned in a bath. Smith had insured her life for a large amount of money. His defence was that his wife had died of natural causes. Evidence was admitted to show that Smith had 'married' two other women and that they too had been found dead in their bath with Smith due to gain from their life assurance policies. As in *Straffen*, the evidence was not admitted to show that Smith had a disposition to commit murder. Its probative force was directed at the plausibility of the defence.

4.7.5 Cross-examining the defendant

Criminal Evidence Act 1898, s 1

'(1) A person charged in criminal proceedings shall not be called as a witness in the proceedings except on his own application.

(2) A person charged in criminal proceedings who is called as a witness in the proceedings may be asked any question in cross-examination notwithstanding

that it would tend to criminate him as to any offence with which he is charged in the proceedings.'

A defendant is not obliged to give evidence. If he chooses to do so then he is liable to be cross-examined in the same way as any other witness. This includes cross-examination on any previous inconsistent statement that may have been made.

Criminal Evidence Act 1898, s 1(3)

'A person charged in criminal proceedings who is called as a witness in the proceedings shall not be asked, and if asked shall not be required to answer, any question tending to show that he has committed or been convicted of or been charged with any offence other than one with which he is then charged, or is of bad character unless –

(i) the proof that he has committed or been convicted of such other offence is admissible evidence to show that he is guilty of an offence with which he is then charged; or

(ii) he has personally or by his advocate asked questions of the witnesses for the prosecution with a view to establish his own good character, or has given evidence of his good character, or the nature or conduct of the defence is such as to involve imputations on the character of the prosecutor, the deceased victim of the alleged crime or the witnesses for the prosecution; or

(iii) he has given evidence against any other person charged in the same proceedings.'

SECTION 1(3)(i)

Section 1(3)(i) enables the prosecution to cross-examine the defendant on the facts behind previous criminal conduct to help prove the offence charged. It is rarely relied on in practice but if it is used it is likely to be in 'similar fact evidence cases'. Before relying on s 1(3)(i) the prosecution must have called evidence of the similar facts as part of its case. If such evidence has been called then the defendant can be cross-examined on those offences if he gives evidence.

SECTION 1(3)(ii)

Section 1(3)(ii) provides:

'He has personally or by his advocate asked questions of the witnesses for the prosecution with a view to establish his own good character, or has given evidence of his good character.'

This provision is largely self-explanatory. If a defendant, while testifying, has put evidence before the court that he is of good character then the prosecution is allowed to cross-examine the defendant on his previous convictions. Such cross-examination is limited to the court, date of conviction and the nature of the conviction. The facts of the previous conviction should not be referred to as they are not relevant. The object of the cross-examination is to rebut the untrue assertion of good character.

Character is indivisible. This means that, if the defendant gives evidence about one aspect of his character, that will allow the prosecution to examine him on other aspects.

Example

Joe is charged with assault. He says in evidence that he is a mild and peace-loving man. This is evidence of good character. The prosecution is permitted to cross-examine Joe about past convictions for dishonesty.

There is obviously an overlap between the common law provisions (see **4.7.3**) and s 1(3)(ii). Two examples will serve to illustrate the point.

Example 1

Alan is on trial for theft. He does not give evidence himself. However, he calls a character witness.

Here, the prosecution will have to call rebutting evidence. The prosecution cannot rely on s 1(3)(ii) as the defendant has not gone into the witness-box to give evidence. Therefore, he cannot be cross-examined.

Example 2

John is charged with an assault occasioning actual bodily harm. He gives evidence of his own good character.

Here, the prosecution could call rebutting evidence but, it will not normally be necessary. John is in the witness-box. He has given evidence-in-chief and can therefore be cross-examined. By giving evidence of his own good character he has lost the basic s 1(3) protection and can therefore be cross-examined on his previous convictions.

Section 1(3)(ii) also provides:

> 'the nature or conduct of the defence is such as to involve imputations on the character of the prosecutor, the deceased victim of the alleged crime or the witnesses for the prosecution.'

This may arise when prosecution witnesses are being cross-examined or when the defendant gives evidence. For example, the defendant may:

(1)   allege that a prosecution witness is biased; or
(2)   allege that police witnesses are fabricating evidence; or
(3)   cross-examine prosecution witnesses on their previous criminal convictions.

If the judge or magistrates find that the attack on the character of a prosecution witness comes within s 1(3)(ii) then the defendant can be cross-examined on his previous convictions.

In *R v Taylor (Nicholas Jones); R v Goodman (Donald Walter)* [1999] Crim LR 407, the Court of Appeal provided guidance on the procedure to be adopted when an accomplice gives evidence for the Crown. An accomplice is a participant in the crime alleged.

Example

John and Warren are jointly charged with an assault occasioning actual bodily harm. Both have previous convictions. John pleads guilty and is now competent and compellable to give evidence for the prosecution at Warren's trial.

At Warren's trial, unless there is a specific request from the defence to refrain, the prosecution ought to read out John's convictions at the beginning of the trial.

If the defence then proceed to cross-examine John on his previous convictions, such a cross-examination would not lead to the loss of Warren's shield under s 1(3)(ii) of the Criminal Evidence Act 1898. This is probably on the basis that nothing new has been revealed to the jury by cross-examining on such admitted facts. However, if the defence goes further and alleges that John has a grudge against Warren or accuses John of fabricating evidence, then the defence has cast imputations on the character of a prosecution witness. The prosecution can then apply to the court for leave to cross-examine Warren on his previous convictions.

Such cross-examination may include the court, date of conviction and the nature of conviction. In *R v McLeod* [1995] 1 Cr App R 591, CA, the court said that similarities in previous defences, rejected by juries in the past (eg an alibi defence) and whether or not the defendant pleaded guilty or not guilty or was disbelieved on oath were also proper matters for cross-examination. The object of cross-examination is to show the court the type of person making the attack on the character of a prosecution witness, that is to say, it is relevant only to the credibility of the defendant as a witness. Hence, previous convictions for offences of dishonesty are, in principle, more damaging than offences of violence (even if the present charge is for an offence of violence).

If cross-examination under this section is permitted, the jury or magistrates should be told that they should not infer guilt from the fact that the defendant is of bad character and that the convictions are relevant only to the credibility of the defendant as a witness.

SECTION 1(3)(iii)

Section 1(3)(iii) provides:

> '[the defendant] has given evidence against any other person charged in the same proceedings.'

This provision will arise where two defendants are on trial together. One defendant, in giving evidence in his own defence, may implicate the other. This may be either through a direct accusation of guilt of the co-defendant or may be evidence that undermines the co-defendant's defence.

The co-defendant is permitted to cross-examine the defendant giving evidence on his previous convictions. If the co-defendant chooses not to exercise this right then the prosecution may do so instead. Cross-examination under s 1(3)(iii) is subject to the same limitations as s 1(3)(ii) and the convictions are again relevant only to the credibility of the defendant as a witness.

THE DISCRETION TO PREVENT CROSS-EXAMINATION

Even if the prosecution can show that cross-examination under s 1(3) is permissible, the judge or magistrates can exercise a discretion to prevent cross-examination of the defendant on his previous convictions (*Selvey v DPP* [1970] AC 304 and the Police and Criminal Evidence Act 1984, s 78).

The use of questioning under s (1)(3)(ii) was considered by the Court of Appeal in *R v McLeod* [1995] 1 Cr App R 591.

(1) The judge has to weigh the prejudicial effect of the questions put to the defendant against the damage done by the attack on the prosecution's witnesses

and has to exercise his discretion so as to secure a fair trial for both the prosecution and defence.

(2)   In the Court of Appeal, it is not enough that the court thinks it would have exercised its discretion differently. It will only interfere with the trial judge's decision if the judge erred in principle or if there was no material on which he could have properly arrived at his decision.

(3)   The primary purpose of cross-examination on previous convictions and on the bad character of the defendant is to show that he is not worthy of belief. It is not, and should not be, to show he has a predisposition to commit the type of offence with which he is charged. However, the mere fact that the previous offences were of a similar type to that charged and may suggest a tendency to commit the offence charged will not make the questioning improper.

(4)   Prolonged cross-examination on previous offences is undesirable. Unless admissible as similar fact evidence, the prosecution should not seek to emphasise similarities between the previous offences and the present offence.

(5)   Similarities of defences rejected by the court on previous occasions could be legitimate questions if they were central to credibility, for example false alibis, a defence that an incriminating substance had been planted, and whether or not the defendant pleaded guilty or was disbelieved having given evidence on oath.

(6)   If the underlying facts show a particularly bad character, the judge should balance the gravity of the attack on the prosecution against the prejudice to the defendant resulting from the disclosure of the facts.

(7)   Objection to a particular line of questioning about underlying facts should be taken early, as this will not normally be a ground for discharging a jury. While it is the judge's duty to keep cross-examination within proper bounds, it will be difficult to contend that there has been an improper exercise of discretion if no objection is taken at the time.

(8)   In every case where the defendant has been cross-examined as to character and convictions, the judge should, in summing up, tell the jury that the purpose of the questioning goes only to credit and that they should not consider that it showed a propensity to commit the offence they were considering.

There is no discretion to prevent cross-examination of one defendant by a co-defendant under s 1(3)(iii) (*Murdoch v Taylor* [1965] AC 574).

Spent convictions

The Rehabilitation of Offenders Act 1974 provides that after a prescribed period of time certain convictions are spent. This means that the convicted person is to be treated as never having been convicted of the spent offence.

The rehabilitation periods vary with the sentence:

Absolute discharge	6 months
Conditional discharge	1 year or period of order if longer
Attendance centre order	1 year after expiry of order
Fine or community sentence	5 years
Custodial sentence of up to 6 months	7 years
Custodial sentence of between 6 and 30 months	10 years

A conviction for an offence which was punished by a custodial sentence exceeding 30 months cannot become spent.

The Act does not apply to evidence admitted in criminal proceedings. Instead, the matter is governed by a Practice Direction issued in 1975. This provides that a spent conviction should be referred to only if it is in the interests of justice to do so. Guidance on the interpretation of the Practice Direction can be found in *R v Nye (Colin Edward)* (1982) 75 Cr App R 247. If a defendant has convictions which are not spent, it will usually be unnecessary to refer to spent convictions. If a defendant has previous convictions which are spent, he may, with the leave of the court, be entitled to put himself forward as a person of previous good character (*R v Bailey* [1989] Crim LR 723).

4.8 FURTHER READING

Textbooks dealing with the general principles of criminal evidence include:

Peter Murphy *Murphy on Evidence* (Blackstone Press, 2000);

Adrian Keane *The Modern Law of Evidence* (Butterworths, 2000);

Richard May *Criminal Evidence* (Sweet & Maxwell, 1999).

Chapter 5

SUMMARY TRIAL

5.1 INTRODUCTION

Magistrates must try a summary offence and have power to try an either way offence with the defendant's consent. This chapter distinguishes the right to advance information of the prosecution case from the rules relating to disclosure of unused material by the prosecution. It examines the statutory scheme for prosecution disclosure of unused material and possible defence disclosure where the defendant pleads not guilty in the magistrates' court. It explains what happens at a pre-trial review and also gives an outline of the procedure followed at a trial in the magistrates' court. The procedure on a plea of guilty in the magistrates' court is examined separately in Chapter 9, 'Sentencing'.

5.2 DISCLOSURE

5.2.1 Duty to provide advance information

This is the obligation on the prosecution to notify the defence of its case, ie the evidence upon which it intends to rely at trial.

The Magistrates' Courts (Advance Information) Rules 1985, SI 1985/601, provide that if the defendant is charged with an offence triable either way, the prosecution must provide the defence either with copies of the prosecution witnesses' written statements or with a summary of the facts and matters about which evidence will be adduced during the course of the prosecution.

For summary only offences, the defence has no legal right to know the prosecution case prior to trial (*R v Kingston upon Hull Justices ex parte McCann* (1991) 155 JP 569) although the defence should still request it. Increasingly, it is CPS practice voluntarily to give advance information.

5.2.2 Duty to disclose 'unused material'

This is the obligation on the prosecution under the Criminal Procedure and Investigations Act 1996 to make available to the defence any material of relevance to the case upon which it does not intend to rely – 'unused material'. It applies when the defendant pleads not guilty in the magistrates' court.

In order for disclosure of such prosecution 'unused material' to be effective, proper procedures must be followed during the investigation so that information, documents and objects are properly recorded and retained. These procedures are set out in the Criminal Procedure and Investigations Act 1996 Code of Practice (the Code).

The Code provides that all material which is obtained in a criminal investigation and which may be relevant to the investigation is retained and revealed to the prosecutor.

The Code is admissible in evidence in all criminal and civil proceedings, and if a court considers that any provision of the Code or any breach of the Code is relevant to any question arising in the proceedings, the court must take that into account when deciding the question (s 26(3), (4)).

The scheme for disclosure where the defendant pleads not guilty in summary trial is described below and a diagram illustrating it appears as **Appendix 1(I)**.

5.2.3 Primary disclosure by the prosecution (s 3)

This applies where the defendant pleads not guilty in the magistrates' court.

In such a case the prosecutor must either:

- disclose to the defence any previous undisclosed prosecution material which the prosecutor considers might undermine the prosecution case; or
- confirm in writing that there is no such material.

Time-limit (ss 12 and 13)

The prosecution must make disclosure as soon as is reasonably practicable after the defendant pleads not guilty in the magistrates' court.

> *Example*
> D is charged with theft. He intends to plead not guilty. Prior to the mode of trial proceedings the prosecution serves the defence with advance disclosure of the prosecution case under the Magistrates' Court (Advanced Information) Rules 1985. At plea before venue, D pleads not guilty. At mode of trial, the magistrates accept jurisdiction and D consents to summary trial. The prosecution must make primary disclosure to the defence of material it does not wish to rely on (unused material) as soon as practicable.

When the prosecutor makes primary disclosure, the prosecutor should send the defendant a notice setting out his rights and duties (Home Office Circular 11/1997, 'Criminal Procedure and Investigations Act 1996', paras 12 and 13). A copy of the notice of rights and duties appears as **Appendix 2(O)**.

Examples of matters which may fall under the duty of primary disclosure

Some examples of undermining material are found in para 7.3 of the Code:

- records of the first description of a suspect given to the police by a potential witness, whether or not the description differs from that of the alleged offender;
- information provided by an accused person which indicates an explanation for the offence with which he has been charged;
- any material casting doubt on the reliability of a confession;
- any material casting doubt on the reliability of a witness;
- any other material which the investigator believes may fall within the test for primary prosecution disclosure in the Act.

Other examples of undermining material were given in the White Paper *Disclosure* (Cm 2864).

- If part of the prosecution case is a statement by a witness that he saw the defendant near the scene of the crime shortly after it was committed, it will be necessary to disclose a statement by another witness that he saw a person of a different description from the defendant at the same time and place.

- If the defendant has told the police in an interview that he was acting in self-defence, it will be necessary to disclose the statement of any witness who supports this but whom the prosecution does not regard as truthful.
- If the victim died of a hammer blow and part of the prosecution case is a forensic test showing that the blood stains on a hammer found buried in the accused's back garden matched those of the victim, it will be necessary to disclose a negative test showing that the fingerprints on the hammer did not match those of the accused.
- If the prosecution is aware that its main witness has a previous conviction, it must disclose it to the defence, since it may affect the weight to be placed on his testimony.
- If the prosecution is in possession of a psychiatric report showing that its main witness has a history of psychiatric disorder with a tendency to fantasise, it should disclose the report since it clearly undermines the credibility of that witness.
- If the prosecution is aware that a prosecution witness has applied for a reward for information leading to the conviction of a person for a criminal offence, it must disclose this to the defence.
- If previous versions of witness statements are inconsistent with the final version served on the defence, they must be disclosed.

Further examples are noted by Ede and Shepherd in their book *Active Defence* (The Law Society, 2000):

- the fact of a witness having been hypnotised;
- the fact of a witness having been coached or rehearsed for a TV programme;
- the fact of a payment to a witness other than as a reward.

5.2.4 Defence disclosure (ss 5 and 6)

Where the defendant pleads not guilty at summary trial, once the prosecution has made primary disclosure the defendant may give a 'defence statement' if he wishes but he has no duty to do so.

The defence statement must be in writing, and must:

- set out in general terms the nature of the defendant's defence;
- indicate the matters on which the defendant takes issue with the prosecution; and
- set out, in the case of each such matter, the reason why the defendant takes issue with the prosecution.

If the 'defence statement' discloses an alibi, the defendant must give particulars of it, including:

- names and addresses of witnesses who the defendant believes are able to give evidence in support of the alibi (includes evidence of alibi given by the defendant himself);
- any information which might help in finding an alibi witness whose name and address is not known to the defendant.

Evidence in support of an alibi is 'evidence tending to show that by reason of the presence of the accused at a particular place or in a particular area at a particular time he was not, or was unlikely to have been, at the place where the offence is alleged to have been committed at the time of its alleged commission'.

If the defendant chooses not to give a statement, the prosecution has no duty of secondary disclosure (see **5.2.3**).

Time-limit

If the defendant chooses to give a statement it must be given to the prosecution and the court within 14 days of the prosecutor complying, or purporting to comply, with the obligation to provide primary prosecution disclosure (Criminal Procedure and Investigations Act 1996 (Defence Disclosure Time Limits) Regulations 1997, reg 2).

The period for making defence disclosure may be extended by as many days as the court specifies, but only if an application is made before the expiration of the relevant period (reg 3(2)).

An application for extension of the period must:

(a) state that the defendant believes, on reasonable grounds, that it is not possible to give a defence statement during the relevant period;

(b) specify the grounds for so believing; and

(c) specify the number of days by which the defendant wishes the period to be extended (reg 3(3)).

There is no limit on the number of applications that may be made, but in each case, the court may grant an extension only if satisfied that the defendant cannot reasonably give a defence statement within the relevant period (reg 4(2), (3)).

5.2.5 Secondary disclosure by the prosecution (s 7)

If the defendant provides a defence statement, the prosecution must either:

(a) disclose to the defence any previously undisclosed prosecution material which might be reasonably expected to assist in the defendant's defence as revealed by the defence statement; or

(b) confirm in writing that there is no such material.

Example

D is charged with theft. The prosecution allege that the offence took place at about 11 pm on a Saturday evening. D says nothing when interviewed by the police but the defence later send to the prosecution a 'defence statement' claiming that D has an alibi: D left his flat at 7 pm that evening to visit a friend and did not return until 3 am on the following morning. The prosecution has evidence that D was seen entering his flat at 3 am on the Sunday morning but not that he was seen leaving it earlier in the evening. The prosecution are under an obligation to disclose the evidence that D was seen entering his flat at 3 am.

Time-limit (ss 12 and 13)

The prosecution must make secondary disclosure as soon as practicable after the defendant gives a defence statement.

5.2.6 Public interest immunity

Certain material must not be disclosed to the defendant.

The most important example of this is where a court, on the application of the prosecution, has ruled that it is not in the public interest to disclose it. Such an application is likely to be on the basis that the material in question falls within one of the categories of 'sensitive' material.

Some examples of 'sensitive' material are found in para 6.12 of the Code:

- material relating to national security;
- material given in confidence;
- material relating to informants, undercover police officers, premises used for police surveillance;
- techniques used in the detection of crime;
- material relating to a child witness (eg material generated by a local authority social services department).

5.2.7 Application to court for disclosure (s 8)

If at any time:

- the defendant has given a defence statement; and
- the prosecution has complied with or failed to comply with secondary disclosure; and
- the defendant has reasonable cause to believe that there is undisclosed prosecution material which might reasonably be expected to assist in his defence,

the defendant can apply to the court for an order requiring the prosecution to disclose that material.

5.2.8 The prosecution's continuing duty of disclosure (s 9)

The prosecution has a continuing duty after primary disclosure and until the defendant is acquitted or convicted to disclose relevant material to the defendant as soon as is reasonably practicable.

5.2.9 Consequences of failure to comply with disclosure requirements (ss 10 and 11)

(a) By the prosecution

If the prosecution fails to comply with the time-limit for disclosure and, because of the delay, D is denied a fair trial, this could constitute grounds for staying the proceedings for abuse of process.

(b) By the defendant

If the defendant gives a defence statement but:

- does not comply with the time-limit for doing so; or
- sets out inconsistent defences in the statement; or
- puts forward a defence at trial which is different from a defence in the statement; or

- adduces alibi evidence at trial without giving adequate details of the alibi or alibi witnesses in the statement,

the court, or, with leave, any other party, may make such comments as appear appropriate; and the court may draw such inferences as appear proper when deciding whether D is guilty.

If the defendant has put forward a defence at trial which is different from a defence in the defence statement, the court must look at the extent of the difference and whether there is any justification for it, before commenting, granting leave to comment, or drawing an inference.

> *Example*
> D is charged with burglary and pleads not guilty. The prosecution makes primary disclosure. D's defence statement indicates a defence of alibi and names X as an alibi witness. At his trial D wishes to call three witnesses X, Y and Z to support his alibi. As no reference was made to Y or Z in his defence statement, by name or otherwise, the court, or, with leave, the prosecution, may comment on this and the court may draw such inferences as appear proper.

The defendant cannot be convicted solely on an inference drawn from his failure to comply with the disclosure provisions.

5.3 PREPARING THE CASE FOR TRIAL

In preparing a case for trial by magistrates, the following steps should be considered.

5.3.1 Interviewing the client

Although outline instructions may have been taken at the police station or to enable a bail application or application for a representation order to be made, detailed instructions must now be taken from the defendant. A pro forma can be used to confirm the formal part of instructions such as name, address, date of birth, family details, etc, but a detailed statement will have to be taken as regards the offence. The solicitor should not be afraid to challenge the client's story in interview as it will most certainly be challenged by the prosecution at the trial.

If advance disclosure of the prosecution case has been given (as it must be with an either way offence, see **6.2**), the statement should also include comments on the prosecution evidence. The statement should be signed and dated by the client.

5.3.2 Interviewing witnesses

The defendant will have provided the names and addresses of relevant witnesses. Witnesses should be interviewed as soon as possible and a full proof of evidence taken from them. Again, when interviewing witnesses, the solicitor should not be afraid to challenge what they say. It is important that inconsistencies be ironed out or explained at this stage rather than in court. The witness's proof of evidence should be signed by the witness and dated.

5.3.3 Writing to the prosecution

A pro forma letter can be sent to the prosecution requesting such of the following information as is appropriate to the case.

(1) In either way offences, advance disclosure of the prosecution case (see **6.2**). There is no right to advance disclosure if the offence is summary only. However, a request for voluntary disclosure in such cases may be looked upon favourably.

(2) Details of the defendant's criminal record. Although details will have been taken from the client, this cannot be relied upon. The prosecution will supply a copy of the record that it will be relying upon in court. This record should be checked against the information given by the client and any inconsistencies cleared up as soon as possible.

(3) A record of any interviews with the defendant.

(4) A copy of the custody record. In some areas the custody record is available directly from the police, but the initial approach may be to the CPS.

5.3.4 Location

If the location of the crime is important to the defence, a visit to the relevant scene should be made and plans and photographs prepared. This action may be necessary, for example, in road traffic cases and in cases where the defendant alleges that a prosecution witness, because of his position, could not possibly have seen the events which he alleges he has seen.

5.3.5 Expert evidence

If expert evidence is necessary, an expert should be instructed at the earliest possible opportunity to prepare a report. Expert evidence may be required on any technical matter that is outside the competence of the magistrates. Expert evidence should be disclosed to the prosecution before the trial. If the defendant is represented under representation order, it is prudent to seek prior authority from the Legal Services Commission Regional Office before instructing the expert. Prior authority is sought by written application outlining the reason for instructing the expert and his fee. If prior authority is granted, the solicitor is certain to recover the cost involved from the Legal Services Commission. If prior authority is refused then the costs will still be recoverable, provided the solicitor can justify the expenditure at the end of the case.

5.3.6 Securing the attendances of witnesses

An application should be made in person or in writing to the clerk to the justices or to a magistrate for a witness summons to be issued for each witness who is to be called. The magistrates' court has a discretion to refuse a witness summons if not satisfied that the application was made as soon as practicable after the defendant pleaded not guilty (Magistrates' Courts Act 1980, s 97(2B)). A summons can be issued only if the clerk or magistrate is satisfied that a witness will not voluntarily attend or produce a document or thing (Magistrates' Courts Act 1980, s 97(1)).

Before applying for a witness summons to be issued, a witness should be asked in writing to confirm that he will attend the trial. If a negative response is received, or no response at all, this will be sufficient evidence for a witness summons to be issued. A letter to the court explaining that it has not been possible to secure the voluntary attendance of the witness will suffice.

A witness summons should be served personally on each witness.

If a magistrate is satisfied by evidence on oath that a witness summons is unlikely to be obeyed, he may, instead of issuing a witness summons, issue a warrant to arrest the witness (Magistrates' Courts Act 1980, s 97(2)).

5.3.7 Dispensing with attendance of witnesses

Criminal Justice Act 1967, s 9

Section 9 of the Criminal Justice Act 1967 provides that a witness's written statement is admissible at a summary trial provided that:

(1) it is in the proper form;
(2) a copy has been served before the hearing on each of the other parties; and
(3) none of the parties has objected within 7 days.

The statement may only contain matters which would have been admissible if the witness had given evidence on oath.

An example of a s 9 statement illustrating the correct form is illustrated at **Appendix 2(N)**. Section 9 statements are used for matters not in dispute. If the other side wishes to challenge the admissibility of the contents of the statement or cross-examine the maker of the statement, they should object.

The s 9 procedure is available to the prosecution and defence.

Criminal Justice Act 1988, ss 23 and 24

Sections 23 and 24 of the Criminal Justice Act 1988, examined in detail at **4.6.3**, provide for the admissibility of documentary hearsay such as a witness statement with leave of the court, provided that there is a prescribed reason for not calling the witness to give evidence.

5.4 PROCEDURE ON A NOT GUILTY PLEA

5.4.1 Preliminary matters

Defect in process

The defendant cannot object to an information, summons or warrant on the ground of any defect in it in substance or form or because of any variation between it and the prosecution evidence. If the variance has misled the defendant, the court must, on his application, adjourn the hearing (Magistrates' Courts Act 1980, s 123).

The practical effect of s 123 is that trivial errors in the information or summons will have no effect at all. This will include misspellings of names or places. Where there is a substantial difference between the information or summons and the evidence to be produced, the defendant is entitled to an adjournment. An example might be an information which alleges that an offence was committed on 1 July and the defendant has alibi evidence to refute the allegation but it transpires that the prosecution evidence will show that the offence was committed on 10 July. The defendant must be allowed an adjournment to reconsider his defence.

Joinder of offences and offenders

Two or more defendants may always be charged in one information with having committed an offence jointly. They will normally be tried together.

Two or more defendants charged on separate informations may be tried together if the defence agrees. The same rule applies if one defendant is charged with more than one offence. If the defence does not agree, the court has power to try two or more informations together if it is of the opinion that it is in the interests of justice to do so because they are founded on the same facts or form part of a series of offences of the same or similar character (*Chief Constable of Norfolk v Clayton (Terence Edward); Chief Constable of Norfolk v Clayton (Eileen Annie); In re Clayton* [1983] 2 AC 473).

> *Example 1*
>
> D is charged with theft, assault and burglary. The offences are unrelated. Unless D consents (and he is unlikely to do so), the offences must be tried individually. They do not fall within the rule in *Clayton*.

> *Example 2*
>
> D is charged with four offences of theft. The allegations all arise from separate incidents of alleged shoplifting, on separate dates, within the same shopping precinct. These cases could be tried together as forming part of a series of offences of the same character. In reaching a decision, the magistrates will have to balance the convenience to the prosecution against the prejudice caused to the defendant.

Exclusion of witnesses

During a criminal trial, witnesses for either side should not sit in court before having been called to give evidence. The reason for this is to minimise the risk of evidence being tailored to suit testimony which has already been given. This rule does not apply to the defendant or to expert witnesses.

5.4.2 Pre-trial review

When a defendant first enters a not guilty plea, the case will usually be adjourned for a pre-trial review (PTR). At the PTR the court will set a date for trial. The court may require the following information to enable a trial date to be fixed:

(1)   a summary of the main issues in the case;
(2)   number of witnesses to give oral evidence;
(3)   number of witnesses whose evidence can be given in writing;
(4)   any facts formally admitted;
(5)   any points of law or admissibility of evidence likely to arise at the trial;
(6)   estimated length of trial; and
(7)   dates of availability of witnesses.

The PTR may be conducted by a justices' clerk.

5.4.3 A not guilty trial

The procedure in the magistrates' court in a not guilty trial is summarised in **Appendix 1(J)**.

The plea

The charge will be read to the defendant and he will be asked whether he pleads guilty or not guilty. The plea must not be equivocal, ie ambiguous. An example is a defendant charged with theft who says, 'Guilty, but I did not intend to steal anything'. When faced with an equivocal plea, the magistrates should endeavour to explain to the defendant in simple language the nature of the charge. The charge should then be put to the defendant again. If the plea remains equivocal, the magistrates should enter a not guilty plea on behalf of the defendant.

The court has a discretion to allow a change of plea from guilty to not guilty at any time before sentence.

Prosecution's opening speech

The prosecution may state the facts of the case and indicate the issues involved and the witnesses who will be called to prove them.

Prosecution calls evidence

This may consist of oral evidence and/or written evidence under the Criminal Justice Act 1967, s 9 or the Criminal Justice Act 1988, s 23 or s 24. Witnesses who give oral evidence will be examined-in-chief, cross-examined and re-examined as described at **4.3**.

Submission of no case to answer

The defence may, at the end of the prosecution case, be in a position to make a submission of no case to answer. Such a submission should be made and upheld where:

(1) there has been no evidence to prove an essential element in the alleged offence; or

(2) the evidence adduced by the prosecution has been so discredited as a result of cross-examination or is so manifestly unreliable that no reasonable tribunal could safely convict on it.

See *Practice Direction (Submission of No Case)* [1962] 1 WLR 227.

If a submission of no case to answer is made, the prosecution has a right of reply.

If the submission is accepted, the charge against the defendant is dismissed. If the submission is rejected, the defence may then present its case and call witnesses.

Defence opening speech

The defence may address the court either before or after calling evidence, but it is more usual for the defence advocate to make a closing speech.

Defence calls evidence

Defence witnesses may be called or their statements admitted in the same way as prosecution evidence. Remember that, if the defendant does give evidence, then he must be called before any other defence witnesses unless the court 'otherwise directs' (Police and Criminal Evidence Act 1984, s 79).

Further prosecution evidence

After the close of its case, the prosecution cannot usually call further evidence without leave. The court may, for example, grant leave for the prosecution to call rebutting evidence on a matter which it could not reasonably have foreseen and of which it had no warning. Examples include alibi evidence or a defendant who adduces evidence of his own good character.

Defence final speech

The defence addresses the court if it has not already made an opening speech. The only matters which can be covered in this closing speech are matters which have been revealed by admissible evidence.

The prosecution may only address the court further with leave. The defence will always address the court last.

Points of law

Either side may address the court on matters of law at any stage in the proceedings as of right. The opponent always has a right of reply.

Verdict

The magistrates' verdict is by a majority. They may be advised by their clerk on matters of law but not on issues of fact.

If the defendant is found guilty, the court will then proceed to sentence.

5.4.4 Costs

A defendant who is convicted can be ordered to pay all, or part, of the prosecution costs. If an order is made it will be for payment of a specified sum.

A defendant who is not represented under a representation order and who is acquitted should normally be awarded costs from central funds. There are exceptions, for example a defendant who by his conduct has brought suspicion upon himself may find that costs are not awarded in his favour.

5.5 FURTHER READING

See, for example:

Archbold: Criminal Pleading Etc (Sweet & Maxwell, 2001);
Blackstone's Criminal Practice (Blackstone Press, 2001);
John Sprack *Emmins on Criminal Procedure* (Blackstone Press, 2000);
Ede and Shepherd *Active Defence* (The Law Society, 2000).

Chapter 6

THE PROSECUTION OF AN OFFENCE TRIABLE EITHER WAY

6.1 INTRODUCTION

An offence triable either way can be tried either in a magistrates' court or in the Crown Court before a judge and jury. The first substantive step in the prosecution will be plea before venue. If the defendant indicates a not guilty plea or refuses to indicate a plea, the mode of trial enquiry will take place. The purpose of this procedure is to determine whether the case will be dealt with by a magistrates' court or by the Crown Court.

6.2 ADVANCE DISCLOSURE OF THE PROSECUTION CASE

Under the Magistrates' Court (Advance Information) Rules 1985, SI 1985/601, a defendant charged with an either way offence is entitled to advance disclosure of the prosecution case. Before a decision is made as to plea before venue and mode of trial, the defence should usually request advance disclosure from the prosecution. Advance disclosure will usually include copies of written statements of prosecution witnesses.

6.3 THE PLEA BEFORE VENUE PROCEDURE

The procedure is as follows. (This is summarised in chart form as **Appendix 1(K)**.)

(1) The charge is read out by the clerk to the justices.

(2) The clerk to the justices will ensure that the defendant is aware of his right to advance disclosure of the prosecution case. If necessary, the hearing will be adjourned to a future date to enable advance disclosure to take place.

(3) (a) The clerk to the justices will explain to the defendant that he may indicate how he would plead if the matter were to proceed to trial.

    (b) The clerk will tell the defendant that if he indicates that he intends to plead guilty he will be treated as having pleaded guilty before the magistrates who may then sentence him. However, the magistrates could still commit him to the Crown Court to be sentenced if they feel that their powers of sentencing are inadequate.

    (c) The clerk will then ask the defendant for his plea.

    (d) If the defendant indicates a guilty plea, the court will proceed as though he had just pleaded guilty at summary trial (see **9.3.2**).

    (e) If the defendant refuses to indicate a plea or indicates that he intends to plead not guilty, the procedure in **6.4** below will be followed.

6.4 THE MODE OF TRIAL PROCEDURE

The procedure is as follows. (This is summarised in chart form as **Appendix 1(K)**.)

(1) The prosecutor will address the court. He will outline the nature of the charge and will indicate in which court the prosecution feels that the case should be tried.

(2) The defence advocate may then address the court. He may indicate where the defence feels the case should be tried.

(3) The magistrates then announce whether they are prepared to deal with the case or whether they feel that the case is suitable only for trial in the Crown Court. The Magistrates' Courts Act 1980, s 19(3) states that the magistrates, in reaching their decision, must take into account:

    (a) the nature of the offence;

    (b) whether the circumstances make the offence one of serious character;

    (c) whether the punishment which a magistrates' court would have power to inflict for it would be adequate; and

    (d) any other circumstances which appear to the court to make it more suitable for the offence to be tried in one way rather than the other.

The defendant's previous convictions are irrelevant for the purpose of deciding mode of trial (*R v Colchester Justices ex parte North East Essex Building Co Ltd* [1977] 1 WLR 1109).

(4) If the magistrates decide that the case is not suitable for summary trial then the defendant has no choice. The case will be adjourned to a future date for committal proceedings to take place.

(5) If the magistrates are prepared to deal with the case then:

    (a) the clerk to the justices will explain to the defendant that he has the right to elect for trial in the Crown Court;

    (b) the clerk will inform the defendant that if he consents to be tried by the magistrates and is convicted, the magistrates may commit him to the Crown Court to be sentenced if they feel that their powers of sentencing are inadequate. (Magistrates cannot imprison a defendant for more than 6 months or, if two or more either way offences are committed, for more than a total of 12 months.) Such a decision may be taken, for example, if facts emerge after mode of trial has been determined (ie usually at a trial of a not guilty plea or a sentencing hearing):

      (i) that show that the offence is so serious that only a custodial sentence would be justified; and

      (ii) that the powers of the magistrates to pass a custodial sentence are inadequate.

    Otherwise, if the magistrates feel at the mode of trial hearing that their powers of sentence are likely to be inadequate they will commit to the Crown Court for trial;

    (c) the defendant makes his decision. If he consents to magistrates' court trial and pleads guilty (having earlier indicated no plea or now having changed his plea), his case may be dealt with immediately. If he consents to magistrates' court trial and pleads not guilty, the case will be adjourned to a pre-trial review (PTR). At the PTR, the magistrates will set a date for trial (see **5.4.2**). If the defendant asks for Crown Court trial, he will not be asked to plead. The case will be adjourned to a future date for committal proceedings to take place.

6.5 PRACTICAL POINTS ON MODE OF TRIAL PROCEDURE

6.5.1 National Mode of Trial Guidelines

In reaching a decision as to whether or not a case should be sent to the Crown Court, the magistrates will bear in mind the National Mode of Trial Guidelines issued by the Lord Chief Justice in 1995. The purpose of the guidelines is to help magistrates decide whether or not to commit either way offences for trial in the Crown Court. Their objective is to provide guidance, not direction. They are not intended to impinge upon a magistrate's duty to consider each case individually and on its particular facts.

6.5.2 Observations in the guidelines

The following general observations are made in the guidelines.

(1) The prosecution version of the facts should be assumed to be correct.
(2) Where cases involve complex questions of fact or law, committal for trial should be considered.
(3) Where two or more defendants are jointly charged with an offence each has an individual right to elect his mode of trial.

> *Example*
> C and D are jointly charged with assault. Both defendants indicate not guilty pleas. The magistrates are prepared to deal with the case. C elects trial by jury. D consents to a summary trial. According to *R v Ipswich Justices ex parte Callaghan* (1995) 159 JP 748, each defendant has the right to elect mode of trial even if it results in not guilty trials before separate courts.

(4) The presumption is that cases will be tried summarily unless:

- one of the relevant circumstances listed below is present; and
- the sentencing powers of the magistrates are considered insufficient.

The guidelines identify certain features of specific either way offences which may make them unsuitable for trial by magistrates.

BURGLARY

Burglary of dwelling-houses involving daytime entry of occupied house; night-time entry of a house normally occupied; part of a series of offences; soiling, ransacking, damage or vandalism; professional hallmarks; unrecovered property of high value (usually above £10,000).

Note that if any person in the dwelling is subjected to violence or the threat of violence, the offence cannot be tried by magistrates (Magistrates' Courts Act 1980, Sch 1, para 28(c)).

Non dwellings – entry of a pharmacy or doctor's surgery; fear caused or violence done to anyone lawfully on the premises; professional hallmarks; substantial vandalism; unrecovered property of high value (usually above £10,000).

ASSAULT OCCASIONING ACTUAL BODILY HARM

Use of a weapon of a kind likely to cause serious injury; violence to the vulnerable, for example the elderly or infirm; more than minor injury caused by kicking, headbutting; serious violence on those whose work brings them into contact with the public, for example police, bus drivers, shopkeepers, publicans; the offence has clear racial motives.

THEFT

Breach of trust by person in a position of substantial authority or in whom a high degree of trust placed; committed in a sophisticated manner; committed by an organised gang; vulnerable victim, for example elderly or infirm; unrecovered property of high value (see 'Burglary' above).

DANGEROUS DRIVING

Alcohol or drugs; grossly excessive speed; racing; prolonged course of dangerous driving; other related offences.

6.5.3 Representations by the defence

Although the defence is given an opportunity to address the court on mode of trial, in many cases this will not be necessary. If the prosecution requests Crown Court trial and the defence agrees, then there is unlikely to be any reason to address the court. This will also be the case if the defence agrees with the prosecution's request for magistrates' court trial. Representations may be necessary if the defence does not agree with the prosecution's arguments. The defence may, for example, request that the magistrates deal with the case, whilst the prosecution requests Crown Court trial.

6.5.4 Defendant changes his mind

A defendant who consents to trial by magistrates may wish to change his mind and go to the Crown Court. This point sometimes arises where the defendant was not legally represented when he made his original decision. The magistrates have a discretion to permit the defendant to change his mind and elect for Crown Court trial at any time before the conclusion of the prosecution evidence (Magistrates' Courts Act 1980, s 25(2)). This discretion may, for example, be exercised in the defendant's favour where he did not understand his legal position or the significance of the choice which he was making. See *R v Birmingham Justices ex parte Hodgson and Another* [1985] 2 All ER 193.

6.5.5 Magistrates' discretion

The magistrates have a discretion to change from Crown Court trial to magistrates' court trial at any time before the conclusion of committal proceedings (see Chapter 7), provided the defendant consents (Magistrates' Courts Act 1980, s 25(3)). This is unlikely to happen very often in practice.

6.6 ADVISING THE CLIENT

If the defendant indicates a guilty plea, the case will be dealt with in the magistrates' court and the defendant will have no choice. If the defendant indicates a not guilty plea, the decision as to whether a case will be tried in a magistrates' court or in the Crown Court will rest with the defendant if the magistrates indicate that they are prepared to deal with the matter. A defendant is entitled to expect advice from his solicitor as to the appropriate court for his case. In formulating this advice, the following factors may be relevant.

6.6.1 Factors in favour of the Crown Court

Likelihood of conviction

Whilst this is subject to knowledge of a local court, it is generally felt that there is a better chance of acquittal in the Crown Court. This may be the case where the defendant is relying on a common defence, such as 'I forgot to pay' in a theft by way of shoplifting case. Magistrates tend to hear the same stories on numerous occasions and may become 'case hardened'. Most jurors are new to the criminal justice system and may be more inclined to believe the defendant's story. If police evidence is to be challenged, magistrates may be familiar with the officer in question and the question may be better raised in the Crown Court before a jury.

Procedure for dealing with the admissibility of evidence

If the admissibility of evidence is to be challenged, the Crown Court provides the better procedure for doing so. Questions of admissibility are decided by the judge in the absence of the jury, so if evidence is ruled inadmissible, the jury will not hear it. In the magistrates' court, the justices are arbiters of fact and law, therefore they will have to hear the evidence (eg that the defendant has made a confession) before ruling on its admissibility.

6.6.2 Factors in favour of the magistrates' court

Speed and stress

A case is likely to be dealt with more quickly in a magistrates' court. The proceedings are less formal than in the Crown Court and may, therefore, be less stressful for the defendant.

Cost

If the defendant is convicted the prosecution will apply for a contribution towards prosecution costs. A Crown Court trial is likely to be more costly than a hearing in the magistrates' court.

If the defendant is represented under a representation order the judge has the power at the conclusion of the case in the Crown Court to order a defendant to pay all or some of the costs of his defence (see **9.2.14**). No such power is available in the magistrates' court.

Sentence

Magistrates' powers of sentencing are limited. A higher sentence may be imposed in the Crown Court. However, it is also necessary to bear in mind the power of a magistrates' court to commit a defendant to the Crown Court for sentencing if the court feels that its powers of sentencing are inadequate. (As to the exercise of this power, see **9.2.16**.)

The advice given to a client as to the appropriate trial court will depend on the facts of the case and which of the factors listed above are considered to be the most important.

6.7 LINKED SUMMARY OFFENCES

If the defendant is to be tried in the Crown Court, a question sometimes arises as to what will happen to other offences with which he is charged but which are purely summary offences.

6.7.1 Criminal Justice Act 1988, s 40(1)

'A count charging a person with a summary offence to which this section applies may be included in an indictment if the charge –

(a)   is founded on the same facts or evidence as a count charging an indictable offence; or

(b)   is part of a series of offences of the same or similar character as an indictable offence which is also charged,

but only if (in either case) the facts or evidence relating to the offence were disclosed to a magistrates' court inquiring into the offence as examining justices.'

The offences to which this section applies are: taking a conveyance, common assault, driving while disqualified and certain offences of criminal damage.

The effect of s 40 is to enable the prosecution, when drafting the indictment for trial in the Crown Court following committal proceedings, to include a purely summary offence provided the conditions in s 40 are satisfied.

Example

D is charged with theft of goods from a motor vehicle and with taking a conveyance. The facts are that he took a vehicle without the owner's consent and stole a quantity of tapes and a radio from the car while it was in his possession. The charges are therefore founded on the same facts. D is committed to the Crown Court for trial on the theft charge. Under s 40, the summary offence of taking a conveyance can also be tried in the Crown Court, provided evidence in support of the charge is included in the notice of prosecution case sent to the Crown Court.

If the defendant is convicted of the summary offence, the Crown Court's sentencing powers are limited to those of the magistrates.

6.7.2 Criminal Justice Act 1988, s 41(1)

'Where a magistrates' court commits a person to the Crown Court for trial on indictment for an offence triable either way or a number of such offences, it may also commit him for trial for any summary offence with which he is charged and which –

(a)   is punishable with imprisonment or involves obligatory or discretionary disqualification from driving; and

(b)   arises out of circumstances which appear to the court to be the same as or connected with those giving rise to the offence, or one of the offences, triable either way,

whether or not evidence relating to that summary offence appears on the depositions or written statements in the case.'

This section does not apply to offences triable only on indictment. Provided the offence committed for trial is triable either way, any summary offence which satisfies the conditions set out above may also be committed for trial.

If the defendant, on conviction for the either way offence, pleads guilty to the summary offence, the Crown Court can sentence for the summary offence, but its powers are limited to those of the magistrates. If the defendant pleads not guilty the summary offence must be remitted to the magistrates' court for trial. The Crown Court has no power to deal with the summary offence in these circumstances.

Example

D is committed for trial in the Crown Court on a charge of assault occasioning actual bodily harm. He also faces a charge of threatening behaviour, under the Public Order Act 1986, s 4, arising out of the same incident. This offence can be added to the indictment in the Crown Court. If D is convicted of the assault charge the Crown Court can sentence him for the public order offence, provided he pleads guilty. If D pleads not guilty to the public order offence or is acquitted on the assault charge, the Crown Court must remit the public order offence back to the magistrates.

The Crown Court is required to inform the clerk of the committing magistrates' court of the outcome of any proceedings under s 41, as proceedings in the magistrates' court in respect of the summary offence will have been adjourned.

6.7.3   Conclusion

Sections 40 and 41 are similar in that they both may allow the Crown Court to deal with linked summary offences when the defendant is before that court in respect of an indictable offence. However, they have the following key differences.

(1)   Section 40 allows the summary offence to be *tried* in the Crown Court, along with the indictable offence.

Section 41 only allows the court to *sentence* for the summary offence if the defendant pleads guilty to it. If he pleads not guilty, the trial must be held in the magistrates' court.

(2)   Section 40 applies if the defendant is committed to the Crown Court for any indictable offence, whether it is either way, or indictable only.

Section 41 only applies if the defendant is committed to the Crown Court for an either way offence.

(3)   Section 40 only enables the Crown Court to try a limited list of the more serious summary offences.

Section 41 may enable the Crown Court to sentence for any summary offence which is punishable with imprisonment or disqualification.

6.8 FURTHER READING

See, for example:

Archbold: Criminal Pleading Etc (Sweet & Maxwell, 2001);
Blackstone's Criminal Practice (Blackstone Press, 2001);
John Sprack *Emmins on Criminal Procedure* (Blackstone Press, 2000).

Chapter 7

COMMITTAL PROCEEDINGS AND SENDING FOR TRIAL

7.1 INTRODUCTION

Offences triable either way (which are not related to indictable only offences) will be the subject of committal proceedings before a magistrates' court. The purpose of committal proceedings is to ensure that there is a case for the defendant to answer in the Crown Court.

There is power to bypass committal proceedings in serious fraud cases and certain sexual or violent offences involving a child witness. Additionally, the prosecution could avoid the holding of committal proceedings by applying to a High Court judge for a voluntary bill of indictment. Such cases are beyond the scope of this book.

Important changes have been introduced by the Crime and Disorder Act 1998. Indictable only offences and related either way offences are no longer subject to committal proceedings.

7.2 TYPES OF COMMITTAL PROCEEDINGS

Offences triable either way (which are not related to indictable only offences) will be subject to committal proceedings.

There are two types of committal proceedings:

(1) committal without consideration of the evidence under Magistrates' Courts Act 1980, s 6(2); and
(2) committal with consideration of the evidence under Magistrates' Courts Act 1980, s 6(1), at which the prosecution must satisfy the magistrates that there is sufficient evidence to put the defendant on trial in the Crown Court.

7.3 PRELIMINARY POINTS

Whichever type of committal proceedings takes place, the following points will always apply.

7.3.1 Conduct of proceedings

Proceedings may be conducted by a single magistrate.

7.3.2 Reporting restrictions (Magistrates' Courts Act 1980, s 8)

Committal proceedings usually take place in open court. The press may be present but any report is restricted to the formal part of the proceedings, that is to say, the names of the defendants and witnesses, the offence charged, and the result of the proceedings. The press are not allowed to report the evidence given at committal proceedings. The main reason for reporting restrictions is to prevent a jury from being prejudiced by what they may read in the newspapers and to attempt to ensure that they decide the case in the Crown Court on the evidence presented at the trial.

A single defendant can insist that reporting restrictions be lifted. A defendant may wish to exercise this right, for example, if publicity is needed to trace a witness whose identity is not known.

7.3.3 Evidence which is admissible at committal proceedings

Only the prosecution can adduce evidence at committal proceedings. To be admissible the evidence must fall within one of the categories set out in Magistrates' Courts Act 1980, ss 5B–5E.

(1) Written statements under the Magistrates' Courts Act 1980, s 5B

The written statement of a prosecution witness is admissible if:

- it purports to be signed by the person who made it;
- it contains a declaration that it is true to the best of the maker's knowledge and belief and that it is made knowing that if it is tendered in evidence he would be liable to prosecution if he wilfully stated in it anything he knows to be false or did not believe to be true; and
- before being tendered in evidence a copy of the statement is given to each of the other parties.

The above conditions are very similar to those in the Criminal Justice Act 1967, s 9 except that the other parties have no right to object to the statement being admitted at committal proceedings.

Any documents or exhibits referred to in the s 5B statements are also admissible at committal proceedings.

(2) Depositions under the Magistrates' Courts Act 1980, s 5C

Depositions are used where a witness will not voluntarily make a written statement or produce a document or exhibit for the prosecution.

Where a magistrate considers that a person is likely to be able to make a written statement or produce a document or exhibit on behalf of the prosecution which will contain or is likely to be material evidence and the person will not do so voluntarily, he (the magistrate) must issue a summons requiring that person to appear before him to give his evidence or produce the document or exhibit (Magistrates' Courts Act 1980, s 97A).

When that person attends court, his evidence will be taken down in writing by the magistrate in the form of a deposition. If that person fails to attend the magistrate can, in certain circumstances, issue a warrant for his arrest.

To be admissible evidence at committal proceedings, a copy of the deposition must be given to all the parties.

Any documents or exhibits included in the deposition are also admissible at committal proceedings.

(3) Statements under the Magistrates' Courts Act 1980, s 5D

These are statements which the prosecution reasonably believes will only be admissible at trial under s 23 or s 24 of the Criminal Justice Act 1988.

In order for the statement to be admissible at committal proceedings, the prosecutor must notify the court and all the parties of his belief and provide them with a copy of the statement.

The magistrates at committal have no power to rule the statement inadmissible.

(4) Documents under the Magistrates' Courts Act 1980, s 5E

These are documents which are admissible by some other enactment (eg a certificate from the Driver and Vehicle Licensing Agency).

7.3.4 Defendant's right to object to written evidence being read at trial

At the same time as the prosecution serves on the defence the evidence to be adduced in committal proceedings, the prosecution must notify the defence of its right to object to written evidence which is admitted in committal proceedings being read at the Crown Court trial without further evidence (see **Appendix 2(P)**).

7.3.5 Pre-committal disclosure of unused material

The prosecution's duty of primary disclosure of 'unused material' under the Criminal Procedure and Investigations Act 1996 applies when the defendant is committed for trial or sent to the Crown Court for trial (see **8.5**). In *R v DPP ex parte Lee* [1999] 2 All ER 737, the Divisional Court held that the 1996 Act did not abolish pre-committal disclosure of 'unused material'. In most cases, prosecution disclosure can wait until after committal without jeopardising the defendant's right to a fair trial. However, the prosecutor must always be alive to the need to disclose material of which he is aware (either from his own consideration of the papers or because his attention has been drawn to it by the defence) and which he, as a responsible prosecutor, recognises should be disclosed at an earlier stage.

7.4 COMMITTAL WITHOUT CONSIDERATION OF THE EVIDENCE (Magistrates' Courts Act 1980, s 6(2))

The procedure is summarised in **Appendix 1(L)**.

7.4.1 Offer of committal

It is up to the prosecution to offer the defence a committal without consideration of the evidence.

The offer of a committal without consideration of the evidence will be made in virtually all cases and will normally be by letter. The prosecution will serve on the defence a bundle of prosecution documents complying with the requirements of ss 5B–5E of the Magistrates' Courts Act 1980. The defence solicitor will consider the statements with his client. Unless there is a good reason for asking for a committal with consideration of the evidence (see **7.6.2**), the defence will accept the prosecution's offer.

7.4.2 Procedure at committal without consideration of the evidence

The court's function is largely administrative and the proceedings will take only a few minutes.

The prosecution and defendant will attend court. A solicitor acting under a representation order will not receive payment for attending a committal without consideration of the evidence unless his presence is necessary. His presence may be necessary, for example, if there is to be a defence application for bail which will be opposed by the prosecution.

The committal proceedings commence with the charge being read to the defendant. No plea is entered as this is not a trial.

The court clerk asks whether the defence wants reporting restrictions to be lifted (see **7.3.2**).

The court clerk will then check that the formalities for a committal without consideration of the evidence have been complied with. The formalities are:

(1) that all the prosecution's evidence falls within ss 5B–5E of the Magistrates' Courts Act 1980; and

(2) copies of the statements and depositions have been served on the defence;

(3) the defendant has a solicitor acting for him (whether present in court or not); and

(4) the defence does not wish to make a submission of no case to answer (see **7.5.1**). If the defence does wish to make such a submission, a committal without consideration of the evidence is not appropriate.

The magistrates do not at any stage read the evidence contained in the prosecution statements.

The defendant is committed for trial to the Crown Court and reminded of his right to object to written evidence which was admitted in committal proceedings being read out at the Crown Court trial without further evidence.

A date will be set for a plea and directions hearing in the Crown Court.

The defence will then deal with the following ancillary matters:

Representation

The defence will make an application for representation to be extended to cover the Crown Court trial. Such an application will usually be granted.

Bail

If the defendant is already on bail, it will be usual for bail to be extended until the Crown Court trial. If the defendant has been in custody until committal proceedings, the defence may be able to make a further bail application to the magistrates (see **3.4.3**).

7.5 COMMITTAL WITH CONSIDERATION OF THE EVIDENCE (Magistrates' Courts Act 1980, s 6(1))

If the defendant is to be committed for trial, the prosecution must show that there is a case to answer.

7.5.1 Procedure

The procedure is summarised in **Appendix 1(M)**.

The charge is read to the defendant but no plea is taken.

The court clerk will ask whether the defence wants reporting restrictions to be lifted.

The prosecution evidence will either be read aloud at the hearing or, if the court directs, orally summarised. No witnesses can be called to give oral evidence.

At the close of the prosecution case, the defence may make a submission of no case to answer. The test to be applied by the magistrates when considering a submission is laid down in the case of *R v Galbraith (George Charles)* [1982] 2 All ER 1060. The magistrates must ask themselves whether the prosecution evidence, taken at its highest, is such that a jury properly directed could not properly convict on it. The practical effect of this test was considered in *Galbraith*:

> '... where the prosecution evidence is such that its strength or weakness depends on the view to be taken of a witness's reliability or other matters which are generally speaking within the jury's province and where one possible view of the facts is that there is evidence on which the jury could properly convict',

then the submission of no case to answer will fail.

For a submission to succeed, therefore, the defence will have to show that the prosecution has failed to adduce evidence in support of an essential element of the offence or that, even taking the best possible view of the prosecution evidence, the case against the defendant is so unreliable that a jury could not convict on it.

If no submission is made or if the submission is rejected, the magistrates will announce that there is a case to answer and commit the defendant to the Crown Court for trial. The magistrates will then remind the defendant of his right to object to written evidence which has been adduced in committal proceedings being read out in the Crown Court without further evidence. If they uphold the submission the magistrates will announce that the submission has been upheld and discharge the defendant.

If the defendant is committed for trial, a date will be set for a plea and directions hearing at the Crown Court. Bail and representation will then be dealt with as on a s 6(2) committal.

Excluding evidence at committal

The Criminal Procedure and Investigations Act 1996 (Sch 1, paras 25 and 26) provides that the magistrates have no power to exclude prosecution evidence at committal proceedings under either s 76(2) or s 78 of the Police and Criminal Evidence Act 1984.

7.6 DECIDING ON THE TYPE OF COMMITTAL PROCEEDINGS

7.6.1 Prosecution decides on committal with consideration of the evidence

If the prosecution decides to have a committal with consideration of the evidence then the defence does not have a choice.

Since the prosecution can no longer use committal proceedings to test its own witnesses by calling them to give oral evidence, it is now very unlikely ever to insist on a s 6(1) committal.

7.6.2 Prosecution decides on committal without consideration of the evidence

If the prosecution offers the defence a committal without consideration of the evidence, the choice as to the type of committal will rest with the defence. Reasons for insisting on a committal with consideration of the evidence include the following.

(1) *Making a submission of no case to answer*
    The circumstances in which this is a realistic possibility were discussed at **7.5.1**.

(2) *To try to persuade the court to commit the defendant for trial on a lesser charge than the one being dealt with at committal*
    For example, a charge of causing grievous bodily harm could be reduced to a charge of assault occasioning actual bodily harm.

If neither of the reasons described above applies to the case then a committal without consideration of the evidence is appropriate. This will be quicker than a s 6(1) committal.

Agreeing to a s 6(2) committal does not in any way prevent the defence from challenging the prosecution witnesses or the admissibility of their evidence at Crown Court.

7.7 SENDING FOR TRIAL PROCEDURE (Crime and Disorder Act 1998, ss 51, 52 and Sch 3)

7.7.1 Cases to which s 51 applies

Where an adult appears or is brought before a magistrates' court charged with an indictable only offence, the court must send him forthwith to the Crown Court for trial:

(a) for that offence; and
(b) for any either way offence or summary offence with which he is charged which fulfills the 'requisite conditions' (s 51(1)).

The 'requisite conditions' are that:

(a) the either way or summary offence appears to the court to be related to the indictable only offence; and
(b) in the case of a summary only offence, it is punishable with imprisonment or involves obligatory or discretionary disqualification from driving (s 51(11)).

An either way offence is related to an indictable only offence if the charge for the either way offence could be joined in the same indictment as the charge for the indictable only offence. A summary offence is related to an indictable only offence if it arises out of circumstances which are the same as or connected with those giving rise to the indictable only offence (s 51(12)).

An adult co-defendant who is charged with a related either way offence must also be sent to the Crown Court for trial (s 51(3)).

If a defendant is sent for trial for a summary offence, the trial of that offence in the magistrates' court shall be treated as if the court had adjourned it and had not fixed the time and place for its resumption (s 51(9)).

A juvenile (an offender under 18) is not liable to be sent to the Crown Court unless he is jointly charged with an indictable offence with an adult. When the adult is sent to the Crown Court under s 51, the magistrates may send the juvenile to the Crown Court as well if the magistrates consider that it is in the interests of justice for him to be tried jointly with the adult defendant. Where they do so, the magistrates may also send the juvenile to the Crown Court to be tried for related offences (s 51(5) and (6)).

7.7.2 The preliminary hearing in the magistrates' court

An adult defendant charged with an offence triable only on indictment will be sent straight to the Crown Court for trial, following a preliminary hearing in the magistrates' court. The purpose of the hearing is to determine whether there is an indictable only offence charged and whether there are related offences which should also be sent to the Crown Court. The court will also consider representation. The magistrates will set the date on which the first preliminary hearing will take place in the Crown Court and will remand the defendant in custody or on bail to appear at the Crown Court.

The preliminary hearing should be before two or more justices. The CPS must be represented by a Crown prosecutor. The preliminary hearing is likely to take place at the next available court sitting after the defendant has been charged.

Section 52(5) provides that the preliminary hearing in the magistrates' court may be adjourned but it is envisaged that, given the limited nature of the court's function under s 51, it will seldom be necessary to adjourn.

7.7.3 Representation

A magistrates' court has the power to grant a 'through representation order' for indictable only offences (and related offences or defendants) that are sent to the Crown Court under s 51.

If an application for representation has not been submitted already representation will be dealt with at the preliminary hearing. The magistrates or the justice's clerk will consider whether the case meets the interests of justice criteria and grant a representation order which covers both representation in the magistrates' court and the Crown Court.

7.7.4 Statement of means for the Crown Court

Only the interests of justice test has to be satisfied before granting a representation order: a representation order is non-means tested. At the conclusion of the case in the Crown Court the judge has the power to order a defendant to pay some or all the costs of his defence (see **9.2.14**).

When the defendant applies for representation to cover proceedings in the Crown Court, the magistrates' court will provide the defendant with Form B (see **Appendix 2(Q)**). This form should be returned to the Crown Court at least four days before the first hearing at the Crown Court which will usually be the preliminary hearing (for cases sent to the Crown Court for trial) or the plea and directions hearing (for cases committed to the Crown Court for trial). Failure to return this form, which provides details of the defendant's means and those of his partner, could result in a defendant's costs order being made at the conclusion of the case for the full defence costs.

7.8 FURTHER READING

For further discussions on criminal proceedings, see, for example:

Archbold: Criminal Pleading, Evidence and Practice (Sweet & Maxwell, 2001);
Blackstone's Criminal Practice (Blackstone Press, 2001);
John Sprack *Emmins on Criminal Procedure* (Blackstone Press, 2000);
Ede and Edwards *Criminal Defence* (The Law Society, 2000).

Chapter 8

PREPARATIONS FOR TRIAL ON INDICTMENT

8.1 INTRODUCTION

This chapter deals with what happens to a case after it has been either committed to the Crown Court for trial or sent to the Crown Court for trial under s 51 of the Crime and Disorder Act 1998. It also deals with the main preparatory steps for Crown Court trial.

8.2 THE INDICTMENT

The indictment is the formal document containing a list of charges against the defendant, to which he pleads guilty or not guilty at the beginning of the Crown Court trial. The offences alleged against the defendant are set out in separate counts of the indictment. Each count must allege only one offence. The indictment must be signed by an officer of the Crown Court. Until the indictment is signed, it is merely a 'bill of indictment'. Bills of indictment are usually drafted by the prosecution and the prosecution will have to deliver the bill to the Crown Court to be signed. Such delivery is known as 'preferment of the bill of indictment'.

The law on drafting indictments is contained principally in the Indictments Act 1915 and the Indictment Rules 1971, SI 1971/1253. Rule 5 (as amended by the Indictments (Procedure) (Modification) Rules 1998, SI 1998/3045) provides that a bill of indictment must be preferred within 28 days of committal to the Crown Court or within 28 days of service of the prosecution case if the case is sent for trial. This period can be extended by application to the court.

8.3 CASES COMMITTED TO THE CROWN COURT FOR TRIAL

8.3.1 Use of statements and depositions of prosecution witnesses at trial

The Criminal Procedure and Investigations Act 1996, s 68 and Sch 2, paras 1 and 2, provide that written statements and depositions which have been admitted in evidence in committal proceedings can be read at the Crown Court trial where all parties agree or where the court considers it to be in the interests of justice to do so (see **4.6.5**).

If the defendant intends to plead not guilty at the Crown Court, the defence must consider whether to object to this prosecution evidence being read to the court. Any objection to the reading out at the trial of a statement or deposition without further evidence shall be made in writing to the prosecutor and the Crown Court within 14 days of the defendant being committed for trial unless the court, at its discretion, permits such an objection to be made outside that period (Crown Court Rules 1982, r 22).

If the defence wishes to challenge the admissibility of the contents of the written statement or cross-examine the maker of the written statement or deposition, the defence should object.

8.3.2 First hearing

The first hearing for a defendant committed for trial at the Crown Court for an either way offence will be the plea and directions hearing (PDH) (see **8.8**). When committing a case to the Crown Court, a magistrates' court will fix a date for a PDH which must take place:

- within 4 weeks of committal if the defendant is in custody; or
- within 6 weeks of committal if the defendant is on bail.

(*Practice Direction (Crown Court: Plea and Directions Hearings)* [1995] 1 WLR 1318.)

8.4 CASES SENT TO THE CROWN COURT FOR TRIAL

8.4.1 Preliminary hearing

The first hearing for a defendant sent for trial for an indictable only offence will be a preliminary hearing. A preliminary hearing is any hearing which takes place before the prosecution has completed service of its case.

The notice specifying the charges upon which the defendant is sent for trial (required by s 51(7) of the Crime and Disorder Act 1998), together with other documents, including the charge, must be sent by the magistrates' court to the Crown Court within 4 days of sending a person to be tried in the Crown Court (Magistrates' Courts (Modification) Rules 1998, SI 1998/3046). The first Crown Court appearance must then take place:

- within 8 days of receipt of that notice where the defendant is sent for trial in custody; or
- within 28 days of receipt of that notice when the defendant is sent on bail.

(Crown Court (Modification) Rules 1998, SI 1998/3047)

The preliminary hearing allows a defendant, who has been sent for trial in custody, to apply to the Crown Court for bail, and allows the judge, having consulted the prosecution, to set a date by which the prosecution is to serve its case on the defence and to set a date for the PDH.

There is nothing to prevent a defendant from making a bail application before the date fixed for the preliminary hearing. It is then for the Crown Court to decide when to allow an earlier hearing to determine bail. If the court so decides, it will depend on the circumstances of the case whether at that hearing it is possible for the court to determine the timetable for the case (in effect bringing forward the date of the preliminary hearing), or whether it will still be necessary to hold a hearing for that purpose on the date originally fixed. If an earlier hearing is arranged, then the s 51(7) notice and associated documents should be sent to the Crown Court in time for the hearing and the CPS should be given as much notice of the hearing as possible.

The Crown Court Rules 1982, SI 1982/1109, r 27 has been modified by the Crown Court (Modification) Rules 1998 to allow the preliminary hearing to take place in chambers. A Practice Direction (Section 51 of the Crime and Disorder Act 1998 – Guidance on listing of preliminary hearings), issued on 22 December 1998 by the Senior Presiding Judge for England and Wales, provides that the preliminary hearing (and any others which take place before the prosecution case is served) should normally be heard in open court as chambers, with the defendant present and the court open to the public. The Crown may be represented at the hearing by a Crown prosecutor and the defence by a solicitor.

8.4.2 Depositions from reluctant witnesses

A provision equivalent to that in s 97A of the Magistrates' Courts Act 1980 (see **7.3.3**) is available. The procedure allows for the taking (before service of the prosecution case) of depositions from reluctant witnesses and this is taken before a magistrate, notwithstanding that the case has been sent to the Crown Court (Crime and Disorder Act 1998, Sch 3, para 4).

8.4.3 Service of prosecution case

The Attorney-General is required to make regulations for the service of documents containing the prosecution evidence on which the charge or charges are based (Crime and Disorder Act 1998, s 51(7), Sch 3, para 1). The Crime and Disorder Act 1998 (Service of Prosecution Evidence) Regulations 1998, SI 1998/3115, set a 'long stop' date of one year from the date the case is sent, for the judge to determine the date by which the evidence is to be served.

It will generally be convenient for the evidence to be served in one bundle. In a complex case, it may be appropriate to serve evidence as it becomes available. If so, the prosecution should notify the defence that more evidence is to be served later and advise the defence once the case has been fully served.

The evidence that is served will form the prima facie case.

The date of service of the prosecution case is relevant for the timing of applications for dismissal, disclosure of evidence the prosecution do not intend to rely on and the preferment of the indictment.

There will usually be another Crown Court hearing after service of the prosecution case (or to find out why the prosecution case has not yet been served). The purpose of this hearing will be to review the case to date and confirm the PDH date. The timing of this hearing will be at the judge's discretion.

8.4.4 Applications for dismissal

Once the prosecution case has been served, the defence may make an application for dismissal (Crime and Disorder Act 1998, Sch 3, para 2). The judge shall dismiss the charge if it appears to him that the evidence against the defendant would not be sufficient for the jury to properly convict him. Detailed provision for this is made in the Crime and Disorder Act 1998 (Dismissal of Charges Sent) Rules 1998, SI 1998/3048. The defence may give notice of intention to make an oral application, or make an application in writing (to which the prosecution may respond with a request for an oral hearing). The notice or written application, accompanied by copies of any material relied on, must be copied to the prosecution, which is allowed 14 days from receipt to make written comments or adduce further evidence. There is provision for the 14-day period to be extended.

The Rules include provision for evidence to be given orally, but only with the leave of the judge, which is to be given only when the interests of justice require.

Reporting restrictions apply which are modelled on the restrictions which apply to the reporting of committal proceedings (see **7.3.2**).

If a defendant succeeds in having the case against him dismissed, no further proceedings on the dismissed charge may be made (other than through a voluntary bill of indictment).

8.4.5 Related either way offences

Sending related either way offences for trial enables the Crown Court to deal with the indictable only offence and related either way offences in the one trial.

Where (following a successful application to dismiss or to discontinue or for any other reason) the indictable only offence which caused the case to be sent to the Crown Court in the first place is no longer on the indictment, consideration must be given to the outstanding related either way offences.

Adult defendants

The Crown Court should deal with outstanding either way offences where there is a guilty plea, or where the case appears suitable for trial on indictment, or where the defendant elects Crown Court trial.

The either way offences should be remitted to the magistrates for trial only where a not guilty plea is indicated (or no indication given), the case is suitable for summary trial and the defendant consents to be so tried (Crime and Disorder Act 1998, Sch 3, paras 7–12).

Procedure

The procedure amounts to an adapted mode of trial hearing, at which the Crown Court determines mode of trial in much the same way as magistrates would do.

(1) The outstanding counts on the indictment that charge either way offences are read to the defendant and the court will invite him to indicate a plea, explaining that if he indicates that he would plead guilty, the court will proceed to deal with him as if the trial had started and he pleaded guilty.
(2) If the defendant indicates that he would plead not guilty or fails to give any indication, the court must next consider whether the case is more suitable for summary trial or trial on indictment, having regard to any representations made by the prosecution or the defendant, the nature of the case, the seriousness of the offence, whether the magistrates' sentencing powers would be adequate, or any other relevant circumstances.
(3) If the court decides that the offence is more suitable for trial on indictment, the case will proceed in the usual way. If, on the other hand, it decides that the case

is more suitable for summary trial, the court must give the defendant the option of electing Crown Court trial.

(4) If the defendant consents to summary trial, the case is remitted to the magistrates. The defendant will be remanded on bail or in custody to appear before the magistrates' court.

Example

D is sent for trial to the Crown Court on a robbery charge. He also faces a charge of assault occasioning actual bodily harm arising out of the same incident. This offence can be sent to the Crown Court as a related either way offence.

At the Crown Court, the robbery charge is dismissed following an application for dismissal. The court will conduct a mode of trial procedure in relation to the assault occasioning actual bodily harm charge.

If D indicates a guilty plea, the court will deal with him as if the trial had started and he had pleaded guilty. The court will proceed to sentence.

If D indicates a not guilty plea, the court will have to decide whether the case is suitable for trial on indictment or summary trial. If the court decides that trial on indictment is more suitable, D has no choice; D will be tried on indictment. If the court decides that summary trial is more suitable then D has a choice. If D consents to summary trial, the case is remitted to the magistrates' court for trial. If not, D will be tried on indictment.

Juvenile defendants

Cases involving juveniles should be remitted to the magistrates' court unless it is necessary that they should be tried in the Crown Court. The circumstances in which the Crown Court should deal with juvenile defendants are where:

- the defendant is charged with an offence which is a grave crime for the purposes of s 53 of the Children and Young Persons Act 1933 and the court considers that it ought to be possible for him to be sentenced under that provision; or
- the juvenile is charged jointly with an adult with an either way offence and it is necessary in the interests of justice that they both should be tried at the Crown Court.

(Crime and Disorder Act 1998, Sch 3, para 13)

8.4.6 Related summary offences

Where a magistrates' court has sent a defendant for trial for offences which include a summary offence, the summary offence will not be included in the indictment and the defendant will not be asked to plead to the summary offence when the trial begins (unless the summary offence has been included in the indictment under s 40 of the Criminal Justice Act 1988, which only applies to a few summary offences; see **6.7.1**).

The Crown Court will deal with a summary offence only if the defendant pleads guilty to it and the defendant has been convicted of the indictable only offence to which it related; in so doing, the court's powers are restricted to those which would have been available to a magistrates' court. In any other circumstances, the summary offence will either be remitted to the magistrates for trial or (if the prosecution do not wish to proceed) be dismissed (Crime and Disorder Act 1998, Sch 3, para 6).

The Crown Court is required to inform the clerk of the 'sending magistrates' court' of the outcome of any proceedings in respect of the summary offence (Sch 3, para 6(7)) as proceedings in the magistrates' court in respect of the summary offence will have been adjourned (see **7.1**).

> *Example*
>
> D is sent for trial in the Crown Court on a charge of robbery. He also faces a charge of threatening behavior, under the Public Order Act 1986, s 4, arising out of the same incident. The s 4 offence is sent to the Crown Court as a related summary offence. If D is convicted of the robbery charge, the Crown Court can sentence him for the public order offence, provided he pleads guilty. If D pleads not guilty to the public order offence or is acquitted of the robbery charge, the Crown Court must remit the public order offence back to the magistrates unless the prosecution decide not to proceed with the public order offence, in which case the Crown Court can dismiss the charge.

8.5 DISCLOSURE

Duty to provide advance information

If the case has been committed to the Crown Court for trial, this duty is met by the papers served on the defence prior to committal to the Crown Court (see **7.4.1**). For those cases sent to the Crown Court for trial, the prosecution will disclose its case at the Crown Court (see **8.4.3**). Any additional evidence which the prosecution later decide to adduce as part of the prosecution case must be brought to the defendant's attention by way of notice of further evidence (see **8.6**).

Duty to disclose 'unused material'

A diagram illustrating disclosure to the defence of any material of relevance to the case upon which the prosecution does not intend to rely ('unused material') in the Crown Court appears as **Appendix 1(N)**.

The prosecution's duty of primary disclosure of 'unused material' will apply where the defendant is committed for trial to the Crown Court or sent to the Crown Court for trial under s 51 of the Crime and Disorder Act 1998. The defence must give a 'defence statement' to the prosecution. If the defendant discloses inconsistent defences or a defence inconsistent with that later advanced at trial, similar consequences will follow to those which result in the magistrates' court (see **5.2.9**).

8.6 NOTICES OF FURTHER EVIDENCE

A witness may be called to give evidence for the prosecution in the Crown Court even though his statement was not served on the defence at committal stage or not served by the prosecution at the Crown Court for cases sent to the Crown Court for trial. It may be, for example, that the evidence only came to light after the plea and directions hearing in the Crown Court.

If the prosecution wishes to call additional evidence, a notice of intention to do so will be served on the defence and the Crown Court. The notice will be accompanied by a copy of the relevant witness statement.

8.7 PREPARING FOR THE PLEA AND DIRECTIONS HEARING

Guilty pleas

If a defendant intends to plead guilty, the defence solicitor should notify the Probation Service, the prosecution and the court as soon as this is known.

Not guilty pleas

The defence solicitor should ensure that the case is sufficiently prepared for the PDH to enable the advocate who appears at the hearing to give the judge the information required to fix a trial date. The amount of information required is such that the case has to be almost ready for a full trial unless it is very complex, in which case further PDHs may be necessary. In particular:

(1) the defence should have checked the availability of defence witnesses for the trial and served witness summonses;

(2) any evidence sought to be admitted by the defence under Criminal Justice Act 1967, s 9 should be served on the prosecution;

(3) any complex issues of law or issues of admissibility of evidence should have been identified;

(4) any factors relevant to mitigation in the event of conviction should have been identified.

A copy of the PDH: Judge's Questionnaire which has to be completed and handed in to the court prior to the commencement of the PDH appears at **Appendix 2(R)**.

8.8 PLEA AND DIRECTIONS HEARING

When committing a case to the Crown Court, a magistrates' court will fix a date for a plea/directions hearing (PDH) in the Crown Court. A PDH must take place:

- within 4 weeks of committal if the defendant is in custody; or
- within 6 weeks of committal if the defendant is on bail.

A PDH will also take place in relation to cases sent to the Crown Court for trial.

At the PDH, a defendant will be required to plead to the charge(s) against him. A defendant who has pleaded guilty may be sentenced at the PDH. If a defendant pleads not guilty, the judge will require the following information:

(1) a summary of the issues in the case;

(2) number of witnesses to give oral evidence;

(3) number of witnesses whose evidence will be given in writing;

(4) any facts formally admitted;

(5) any alibi which should have been disclosed to the prosecution;

(6) any points of law or admissibility of evidence likely to arise at the trial;

(7) estimated length of trial;

(8) dates of availability of witnesses;

(9) dates of availability of the advocates.

See *Practice Direction (Crown Court: Plea and Directions Hearings)* [1995] 1 WLR 1318.

If a date is not fixed for the not guilty trial, then the case will be placed in the warned list.

In the majority of cases committed for trial in the Crown Court, the only pre-trial hearing will be a PDH.

8.9 PRE-TRIAL RULINGS

Section 40 of the Criminal Procedure and Investigations Act 1996 allows a judge, at any hearing which takes place before trial (eg PDH), to rule on the admissibility of evidence and on any question of law relating to the case.

The ruling can be made on the application of the prosecution or the defence or on the judge's own motion.

It will bind the parties at trial unless it is discharged or varied.

A ruling can be discharged or varied on the judge's own motion or on an application by the prosecution or the defence if the judge considers that it is in the interests of justice to do so. The prosecution or defence can only apply for a discharge or variation if there has been a material change of circumstances since the ruling was made.

> *Example*
> At PDH, the judge could now be asked to rule on the admissibility of a statement which the prosecution or the defence seeks to adduce at trial under s 23 of the Criminal Justice Act 1988. If the judge ruled it to be inadmissible that ruling would be binding unless it was subsequently discharged in the interests of justice.

8.10 PREPARATORY HEARINGS

Part III of the Criminal Procedure and Investigations Act 1996 creates a statutory scheme of preparatory hearings (PHs) for long or complex cases which are to be tried in the Crown Court.

A judge, on his own motion, or on the application of the prosecution or the defence, can order that a PH be held if he considers that it is likely to bring substantial benefits because of the complexity or likely length of the case.

The PH will take place before the jury are sworn in and can be used for any of the following purposes:

- to identify important issues for the jury;
- to help the jury's understanding of the issues;
- to speed up the proceedings before the jury;
- to help the judge's management of the trial.

The plea will be taken at the start of the PH unless it has already been taken.

At the PH, the judge can rule on the admissibility of evidence and on any other question of law.

Under s 31, the judge can also exercise powers to help identify, simplify and narrow the issues of dispute, for example he can require the prosecution or the defence to provide a detailed case statement.

Any order or ruling made by the judge is binding throughout the trial unless he decides on the application of the prosecution or the defence that it is in the interests of justice to vary or discharge it.

Inferences

If either party departs from the case disclosed as a result of a requirement under s 31, or fails to comply with a s 31 requirement, the judge or, with leave of the judge, any other party, may comment on this at the trial and the jury may draw such inferences from it as appear proper.

Appeals

It is possible, in certain circumstances, to appeal against the judge's ruling on the admissibility of evidence or a question of law to the Court of Appeal and then to the House of Lords.

8.11 BRIEFING COUNSEL

If counsel is to be instructed in the Crown Court, counsel's clerk should be notified as soon as the case has been committed to the Crown Court or sent for trial to the Crown Court. The Law Society recommends that solicitors should aim to deliver a brief to counsel 3 weeks before the PDH.

On receipt of the brief, counsel may require a conference prior to the PDH.

An example of a brief to counsel appears as **Appendix 2(S)**. It covers counsel attending the PDH and trial. A brief should be as full as possible and should be broken down into sections:

> Introduction – this deals with the defendant, the charge, the history of the case, bail arrangements and which prosecution witnesses must attend the trial to give oral evidence
> Prosecution case – this contains a summary of the evidence to be given by each witness
> Defence case – this contains a summary of the defence evidence
> Evidence – any major point likely to arise at the trial should be highlighted for the benefit of counsel
> Mitigation – any facts relevant to mitigation in the event of a conviction should be mentioned.

8.12 TRIAL ON INDICTMENT

Procedure in the Crown Court on a not guilty plea is summarised in **Appendix 1(O)**.

A trial on indictment begins with the arraignment at the PDH, which consists of putting the counts in the indictment to the defendant so that he can plead guilty or not guilty.

If there is a plea of not guilty the trial takes place before a judge and a jury in the presence of the defendant (unless, for example, he is disruptive). The order of proceedings is similar to that in a magistrates' court, except that the prosecution must make an opening speech and will also address the jury at the conclusion of the defence case before counsel for the defence. The judge will then sum up to the jury.

The judge hears argument on points of law and evidence in the absence of the jury and may direct the jury to acquit if, for example, there is a successful submission of no case to answer. The test to be applied by the judge when considering a submission is laid down in the case of *R v Galbraith (George Charles)* [1992] 2 All ER 1060 (see **7.5.1**).

The verdict whether guilty or not guilty is decided by unanimous vote of the jury, although a majority verdict of 11:1, or 10:2 will be accepted if, after 2 hours, unanimity is not possible. If the jury fails to agree there may be a new trial before a new jury.

The judge decides on sentence and has wider powers of sentencing than the magistrates.

8.13 FURTHER READING

For further discussions on criminal proceedings, see, for example:

Archbold: Criminal Pleading, Evidence and Practice (Sweet & Maxwell, 2001);
Blackstone's Criminal Practice (Blackstone Press, 2001);
John Sprack *Emmins on Criminal Procedure* (Blackstone Press, 2000);
Ede and Edwards *Criminal Defence* (The Law Society, 2000).

Chapter 9

SENTENCING

9.1 INTRODUCTION

This chapter deals with the law, practice and procedure of sentencing of offenders who are aged 18 or older. Offenders under the age of 18 are dealt with in the youth court. A brief outline of the sentencing powers of the youth court is contained in Chapter 10.

A large part of a solicitor-advocate's time is taken up with the sentencing process, either following a guilty plea by his client or on conviction at a summary trial. Solicitors also have limited rights of audience in the Crown Court on sentencing matters (see **1.4.2**) and in any event must brief counsel who is appearing in the Crown Court on any matter that will be relevant to sentence in the event of the client pleading guilty or being convicted by a jury.

This chapter deals with:

(1) powers of the court;
(2) procedure on sentencing; and
(3) mitigation.

9.2 THE POWERS OF THE COURT

The Powers of Criminal Courts (Sentencing) Act 2000 (PCC(S)A 2000) provides a structured approach to sentencing. The standard penalty is a fine. If the offence is too serious for a fine a 'community sentence' will be given (eg community punishment orders or community rehabilitation orders). If the offence is considered too serious for a community sentence, then, and only then, should a custodial sentence be imposed. A diagram illustrating the PCC(S)A 2000 sentencing scheme appears as **Appendix 1(P)**.

In deciding the seriousness of the offence, the court may take into account:

(1) the present offence;
(2) any associated offences (as defined below);
(3) previous convictions (see below); and
(4) racial aggravation (see below).

Associated offences

An associated offence is one in which the defendant has been convicted in the same proceedings or sentenced at the same time, or an offence which the defendant has asked the court to take into consideration when passing sentence (see **9.3.2** for offences taken into consideration).

Example

D is convicted of three offences of theft. In applying the seriousness test, the court will look at the most serious offence first. If only a custodial sentence is justified for this offence then the seriousness test is satisfied. If one offence alone is not serious enough for a custodial sentence then the court may look at all three offences together in deciding whether only a custodial sentence is justified.

Previous convictions

By PCC(S)A 2000, s 151(1), a court may, in applying the seriousness test:

> 'take into account any previous convictions of the offender or any failure of his to respond to previous sentences.'

Example

D is convicted of theft from an employer. He has two previous convictions for similar offences and committed the current offence whilst on a community rehabilitation order.

The court may take previous convictions and the failure to respond to the community rehabilitation order into account in determining seriousness.

Section 151(2) also provides that:

> 'In considering the seriousness of any offence committed whilst the offender was on bail, the court shall treat the fact that it was committed in those circumstances as an aggravating factor.'

Racial aggravation

If an offence is 'racially aggravated' the court must treat that fact as an aggravating factor and must state in open court that the offence was so aggravated (PCC(S)A 2000, s 153).

The Crime and Disorder Act 1998, s 28(1) provides that an offence is racially aggravated if:

> '(a) at the time of committing the offence, or immediately before or after doing so, the offender demonstrates towards the victim of the offence hostility based on the victim's membership (or presumed membership) of a racial group; or
>
> (b) the offence is motivated (wholly or partly) by hostility towards members of a racial group based on their membership of that group.'

'Membership' includes association with members of that group.

'Racial group' means a group of persons defined by reference to race, colour, nationality (including citizenship) or ethnic or national origins (Crime and Disorder Act 1998, s 28(4)).

Section 153 of the PCC(S)A 2000 will not apply if the defendant has been charged with one of the racially aggravated offences under ss 29–32 of the Crime and Disorder Act 1998 (assault, criminal damage, public order offences and harassment).

9.2.1 Custodial sentences

Offenders aged 18–21 are sent to young offender institutions. Offenders aged 21 or above are sent to prison.

Where the court intends to impose a sentence of imprisonment for the first time or impose detention in a young offender institution, the offender must be legally represented at the time of sentence unless he has been given the opportunity to apply for representation and has failed to do so.

Qualification for a custodial sentence (PCC(S)A 2000, s 79)

The court cannot impose a custodial sentence unless one of the following applies.

THE SERIOUSNESS TEST

A court may impose a custodial sentence if it considers that the offence (or the combination of the offence and one or more offences associated with it) is so serious that only a custodial sentence can be justified for it.

In *R v Howells and Others* [1999] 1 Cr App R (S) 335, the Court of Appeal gave some guidance on the interpretation of the seriousness test when approaching cases which are on or near the custody threshold. In such cases, the courts would usually find it helpful to begin by considering the nature and extent of the defendant's criminal intention and of any injury or damage caused. Other things being equal, an offence which was deliberate and premeditated would be more serious than one which was not. An offence resulting in physical or mental trauma would generally be more serious than one that resulted in financial loss. Previous convictions and failure to respond to non-custodial sentences may be taken into account and the commission of an offence whilst on bail is to be treated as an aggravating factor. In deciding whether to impose a custodial sentence in a borderline case, the court would ordinarily take account of matters relating to the offender, such as:

(1) an admission of guilt;
(2) hard evidence of remorse (shown for example by an expression of regret to the victim and the offer of compensation);
(3) evidence of a determination to take steps to deal with an addiction to drink or drugs;
(4) youth and immaturity;
(5) previous good character (absence of a criminal record);
(6) positive good character (such as solid employment record or faithful discharge of family duties);
(7) physical or mental disability;
(8) whether or not the offender had previously served a custodial sentence.

Courts should always bear in mind that criminal sentences in almost every case are intended to protect the public, whether by punishing the offender or reforming him, or by deterring him and others, or all of these things. The sentence imposed should be no longer than is necessary to meet the penal purpose which the court had in mind.

The above guidelines are useful but it cannot be said that they offer a test to determine when the custody threshold has been reached in individual circumstances. Guidance on this question must still be found in decisions of the Court of Appeal in particular kinds of cases.

VIOLENT AND SEXUAL OFFENCES

The second ground for qualification for a custodial sentence is that the offence is a violent or sexual offence and the court considers that only a custodial sentence would be adequate to protect the public from serious harm from the defendant. This means that the court considers that unless the defendant is imprisoned he is likely to commit further offences which would lead to death or serious physical or psychological injury to a member of the public.

The previous convictions of the defendant may be relevant on this ground in showing, for example, a history of violent or sexual offences of increasing severity. This may lead the court to the conclusion that the ground of protection of the public is satisfied. Because protection of the public is likely to require a long custodial sentence, the ground is unlikely to be used by magistrates.

REFUSAL OF A COMMUNITY SENTENCE

A custodial sentence may be imposed if the defendant refuses to consent to a community sentence (see **9.2.4**) where his consent is required.

Aggravating and mitigating factors

In applying the seriousness test, the court must also have regard to any aggravating and mitigating factors about the offence and (in the case of violent and sexual offences) the offender (PCC(S)A 2000, s 81(4)).

Criteria for deciding length of term of imprisonment (PCC(S)A 2000, s 80)

The sentence must be:

(1) for such term as the court considers is commensurate with the seriousness of the offence or the combination of the offence and one or more offences associated with it; or

(2) where the offence is a violent or sexual offence, for such longer term as the court considers necessary to protect the public from serious harm from the defendant. (This cannot exceed the statutory maximum for the offence.)

Any aggravating or mitigating factors will also be taken into account in determining length of sentence (PCC(S)A 2000, s 81(4)).

A person aged 21 or over may be sentenced to imprisonment:

(1) by the Crown Court up to the maximum fixed by statute;

(2) by a magistrates' court for up to 6 months, unless statute fixes a lower maximum. Magistrates may, however, impose consecutive sentences up to a maximum of 12 months in aggregate when dealing with two or more either way offences (Magistrates' Courts Act 1980, ss 31, 133(2)).

The maximum sentence in a young offender institution for a person aged between 18 and 21 is the same as for imprisonment.

9.2.2 Suspended sentence of imprisonment (PCC(S)A 2000, ss 118–125)

The Crown Court may suspend a term of imprisonment not exceeding 2 years for between 1–2 years inclusive ('the operational period').

A magistrates' court may suspend imprisonment for the same operational period, but the term will be subject to their maximum.

It is not possible to suspend detention in a young offender institution.

A suspended sentence can be imposed only if the court first decides to imprison but then feels that it can be suspended because of the exceptional circumstances of the case. This is a very important principle. A suspended sentence should not be used in an attempt to frighten a petty offender who does not qualify for imprisonment. The decision of the sentencing court should be that the defendant qualifies for imprisonment, but because of the exceptional circumstances of the case the sentence may be suspended.

Frequently invoked mitigating circumstances cannot be regarded as exceptional. In *R v Okinikan* (1993) 14 Cr App R (S) 453, the Court of Appeal held that:

> 'taken on their own, or in combination, good character, youth and an early plea are not exceptional circumstances justifying a suspended sentence…. They may amount to mitigation sufficient to persuade the court that a custodial sentence should not be passed or reduce its length.'

Decisions where the Court of Appeal has held that exceptional circumstances exist include *R v Cameron (John McDougal)* (1993) 14 Cr App R (S) 801 (assault occasioning actual bodily harm on son by father; local authority supported their being reunited), *R v French (Julie Ann)* (1994) 15 Cr App R (S) 194 (fraud; severe financial and emotional difficulties; psychiatric care), *R v Khan (Ashraf Ullah)* (1994) 15 Cr App R (S) 320 (fraud; paranoid psychosis) and *R v Weston (Arnold)* [1996] 1 Cr App R (S) 297 (indecent assault on young girl; arthritic defendant in early retirement with disabled and depressed wife).

Where a court passes a suspended sentence for a term of more than 6 months, the court may make a suspended sentence supervision order. This is an order placing the offender under the supervision of a supervising officer (usually a member of the Probation Service) for a period which is specified in the order and does not exceed the operational period of the order (PCC(S)A 2000, s 122).

Activation of a suspended sentence

If an offender is subsequently convicted of an imprisonable offence committed during the operational period, the suspended sentence must normally be ordered to take effect with the original term unaltered. The court must normally activate the suspended sentence in full, unless it is of the opinion that it would be unjust to do so in view of the circumstances which have arisen since the sentence was passed, including the facts of the subsequent offence (s 119).

If the court is of the opinion that it would be unjust to activate the suspended sentence in full, there is power to activate the suspended sentence:

* for a lesser period;
* to vary the length of the operational period (so that it lasts until a date not more than 2 years from the date of variation); or
* to make no order at all.

Relevant factors that may be taken into account by a court include: whether the new offence before the court is both trivial in nature and unconnected with the original offence that led to the imposition of the suspended sentence; and whether the new offence has been committed towards the end of the operational period.

If activated, the original sentence will normally run consecutively to any term imposed for the second offence. If not activated in full, the reasons for the court's decision must be given.

Magistrates may deal with breach of a suspended sentence imposed by any magistrates' court. If the suspended sentence was imposed by the Crown Court, only the Crown Court may deal with the matter.

9.2.3 Community sentences (PCC(S)A 2000, ss 33–36)

A community sentence is a sentence composed of one or more of the following orders:

> Community rehabilitation orders
> Community punishment orders
> Community punishment and rehabilitation orders
> Drug treatment and testing orders
> Curfew orders
> Attendance centre orders (offenders under 21 only).

Before imposing a community sentence, the court must consider that:

(1) the offence (or combination of the offence and one or more associated offences) is serious enough to warrant it; and

(2) the order or orders are the most suitable for the offender; and

(3) the restrictions on the offender's liberty imposed by the order or orders are commensurate with the seriousness of the offence or the combination of the offence and other offences associated with it.

In assessing the seriousness of the offence, the courts are subject to the same rules as for imprisonment (see **9.2**).

Community sentences may be an effective way of dealing with offenders convicted of crimes against property and less serious offences of violence. As a general principle, a court must be satisfied that the offence is too serious for a financial penalty.

9.2.4 Community rehabilitation orders (Criminal Justice and Court Services Act 2000, s 43, PCC(S)A 2000, ss 41–45 and Schs 2 and 3)

A community rehabilitation order is likely to be appropriate where an offender needs advice and assistance to overcome the reasons for offending. The offender is placed under the supervision of a probation officer and 'additional requirements' can be imposed. These include requirements to undergo treatment for psychiatric problems or alcohol dependency. The offender can be required to live in a particular place, including an approved hostel or other institution, which will provide close supervision. Attendance at a community rehabilitation centre can also be required. Such centres help the offender face up to the consequences of offending.

A court may place the defendant on a community rehabilitation order from 6 months to 3 years for any offence where it considers it desirable in the interests of:

(1) securing the offender's rehabilitation; or

(2) protecting the public from harm from him; or

(3) preventing the commission of further offences by him.

The defendant must consent to the community rehabilitation order if the proposed order imposes a requirement for psychiatric treatment or alcohol dependency treatment.

A community rehabilitation order may be combined with a fine but not with imprisonment, immediate or suspended.

9.2.5 Community punishment orders (Criminal Justice and Court Services Act 2000, s 44, PCC(S)A 2000, ss 46–50 and Sch 3)

A community punishment order (CPO) requires an offender to participate in community projects of various kinds, supervised by the Probation Service. The maximum number of hours that can be imposed is 240. The minimum number of hours is 40. A CPO may be appropriate where the court feels that the offender should be deprived of leisure time or should make reparation to the community for his offending.

A community punishment order can be imposed only if:

(1) the defendant has been convicted of an imprisonable offence; and

(2) the court is satisfied that the offender is a suitable person to do the work and that appropriate work is available.

A suspended sentence of imprisonment should not be imposed as well as a CPO, but a defendant given a CPO may also be fined.

9.2.6 Community punishment and rehabilitation orders (Criminal Justice and Court Services Act 2000, s 45, PCC(S)A 2000, s 51 and Sch 3)

A community punishment and rehabilitation order is an order which requires the defendant to be under the supervision of a probation officer for a minimum period of 12 months and a maximum period of 3 years and to perform unpaid work for a minimum of 40 hours and a maximum of 100 hours.

A community punishment and rehabilitation order may be suitable where the court feels that an offender should be punished by deprivation of leisure time and given assistance in overcoming the root cause of his offending.

The defendant must have been convicted of an imprisonable offence and the court must consider that a community punishment and rehabilitation order is desirable in the interests of:

(1) rehabilitating the defendant; or

(2) protecting the public from harm; or

(3) preventing the commission of further offences.

9.2.7 Drug treatment and testing orders (PCC(S)A 2000, ss 52–58 and Sch 3)

This order is available for defendants aged 16 or over and can last from 6 months to 3 years. The court can make the order if it is satisfied that the defendant is dependent on drugs and is susceptible to treatment. The defendant must consent to the order. (Remember that refusal of consent is a ground for imposition of a custodial sentence.) A treatment provider's assessment must accompany or be incorporated into the pre-sentence report. The court has to be satisfied that the defendant is susceptible to treatment and that there is a place on a treatment programme.

The court can require the defendant to submit to treatment to reduce or eliminate his dependency, for example, by attending a clinic or taking methadone. The court can impose a testing requirement specifying how many tests the defendant must submit to each month. The tests will be taken by the treatment provider who will submit the results to the supervising probation officer, who will report them to the court.

The court can review the defendant's progress no more frequently than once a month. At each review, the court will receive a written report from the offender's probation officer which will include drug test results. The court may amend the order at a review hearing with the defendant's consent. If the defendant does not consent, the court may revoke the order and re-sentence the offender.

9.2.8 Curfew orders (PCC(S)A 2000, ss 37–40 and Sch 3)

A curfew order is an order requiring the defendant to stay for specified periods in specified places. It can last for a maximum period of 6 months. If the defendant is aged under 16, the maximum period is 3 months. A period of curfew cannot last for less than 2 hours or more than 12 hours during any one of the days specified. An example would be an order requiring the defendant to stay indoors at home between the hours of 8 pm and 6 am. This may be appropriate, for example, to keep the offender out of public houses or night clubs. If a curfew order is made, the court will appoint a person to monitor the defendant's whereabouts.

A curfew order can be imposed if the defendant has been convicted of any offence (it need not be imprisonable). A court cannot make a curfew order unless it is situated in an area with facilities for monitoring the whereabouts of the offender.

Section 38 of the PCC(S)A 2000 provides that a curfew order may, in addition, include requirements for securing electronic monitoring ('tagging') of the defendant's whereabouts during the curfew period specified in the order.

9.2.9 Attendance centre orders (PCC(S)A 2000, ss 60–62 and Sch 5)

An attendance centre order requires the offender to attend a specified place and take part in supervised activities.

A typical order will require the offender to attend a centre for 3 hours on a number of Saturday afternoons, depriving him of leisure time.

The consent of the defendant is not required and the sentence is only available for an offender under the age of 21.

9.2.10 Breach of a community sentence and re-offending (PCC(S)A 2000, ss 39, 43, 48, 51, 56 and Sch 3, paras 3–6 and 10–14)

Breach of community sentence – by failure to comply

Breach is confined to a failure to comply with the terms of the community sentence.

Failure to comply with community sentence requirements (eg not turning up for work on a community punishment order) can lead to the court punishing the breach and allowing the order to continue or revoking the order and re-sentencing for the offence.

Magistrates may deal with breach of a community sentence imposed by any magistrates' court. Breach of a Crown Court community sentence must be dealt with by the Crown Court.

Further offence during community sentence

Commission of a further offence during the currency of a community sentence does not amount to breach of that sentence.

The new offence must be dealt with according to its own seriousness. Once sentence for that offence has been decided upon then the court should consider the effect of the new sentence on the existing community sentence.

'Existing' means still in existence at the time the new offence is disposed of. Thus, if the community sentence, which was in existence when the new offence was committed, has subsequently expired or been completed, then it is no longer existing and the court has no power to deal with it.

All magistrates' courts have the power to allow the community sentence to continue or revoke the community sentence without re-sentencing the defendant for the original offence. If the same magistrates' court imposed the community sentence, then the court has the power to revoke the community sentence and re-sentence for the original offence.

The Crown Court can deal with a community sentence made either by a magistrates' court or a Crown Court. The court has the power to allow the community sentence to continue, revoke without re-sentencing or revoke and re-sentence for the original offence.

9.2.11 Fines (PCC(S)A 2000, ss 126–129 and 135–142)

Where the Crown Court or magistrates' court decides that a fine is the appropriate sentence for an offence, PCC(S) A 2000, s 128 provides that:

(a) before fixing the amount of any fine, a court shall inquire into the financial circumstances of the offender;

(b) the amount of any fine fixed by a court shall be such as, in the opinion of the court, reflects the seriousness of the offence;

(c) in fixing the amount of any fine, a court shall take into account the circumstances of the case including, among other things, the financial circumstances of the offender so far as they are known, or appear, to the court.

(d) the requirement to take into account the financial circumstances of the offender applies whether this has the effect of increasing or reducing the amount of the fine.

The court has power to order an offender to provide a statement of means before passing sentence.

9.2.12 Absolute or conditional discharge (PCC(S)A 2000, ss 12–15)

In order to impose either an absolute or conditional discharge, the court must be satisfied that, having regard to the circumstances and nature of the offence and character of the defendant, punishment is inexpedient. A conditional discharge may be imposed, for example, where a person of previous good character commits a petty theft. The court may feel that a court appearance with the attendant publicity is punishment enough. An absolute discharge is sometimes imposed where the court feels that the defendant, although technically guilty of an offence, is morally blameless.

A person can be conditionally discharged for a period not exceeding 3 years. If he commits any offence during that time he may be sentenced for the original offence.

9.2.13 Motoring penalties

Endorsement of driving licences (Road Traffic Offenders Act 1988, s 44)

Dangerous driving, careless driving and aggravated vehicle-taking all carry obligatory endorsement of the driving licence with particulars of the conviction (see **1.6**).

The licence must also be endorsed with the appropriate number of penalty points, unless at the same time the defendant is disqualified from driving.

Where a licence is ordered to be endorsed, particulars of the endorsment are recorded on the licence and also recorded centrally at the Driver and Vehicle Licensing Agency (DVLA) at Swansea.

Where the defendant is convicted of two or more endorsable offences committed on the same occasion the court will endorse the highest number of points unless it thinks fit to order otherwise (Road Traffic Offenders Act 1988, s 28(4)). In such circumstances, the court must state its reasons in open court.

> *Example*
> D is convicted of speeding (3 to 6 penalty points) and using a vehicle with defective brakes (3 penalty points), both offences being committed on the same occasion. The court takes the view that the speeding offence merits 6 points. Only 6 points will go on his driving licence unless the court thinks fit to order otherwise. The court may endorse points for both offences if it is satisfied that D has been driving with defective brakes for a number of months.

Disqualification for the offence itself (Road Traffic Offenders Act 1988, s 34)

OBLIGATORY DISQUALIFICATION

A number of offences, including dangerous driving and aggravated vehicle-taking, carry obligatory disqualification. Where an offence carries obligatory disqualification the court must generally order the defendant to be disqualified from driving for at least 12 months.

DISCRETIONARY DISQUALIFICATION

Where an offence carries discretionary disqualification for committing the offence itself, the court may order the defendant to be disqualified for such period as it thinks fit. Careless driving, taking a conveyance and theft of a motor vehicle carry discretionary disqualification.

INTERIM DISQUALIFICATION

Section 26 of the Road Traffic Offenders Act 1988 enables a magistrates' court, when committing a defendant to the Crown Court under certain statutory provisions for sentencing, deferring sentence or adjourning for sentence, to impose an interim period of disqualification from driving for an offence involving obligatory or discretionary disqualification. This can last until the case is concluded.

DISQUALIFICATION UNDER PCC(S)A 2000, s 146

Where a defendant is convicted of any offence, the court may order him to be disqualified from driving for such period as it thinks fit. That no vehicle was used in the commission of the offence is irrelevant. The disqualification may be in addition to dealing with him in any other way or may be instead of any other sentence.

DISQUALIFICATION UNDER PCC(S)A 2000, s 147

Where a defendant is convicted on indictment of an offence carrying imprisonment of 2 years or more, or is committed for sentence, under s 38 or s 38A of the Magistrates' Courts Act 1980 to be sentenced for such an offence, the Crown Court may disqualify him for such period as it thinks fit if satisfied that a motor vehicle was used in committing the offence. This applies even if the offence is not endorsable, and even if the defendant disqualified had not himself used the vehicle (ie it was used by an accomplice).

Disqualification under the penalty points system (Road Traffic Offenders Act 1988, Part II)

A defendant will be liable to disqualification for at least 6 months if the penalty points to be taken into account number 12 or more.

Where the defendant is convicted of an offence which carries obligatory endorsement the penalty points to be taken into account are:

(1) any points attributed to the offence of which he is convicted, disregarding any offence in respect of which an order for disqualification for committing the offence itself is made (see above); *plus*

(2) any points previously endorsed on his licence in respect of offences committed within the 3 years immediately preceding the commission of the most recent offence.

Note that any penalty points endorsed on the defendant's licence prior to a previous disqualification under the points system must be ignored. Only a disqualification for accumulating 12 or more penalty points has the effect of 'wiping the slate clean', ie removing all existing penalty points from the licence; all other disqualifications leave them undisturbed.

Example 1

D is convicted of careless driving. The offence was committed on 1 April 2000. He has the following endorsement on his licence: careless driving committed on 31 March 1998, 5 points.

If D is disqualified for the offence itself, his licence will not be endorsed with any penalty points. If he is not disqualifed for the offence itself, between 3 and 9 points will be awarded. If the number of points awarded are 7 or more, D is liable to be disqualified under the points system.

Example 2

D is convicted of careless driving. The offence was committed on 1 June 2001. He has the following endorsements on his licence:

Offence	Date of Offence	Sentence
Speeding	1 October 2000	4 points
Speeding	1 March 2000	(disqualified for 6 months under penalty points system)
Careless driving	1 July 1999	8 points
Speeding	1 July 1998	3 points

If D is disqualified for the current offence of careless driving itself, his licence will not be endorsed with any penalty points. If he is not disqualified for the offence itself, he will be awarded 3 to 9 points. The only relevant points on the licence to date which are to be taken into account are the 4 points awarded on 1 October 2000. Although all the other points were awarded for offences committed within 3 years of the date of commission of the current offence, they are not taken into account as D was disqualified for these under the penalty points system. Therefore, if the number of points awarded for the current offence of careless driving is 8 or more, D is liable to be disqualified under the points system.

The disqualification under the points system must be for a minimum period. If the defendant has no previous disqualification of 56 days, or none imposed within 3 years of the commission of the most recent offence for which penalty points are to be taken into account, then the period is 6 months. If there is one such disqualification in the 3 years, the period is a minimum of one year. If there are two or more such disqualifications imposed within 3 years of the most recent offence, then the minimum period is 2 years. Disqualifications under the Road Traffic Offenders Act 1988, s 26, the PCC(S)A 2000, s 147, and those imposed for theft of a motor vehicle or taking a conveyance without the consent of the owner are not to be taken into account.

The Road Traffic (New Drivers) Act 1995 provides a 'probationary period' for a newly qualified driver of 2 years, beginning with the day on which he becomes a newly qualified driver. If such drivers accumulate six or more penalty points during that period, the court notifies the DVLA. The DVLA then issues a notice of revocation of the driving licence and requires the surrender of the existing driving licence, if still in the driver's possession. The driver is invited to apply for a provisional licence. A full driving licence may not be granted until the driver has passed another driving test.

Relationship between disqualification for the offence itself and disqualification under the penalty points system

It is not possible to be disqualified under both provisions for the one offence.

The court will consider penalty points disqualification before discretionary disqualification for the one offence unless the court is unable to disqualify the defendant under the penalty points system (Road Traffic Offenders Act 1988, s 34(2)).

It has yet to be authoritatively decided as to whether disqualification can arise under both provisions when the defendant is being dealt with for more than one offence.

Avoiding disqualification or endorsement

OBLIGATORY DISQUALIFICATION OR OBLIGATORY ENDORSEMENT ARISING OUT OF THE OFFENCE ITSELF

Obligatory penalties can be avoided if the defendant can show the existence of 'special reasons'. Special reasons may avoid endorsement or disqualification or secure a reduced period. There is no statutory definition of special reasons. A special reason is one that is:

(1) a mitigating circumstance;
(2) which does not constitute a defence to the charge;
(3) connected with the commission of the offence not personal to the offender; and
(4) which the court ought properly to take into account when considering sentence

(*R v Crossan* [1939] NI 106; *Whittall v Kirby* [1946] 2 All ER 552; *R v Wickins* (1958) 42 Cr App R 236).

Therefore, the fact that the defendant was driving dangerously because of an emergency may constitute a special reason. The fact that the defendant would lose his job if disqualified is not a special reason: it is personal to the offender and is not connected with the commission of the offence itself.

It is possible for the court to find the reasons special enough to avoid obligatory disqualification but not special enough to avoid obligatory endorsement. If that is the case, the court will endorse the defendant's driving licence with penalty points. If the defendant already has sufficient penalty points on his driving licence, then he may find himself liable to be disqualified under the penalty points system.

> *Example*
> The defendant is charged with driving with excess alcohol which carries an obligatory disqualification. The defendant argues special reasons. The court finds the reasons special enough to avoid obligatory disqualification but not special enough to avoid obligatory endorsement. The defendant already has 9 points on his licence and so is liable to be disqualified under the penalty points system as 3–11 points must be endorsed on the defendant's driving licence for the offence.

The defendant must prove special reasons exist on the balance of probabilities. If the court finds special reasons, they must be stated in open court (and in magistrates' courts, recorded in the court register) (Road Traffic Offenders Act 1998, s 47(1)).

DISCRETIONARY DISQUALIFICATION FOR THE OFFENCE ITSELF

Whenever the court has a discretion to disqualify, mitigating factors can be put to the court with a view to avoiding disqualification or reducing the period. Mitigating factors are any factors which are relevant to the offence before the court. They can be connected with the circumstances of the offence itself or be personal to the offender. Therefore, unlike special reasons, factors such as loss of job on disqualification can be taken into account.

DISQUALIFICATION UNDER THE POINTS SYSTEM

If the court is satisfied that there are mitigating circumstances, it may decide not to disqualify under the points system or to reduce the period. All circumstances can be taken into account (both those connected with the offence and those personal to the offender) except:

(1)   the triviality of the present offence;
(2)   hardship (unless it is exceptional);
(3)   mitigating circumstances taken into account to avoid disqualification (or reduce the period) under the points system within the preceding 3 years (Road Traffic Offenders Act 1988, s 35(4)).

Example 1

James is liable to disqualification under the points system. He puts forward the fact that if disqualified he will lose his job. This can be taken into account only if the court is satisfied that loss of his job would constitute exceptional hardship.

Example 2

Joan is liable to disqualification under the points system. She avoided a points disqualification 18 months ago on the basis that disqualification would cause exceptional hardship due to the fact that she lives in an isolated area, with no public transport, and suffers from arthritis, making walking difficult. She cannot put forward these factors again at the current hearing.

The defendant must prove mitigating circumstances exist on the balance of probabilities. If the court finds mitigating circumstances, they must be stated in open court (and in the magistrates' court recorded in the court register) (Road Traffic Offenders Act 1988, s 47(1)).

9.2.14 Ancillary orders

A court has power to make the following ancillary orders.

Compensation orders (PCC(S)A 2000, ss 130–134)

The defendant can be ordered to pay compensation to the victim of an offence. Compensation cannot normally be ordered in respect of motoring offences. Magistrates can make an order of up to £5,000 per offence. There is no limit in the Crown Court, but the court must have regard to the defendant's means.

Forfeiture orders (PCC(S)A 2000, ss 143–145)

A court may order forfeiture of any property which was in the defendant's possession or control at the time of apprehension if the property was used for committing or facilitating any offence or was intended by him to be so used or was in his unlawful possession.

Confiscation orders (Crime and Disorder Act 1998, s 3)

A magistrates' court has the power to make a confiscation order in respect of the proceeds of crime if it commits a defendant to the Crown Court for sentence under s 3 or s 4 of the PCC(S)A 2000. The Crown Court may make a confiscation order in respect of the proceeds of crime (Criminal Justice Act 1988, ss 71–102). This is subject to detailed conditions beyond the scope of this book.

Prosecution costs (Prosecution of Offences Act 1985, s 18)

If the defendant is convicted of any offence, the court may order the defendant to pay to the prosecution such costs as are just and reasonable and must specify the amount.

Defence costs (Access to Justice Act 1999, s 17 and the Criminal Defence Service (Recovery of Defence Costs Orders) Regulations 2001, SI 2001/856)

A defendant who is not represented under a representation order and who is acquitted should normally be awarded costs from central funds (Prosecution of Offences Act 1985, s 16). There are exceptions, for example a defendant who by his conduct has brought suspicion upon himself, and has misled the prosecution into thinking that the case against him is stronger than it is, may find that costs are not awarded in his favour. (See further *Practice Direction (Crime: Costs)* [1991] 1 WLR 498, as amended by *Practice Direction (Costs in Criminal Proceedings) (No 2)* [2000] 1 Cr App R 60.)

At the conclusion of a case in the Crown Court the judge has the power to order a defendant who is represented under a representation order to pay some or all the costs of his defence (a recovery of defence costs order (RDCO)).

The judge has to consider making an RDCO at the end of the case and after all other financial orders and penalties that may be made. The judge will consider whether it is reasonable in all the circumstances of the case, including the means of the defendant to do so. The order is not dependent on the defendant being convicted and does not form part of his sentence, although an order against an acquitted defendant would be exceptional. The order can be for any amount up to the full costs incurred in representing the defendant and can include costs incurred in other courts.

An RDCO may not be made against a defendant who:

- only appears in the magistrates' court;
- has been committed for sentence to the Crown Court;
- is appealing against sentence in the Crown Court;
- has been acquitted other than in exceptional circumstances.

The defendant must complete Form B (see **Appendix 2(Q)**) and return it to the Crown Court at least four days before the first hearing at the Crown Court. The Crown Court will then refer the financial resources of the defendant to the Legal Services Commission who will prepare a report for the judge outlining the income and capital available to the defendant. The report will also be made available to the defence. The judge will then consider the report at the conclusion of the case and determine whether to make a RDCO. The judge may require the solicitor representing the defendant to provide an estimate of the costs likely to be incurred in the proceedings. If it later turns out that the actual costs incurred were less than the amount of the RDCO, then the balance must be repaid.

In deciding how much should be paid under an RDCO the judge will take into account the resources of the defendant together with the resources of his partner. The resources of other people who have been making funds available to the defendant can also be considered. Generally an order will not be made against the first £3000 of any capital available. The defendant's main dwelling may be treated as capital for the purposes of an RDCO but the first £100,000 of any equity (ie the market value less any outstanding mortgages) in that property will be disregarded. In most cases, RDCOs will be made on the basis of capital rather than income. Income will only be taken into account if the defendant's gross annual income exceeds £24,000.

The Crown Court has the power to make an order freezing the defendant's assets where it is appropriate to do so in support of the RDCO provisions. An RDCO may provide for payment to be made forthwith or by instalments. Payments are made to the Legal Services Commission. The Legal Service Commission may enforce an order as if it was a civil debt.

9.2.15 Deferment of sentence (PCC(S)A 2000, ss 1 and 2)

A court may defer sentence for up to 6 months. When the defendant appears to be sentenced, the court has the same powers of sentence as it had on conviction. If the defendant is convicted of any offence during the period of deferment, he may be sentenced for the deferred sentence at the same time.

This is a useful provision and can be used, for example, where the defendant claims that a recent change in circumstances in his life will mean that he is unlikely to offend again. If he has the offer of a job, or is about to be married, the court may decide to defer sentence for a period of up to 6 months to see how the defendant reacts to the change in his circumstances. If the reaction is favourable, a custodial sentence should not normally be imposed at the end of the period of deferment.

When imposing a deferred sentence, the court should specify what conduct is expected of the defendant and what sentence it is minded to impose if he does not comply. The court can defer sentence only once.

9.2.16 Committal to the Crown Court for sentence

PCC(S)A 2000, s 3

A magistrates' court may commit an offender of 18 years of age or above to the Crown Court for sentence if:

(1) it has convicted him of an offence triable either way; and either
(2) the offence (or the combination of the offence and one or more associated offences) was so serious that greater punishment should be inflicted for the offence than the court has power to impose; or
(3) in the case of a violent or sexual offence, a prison sentence or a term longer than the court has power to impose is necessary to protect the public from serious harm from him.

The Crown Court may then deal with the defendant as if he had been convicted on indictment.

At plea before venue, the defendant is asked to indicate a plea.

If the defendant indicates a guilty plea, the magistrates may still commit the defendant to the Crown Court for sentence if they consider their sentencing powers inadequate.

Example 1

D is charged with assault occasioning actual bodily harm. D indicates a guilty plea. The plea before venue procedure comes to an end and the magistrates proceed to sentence.

When the prosecution summarise the facts, the magistrates learn that the defendant attacked a bus driver who sustained extensive injuries. D may be committed to the Crown Court for sentence.

Example 2

D is charged with theft. D indicates a guilty plea. The plea before venue procedure comes to an end and the magistrates proceed to sentence.

The prosecutor hands into the court a list of D's previous convictions. D has numerous previous convictions for dishonesty offences. This may now be a suitable case for committal for sentence to the Crown Court.

In *R v Warley Magistrates' Court ex parte DPP; R v Staines Magistrates' Court ex parte DPP; R v North East Suffolk Magistrates' Court ex parte DPP; R v Lowestoft Justices ex parte DPP* [1998] 2 Cr App R 307, the Divisional Court considered the plea before venue procedure and committal for sentence. In deciding whether the powers of punishment were adequate, the magistrates should take into account the sentencing discount granted on a guilty plea. Where it was obvious that the gravity of the offence required punishment that would exceed the magistrates' powers, they should commit to the Crown Court without seeking any pre-sentence report or hearing mitigation. The defence should, however, be allowed to make a brief submission in opposition to this course of action and the prosecution should be allowed to reply.

If the defendant indicates a not guilty plea, the magistrates hear representations from the prosecution and the defence as to mode of trial. If the offence is so serious that the magistrates do not have sufficient sentencing powers, this will usually be revealed at the mode of trial enquiry and the magistrates will commit to the Crown Court for trial. A decision to commit for sentence is likely to be based on factors which were unknown at the mode of trial enquiry.

Example 3

D indicates a not guilty plea, the magistrates accept jurisdiction, and the defendant consents to summary trial. Having been convicted he asks for 16 other offences to be taken into consideration (TIC) (see **9.3.2**). The 'TICs' were not known at the mode of trial enquiry. D may be committed to the Crown Court for sentencing.

Example 4

Having indicated a not guilty plea, D is convicted by the magistrates. At the mode of trial enquiry, it appeared that the offence involved unoccupied premises. It later transpires that part of the premises consisted of a dwelling and the victim was frightened by D. This may now be a suitable case for committal for sentence to the Crown Court.

PCC(S)A 2000, s 4

This provision deals with the situation where the magistrates' court has committed a defendant for trial for some offences, but has to deal with him for other related either way offences. In this context, one offence is related to another if they can both be tried on the same indictment. If the defendant committed for trial has indicated an intention to plead guilty to those related offences, he must by virtue of the mode of trial procedure, be treated as if he has pleaded guilty to them (see **6.3**). Section 4 gives the magistrates power to commit the defendant to the Crown Court for sentence for the related offences, even if they do not meet the requirements laid down in s 3, ie that the offence is so serious that the magistrates' powers of punishment are inadequate or (in the case of a violent or sexual offence) that a longer sentence than they have power to impose is necessary to protect the public from serious harm from him.

> *Example*
> The defendant is charged with aggravated vehicle taking and theft of a radio cassette player from the same vehicle.
>
> At mode of trial, the defendant indicates a plea of not guilty to the theft charge. The magistrates accept jurisdiction and the defendant elects trial by jury.
>
> The defendant indicates a guilty plea to the aggravated vehicle taking charge which means that the magistrates will proceed to sentence.
>
> Instead of sentencing the defendant, the magistrates can commit the defendant for sentence for the aggravated vehicle taking charge under s 4 even though it does not meet the requirements for committal for sentence under s 3.

The powers of the Crown Court to sentence the defendant for the offence committed under s 4 depend on whether it convicts him of the original offence, ie the theft offence in the above example. If it convicts him of the original offence, then the Crown Court will have the power to impose any sentence which it would have power to impose if the defendant had been convicted on indictment. If not, the Crown Court's powers to deal with the defendant in respect of offences for which he has been committed for sentence are limited to those of the magistrates.

Committal for sentence – bail or custody

In most cases where a plea of guilty is made at the plea before venue, it will not be usual to alter the position as regards bail or custody. When a defendant who has been on bail pleads guilty at the plea before venue, the practice should normally be to continue bail, even if it is anticipated that a custodial sentence will be imposed at the Crown Court, unless there are good reasons for remanding the defendant in custody. If the defendant is in custody, then after entering a plea of guilty at the plea before venue, it will be unusual, if the reasons for remanding in custody remain unchanged, to alter the position (*R v Rafferty* [1999] 1 Cr App R 235).

9.3 SENTENCING PROCEDURE

Following a guilty plea or conviction of the defendant, it will often be necessary for the court to adjourn for reports to be prepared to assist the court in sentencing.

9.3.1 Pre-sentence reports

Pre-sentence reports are ordered by the court and made by a probation officer or social worker. The purpose of the report is to assist the court in deciding the most suitable method of dealing with the offender. If a custodial sentence is being considered by the court, the report should contain detailed information about how the offender could be punished in the community.

Pre-sentence reports will often be ordered before:

(1)   imposing any custodial sentence unless the offence (or an associated offence) is triable only on indictment and the court is of the opinion that it is unnecessary;

(2)   making a community rehabilitation order with additional requirements (see **9.2.4**);

(3)   making a community punishment order;

(4)   making a community punishment and rehabilitation order;

(5)   making a drug treatment and testing order.

A court need not obtain a pre-sentence report if it considers that it is unnecessary to do so. There will be cases, for example, when a custodial sentence is inevitable irrespective of the content of a pre-sentence report. A court may feel that a report is, therefore, not necessary. Courts are unlikely to impose a community sentence without a pre-sentence report because of the need to consult with the agencies responsible for supervision of the sentence (eg the Probation Service).

Copies of a pre-sentence report should be given by the court to the offender or his solicitor and to the prosecutor.

9.3.2 Procedure

Magistrates' court sentencing procedures are illustrated in a flowchart at **Appendix 1(Q)**.

Unless the defendant pleaded not guilty and sentencing is following immediately after trial, the prosecution will summarise the facts of the case.

Although the defendant pleads guilty, he may still dispute some prosecution allegations. If the dispute is substantial the court must either accept the defence account, and sentence accordingly, or give the parties the opportunity of calling evidence so that the dispute may be resolved (*R v Newton (Robert John)* (1983) 77 Cr App R 13). If evidence is called this is known as a '*Newton* hearing'.

> *Example*
> Fred pleads guilty to s 47 actual bodily harm. The prosecution alleges that he was the aggressor and launched an unprovoked attack. Fred says that he only attacked the other man after being subjected to racial abuse. The difference would have a major effect on the sentence the court would impose, and so the court must either hold a *Newton* hearing or accept Fred's account as true.

The prosecution will present details of the defendant's background and a record of his previous convictions to the court. When considering the seriousness of the offence, the court can take into account any previous convictions of the offender or any failure of his to respond to previous sentences. If the offence was committed whilst on bail, the court must treat that as an aggravating factor.

The prosecution will give details of other offences to be taken into consideration. In addition to the offence or offences charged, the defendant may have committed a number of other crimes. It is likely to be in the defendant's interest that all matters outstanding against him should be dealt with at the same time. The defendant can ask a court to take other offences into consideration on sentence. These should be offences of a similar or less serious nature. When sentencing the defendant, the court has the power to sentence only in respect of the offences with which he is convicted. The effect of asking for other offences to be taken into consideration is that the court is entitled to take them into account when passing sentence. If the defendant qualifies for a custodial sentence (see **9.2.1**), a number of TICs may increase the length of the sentence. In practice, the overall effect on the sentence is unlikely to be great, particularly when the offence charged is the most serious one.

If an offence is taken into consideration the defendant cannot subsequently be prosecuted for it. It is not a conviction but compensation can be awarded to the victim of a 'TIC' offence.

The practice involved in asking for other offences to be taken into consideration is that the defendant will be given a form by the police giving details of the various offences. He will sign the form and will be asked to admit before the court that he wishes the other offences to be taken into consideration on sentence. An example of a 'TIC' form appears at **Appendix 2(T)**.

Pre-sentence report and means enquiry form

If a report has been ordered it will now be made available to the court. In a magistrates' court, the defence will also have to produce a completed means enquiry form. This will be used by the court if a financial penalty is being considered.

The defence speech in mitigation is presented to the court (see **9.4**). Sentence is passed.

9.4 THE PLEA IN MITIGATION

9.4.1 The purpose of the plea in mitigation

The role of the defence solicitor in presenting a plea in mitigation to the court is either to reduce the severity of the sentence to be passed or, in appropriate cases, to persuade the court that punishment, as such, would be inexpedient and that a sentence which will help the defendant should be passed. The objective of the plea in mitigation is to ensure that a sentence is passed by the court which is appropriate both to the circumstances of the offence and to the circumstances of the defendant. The aim is to obtain the most lenient punishment which can reasonably be imposed.

9.4.2 Assessing the likely sentence

A common fault of young solicitor advocates is to 'talk up' a sentence. In other words, the advocate has not made any attempt to assess the likely range of penalties to be imposed for the offence and addresses the court on potential penalties which may be wholly inappropriate. The starting point for any plea in mitigation is to attempt to make a realistic assessment of the likely range of sentences which will be in the mind of the court.

A useful starting point in the magistrates' court is to consult the Magistrates' Association Sentencing Guidelines. If more than one offence is being dealt with, it is also necessary to bear in mind that the overall sentence should be kept in proportion to the 'totality' of the offending behaviour. This simply means that care should be taken in sentencing for several minor offences to avoid an overall sentence that would be more appropriate to a much more serious crime.

Extracts from the Sentencing Guidelines appear in **Appendix 3**, and should be consulted when a plea in mitigation is being prepared.

9.4.3 The plea in mitigation

When making a plea in mitigation, the advocate should address the court on the circumstances of the offence, the circumstances of the offender and the sentence he is seeking to persuade the magistrates to impose. An effective plea in mitigation will try to 'sell' a particular sentence by reference to the mitigating factors available. Whatever the advocate says about the offence and the offender should be designed to persuade the magistrates to impose a particular sentence.

The court may have ordered a pre-sentence report. The advocate should note any comments contained in the report about the offence, the defendant's background and any recommendation on sentence.

The court may hear character witnesses or receive letters or references on the defendant's behalf.

When the defendant wishes to avoid obligatory disqualification or endorsement for a driving offence, he will give evidence on oath of special reasons or mitigating circumstances.

The following are matters commonly dealt with by the advocate in his plea in mitigation.

The offence

AGGRAVATING FEATURES

The advocate should identify any aggravating features which would normally encourage a court to take the view that a sentence at the higher end of the scale should be appropriate and see if it is possible to disassociate the defendant's case from those features.

Under the PCC(S)A 2000, failure to respond to previous sentences may be taken into account when considering the seriousness of the offence, and if the offence is committed whilst on bail the court must treat that as an aggravating factor (see **9.2**). The court 'should identify any convictions relevant for this purpose and then consider to what extent they affect the seriousness of the present offence'

(Magistrates' Association Guidelines, p iii). Offences of a similar nature are therefore liable to weigh more heavily against the defendant than those of a different character.

It may therefore be necessary for the advocate to explain the circumstances of the previous offences and the defendant's failure to respond to previous sentences.

MITIGATING FEATURES

The advocate should identify whether there are any mitigating factors which should be brought to the attention of the court to reduce the seriousness of the offence. For example, if the offence is an offence against the person, provocation can be relevant mitigation.

The offender

The Magistrates' Association Sentencing Guidelines set out some examples of offender mitigation but there are frequently others to be considered in individual cases.

AGE

The younger the offender, the more likely a court will be to pass a sentence designed to help the offender rather than punish him. Equally, a defendant of advanced age may receive more sympathetic treatment than would otherwise be the case.

HEALTH (PHYSICAL OR MENTAL)

One of the most common explanations given to a court for criminal conduct is that the defendant was under the effects of drink or drugs. As a basic rule, the voluntary ingestion of drink or drugs will not be good mitigation. If, on the other hand, there is evidence that the defendant is an alcoholic or a drug addict, this may point towards the need for a sentence which will overcome these problems, as opposed to the imposition of a punitive penalty.

CO-OPERATION WITH THE POLICE

If a defendant has assisted the police with their enquiries by naming others involved in the crime or by revealing the whereabouts of stolen property which is subsequently recovered, this may be effective mitigation.

The fact that the defendant confessed when being questioned by the police can also be presented in a favourable light as the defendant has not wasted time during the investigation process.

VOLUNTARY COMPENSATION

A defendant who voluntarily makes good the damage which has been caused, or who makes voluntary payments of compensation may get credit from the court for this. The motive behind the reparation is obviously important. It is far easier for a wealthy person to make voluntary payments of compensation than for a person of limited means. The court will therefore look not only at whether reparation has been made, but also the reasons for it.

REMORSE

Evidence of remorse is undoubtedly effective mitigation in many cases. The fact that an advocate apologises to the court on behalf of his client is unlikely to have any great effect. The court is likely to be more impressed with tangible signs of remorse for example, the defendant taking positive steps to tackle the problems which led him to commit the offence.

OTHER OFFENDER MITIGATION

The defendant's advocate will explain to the court the defendant's reasons for committing the offence. If the offence is one involving dishonesty, the fact that the defendant was in serious financial difficulty can be put forward, although it must be appreciated that a mere plea 'that the defendant found it difficult to live on benefit' is unlikely to meet with any sympathy. A stressful home background which has driven the defendant to committing an offence can validly be put forward.

The advocate should explain why the defendant committed the offence in a way that puts the offence in the context of the defendant's life generally. The court will want to try and understand the defendant and why he committed the offence.

If the defendant has been convicted following a plea of not guilty, it will not usually be appropriate to then explain to the court why the defendant committed the offence.

A person of previous good character should be given credit for this fact. The defendant should be given some credit if he has no previous convictions for the kind of offence for which he has been convicted. For example, the advocate might say in mitigation that, although the defendant has a record for dishonesty offences, he has no history of violence so that, in relation to the assault, he should be treated as a person of good character. The defendant should also be given some credit if there has been a substantial gap between the present offence and the last one, indicating that the offender has made a genuine attempt to 'go straight'.

The defendant's present situation is of great importance. The court will be looking for evidence of the defendant's stability, a regular home and job, and people who will be supportive to the defendant. The advocate will need to compare the defendant's present situation with the time the offence was committed.

The mere fact that the defendant or his family will be upset by the imposition of a custodial sentence is unlikely to have any effect on the court. If, however, it can be shown that there are exceptional circumstances, the effect of imprisonment can, in appropriate cases, be effective mitigation. If the defendant's partner is seriously ill, for example, a court may decide not to impose an immediate custodial sentence. This, of course, will depend on the nature of the offence. It must be appreciated that some offences are so serious that custody is inevitable.

If conviction will result in dismissal from employment, this factor may be taken into account by the court, although if the offence is related to the defendant's employment it will be less effective mitigation.

In driving offences, the loss of licence will inevitably lead to hardship and this can be taken into account to avoid discretionary disqualification for the offence but not to avoid disqualification under the points system unless such hardship is exceptional.

When a fine is a possibility, the advocate will need to obtain considerable detail about the defendant's financial position (eg income after tax, outgoings out of income, any capital) in order to help the court fix the fine at a proper level. In the magistrates' court, the defence will have to produce a completed means enquiry form. The advocate will also need to take the defendant's instructions on how much time the defendant will need to pay any fine imposed and the level of weekly instalments he could meet.

Sentence

The PCC(S)A 2000, s 152 requires a court to take into account in deciding the sentence to pass on an offender who has pleaded guilty:

(1) the stage in the proceedings for the offence at which the offender indicated his intention to plead guilty; and

(2) the circumstances in which the indication was given.

The object of this provision is to save court time and spare, for example, victims of crime the anxiety of giving evidence. Section 48 may result in a discount being given on a custodial sentence or the number of hours to be served under a community punishment order being reduced.

Example 1

Joe is arrested at the scene of a burglary. He is caught 'red handed' by the police. The circumstances of the case make it unlikely that any credit will be given for a guilty plea. A guilty plea is almost inevitable on the facts.

Example 2

Peter is arrested for theft. The evidence against him is largely circumstantial. He makes a full confession to the police and, on his first appearance before a court, indicates his intention to plead guilty. Peter will get full credit for his early guilty plea in these circumstances.

The possible sentencing options should be addressed and the advocate should identify the advantages of the sentence he is arguing for and any detrimental effects of those he is arguing against.

The advocate should also deal with any ancillary orders, for example, compensation, forfeiture, and costs, which the prosecution may have applied for.

The mitigating factors which are set out above are not exhaustive but are some of the most commonly used.

9.5 SENTENCING GUIDELINES

Under ss 80 and 81 of the Crime and Disorder Act 1998, the Court of Appeal can give guidance on sentences imposed for indictable offences. A duty is imposed on the Court of Appeal to consider whether to frame guidelines, or to revise existing guidelines. In considering guidelines, the Court of Appeal must have regard to the need to promote consistency in sentencing, the pattern of sentencing for similar offences, the cost and effectiveness of different offences and the need to promote public confidence in the criminal justice system. This duty is supplemented by the creation of a new body, the Sentencing Advisory Panel, which, on its own initiative, may propose to the Court of Appeal that guidelines for particular categories of offence be adopted or revised and must do so if directed by the Home Secretary. In either situation, it will consult, consider and formulate views and furnish information to the Court of Appeal. The Panel is appointed by the Lord Chancellor.

For offences sentenced in the magistrates' court, the Magistrates' Association has issued guidelines.

Extracts from the Magistrates' Association Sentencing Guidelines are set out in **Appendix 3**.

9.6 FURTHER READING

See, for example:

Archbold: Criminal Pleading, Evidence and Practice (Sweet & Maxwell, 2001);
Blackstone's Criminal Practice (Blackstone Press, 2001);
John Sprack *Emmins on Criminal Procedure* (Blackstone Press, 2000);
Michael Fritton and David Roberts *The Advocates' Sentencing Guide* (The Law Society, 1998);
Wallis and Halnan *Wilkinson's Road Traffic Offences* (FT Law & Tax, 2000).

Chapter 10

THE YOUTH COURT

10.1 GENERAL

Defendants under the age of 18 must be dealt with in the youth court unless:

(1) they are charged with homicide, in which case they must be committed to the Crown Court;

(2) they are charged jointly with an adult and the court considers it necessary in the interests of justice for both to be tried in the Crown Court; or

(3) a defendant aged 10 to 17 inclusive is charged with indecent assault or an offence which carries a maximum penalty of 14 years or more for an adult or the defendant is aged 14–17 inclusive and is charged with causing death by dangerous driving, or causing death by dangerous driving whilst under the influence of drink or drugs, and the court considers that, if he or she is convicted, no disposal would be appropriate other than a term of detention under PCC(S)A 2000, s 91, in which case the matter should be sent to the Crown Court. (Section 91 of the PCC(S)A 2000 permits a period of detention in excess of the normal maximum that can be imposed on an offender aged under 18, ie 24 months.)

10.2 SENTENCING

A detailed consideration of sentencing in the youth court is beyond the scope of this book. For the most part, sentencing principles are similar to the sentencing principles that apply in the adult court.

10.2.1 Detention and training orders (PCC(S)A 2000, ss 100–107)

A detention and training order requires the offender to be subject to a period of detention and training followed by a period of supervision. The court will be able to impose a detention and training order on those aged 15–17 inclusive, convicted of an imprisonable offence sufficiently serious to justify custody, and on those aged 12–14 inclusive, convicted of an imprisonable offence sufficiently serious to justify custody who are, in the opinion of the court, persistent offenders.

Subject to the limitation as to overall length, the period of a detention and training order shall be 4, 6, 8, 10, 12, 18, or 24 months. The total length of the order (comprising both the period of detention and training and also the period of supervision) may not exceed the maximum term of imprisonment that a Crown Court could impose on an adult offender (PCC(S)A 2000, s 101(2)).

10.2.2 Community sentences

Community rehabilitation orders (Criminal Justice and Court Services Act 2000, s 43, PCC(S)A 2000, ss 41–45 and Schs 2 and 3)

A community rehabilitation order is available for offenders of a minimum age of 16.

Community punishment (Criminal Justice and Court Services Act 2000, s 44, PCC(S)A 2000, ss 46–50 and Sch 3)

Community punishment orders are available for offenders aged at least 16.

Community punishment and rehabilitation orders (Criminal Justice and Court Services Act 2000, s 45, PCC(S)A 2000, s 51 and Sch 3)

Community punishment and rehabilitation orders are available for defendants aged at least 16.

Curfew orders (PCC(S)A 2000, s 59 and Sch 3)

Curfew orders are available for offenders of a minimum age of 10.

Drug treatment and testing orders (PCC(S)A 2000, ss 52–58 and Sch 3)

Drug treatment and testing orders are available for defendants aged 16 or over.

Attendance centre orders (PCC(S)A 2000, ss 60–62 and Sch 5)

Attendance centre orders are available for offenders of a minimum age of 10.

Action plan orders (PCC(S)A 2000, ss 69–72 and Sch 7)

These are designed to give the offender a short but intensive programme of work with the offender, and his parents, to tackle the causes of offending at an early age. The court can impose such an order where it thinks that this will prevent reoffending or will rehabilitate the offender. The offender must comply with a 3-month action plan. The plan will impose certain requirements regarding the offender's behaviour and whereabouts. The order cannot be combined with custody or any other community sentence. Action plan orders are available for offenders aged 10 to 17 inclusive.

Supervision orders (PCC(S)A 2000, ss 63–68 and Sch 7)

A supervision order may be made on an offender aged under 18, placing him under the supervision of a local authority or a probation officer or a member of a youth offending team. In many ways, a supervision order is the equivalent for children or young persons of a community rehabilitation order. The basic supervision order may be supplemented, where appropriate, with various requirements: for example, making reparation to a specified person. It is not possible, however, to combine a reparation order (see below) with a supervision order. If an offender is suitable to be made the subject of a supervision order, a reparation element should form a requirement of such an order. Before making such requirements, the court should consider the views of the victim. There is no specified minimum period to a supervision order and the maximum period is 3 years.

10.2.3 Reparation orders (PCC(S)A 2000, ss 73–75 and Sch 8)

A reparation order may require an offender to, inter alia, write a letter of apology to the victim, apologise to the victim in person, or repair criminal damage. This is not a community sentence. It cannot be combined with custody or a community sentence but can be made a requirement of a supervision order (see above). If, in any case, the court has power to make a reparation order but does not do so, it shall give reasons as to why it does not make the order. It is intended that courts consider the making of the order in any case in which a compensation order is not imposed.

10.2.4 Fines and discharges

Fines and discharges are available in the youth court. Parents may be ordered to pay fines imposed in respect of offenders under the age of 18 (PCC(S)A 2000, s 137).

10.2.5 Referrals to youth offender panels (PCC(S)A 2000, ss 16–32 and Sch 1)

Referral to a youth offender panel is available for young people convicted for the first time. Its primary aim is to prevent re-offending. The youth offender panel is composed of people with an interest or expertise in dealing with young people.

The youth offender panel will work with the young offender and his family to establish a programme of behaviour for the young offender to follow. The programme will be guided by the following three principles:

(1) making reparation to the victim;
(2) achieving reintegration into the law-abiding community;
(3) taking responsibility for the consequences of offending behaviour.

10.3 FURTHER READING

See, for example:

Archbold: Criminal Pleading, Evidence and Practice (Sweet & Maxwell, 2001);
Blackstone's Criminal Practice (Blackstone Press, 2001);
John Sprack *Emmins on Criminal Procedure* (Blackstone Press, 2000);
Michael Fritton and David Roberts *The Advocates' Sentencing Guide* (The Law Society, 1998).

Chapter 11

APPEALS

11.1 APPEALS FROM THE MAGISTRATES' COURT AND YOUTH COURT

A flowchart summarising appeals from the magistrates' court and youth court appears as **Appendix 1(R)**.

11.1.1 To the Crown Court

The defendant may appeal against conviction or sentence, but if he pleaded guilty he may only appeal against sentence unless he claims his plea was equivocal (Magistrates' Courts Act 1980, s 108).

If the Crown Court is satisfied that the plea was equivocal, it will remit the case to the magistrates' court with a direction that a plea of not guilty be entered.

Notice of appeal must be given both to the justices' clerk and the prosecution within 21 days of sentence. The Crown Court has power to grant leave to appeal out of time, but this is rarely exercised. An example of a notice of appeal appears in **Appendix 2(U)**.

Appeals against conviction and/or sentence will be heard by a Crown Court judge or a recorder sitting with between two and four magistrates. The appeal will take the form of a re-hearing. If the appeal is against conviction, all of the evidence will be heard again. If the appeal is against sentence, the prosecution will outline the facts of the case to the court who will decide what the appropriate sentence is.

On an appeal to the Crown Court, the court may:

(1) confirm, reverse or vary the magistrates' decision; or
(2) remit the matter (eg on an equivocal plea) with its opinion thereon to the magistrates; or
(3) make such other order in the matter as the court thinks just and by such order exercise any power which the magistrates might have exercised. This means, for example, that orders for costs and compensation can be made.

The Crown Court may issue any sentence, which may be heavier or lighter than that of the magistrates, provided the sentence is one which the magistrates' court had power to issue. It is important, therefore, to point out to a defendant who wishes to appeal to the Crown Court that his sentence could be increased up to the maximum sentencing powers of the magistrates' court which originally dealt with the case.

11.1.2 To the High Court (Queen's Bench Division) by case stated

Either the defence or the prosecution may appeal from the decision of a magistrates' court to the High Court (Queen's Bench Division). The right of appeal is available where the magistrates' decision is wrong in law or was given in excess of the magistrates' jurisdiction (Magistrates' Courts Act 1980, s 111). The High Court may affirm, reverse or vary the decision of the magistrates or remit the case to the magistrates' court with its opinion. The procedure for the appeal is not a re-hearing. The appeal will be decided after hearing arguments on points of law put forward by the parties.

11.2 APPEALS FROM THE CROWN COURT

A flowchart summarising appeals from the Crown Court following a trial on indictment appears as **Appendix 1(S)**.

A defendant may appeal against conviction to the Court of Appeal only with leave of the Court of Appeal or where the trial judge has issued a certificate of fitness for appeal. This applies whether the appeal is on a question of fact, a question of law or a mixed question of fact and law (Criminal Appeals Act 1995, s 1).

The test for granting leave to appeal is whether the court feels that the conviction is unsafe. In practice, this comes down to the question of whether there is a real danger that the defendant might have been prejudiced.

As a result of the decision in *Condron and Another v United Kingdom* (see **2.9.6**) where the procedure at trial is held to be in violation of Article 6 (right to a fair trial), a conviction will be deemed unsafe.

A defendant may appeal his sentence with leave of the Court of Appeal. The Court of Appeal cannot increase the sentence but may either confirm or reduce it.

The prosecution cannot appeal to the Court of Appeal against the acquittal of a defendant or against the sentence imposed on the defendant. However, if it appears to the Attorney-General that the sentencing of a person in the Crown Court has been unduly lenient he may, with the leave of the Court of Appeal, refer the case to the Court of Appeal to review the sentencing of that person. On such a referral, the Court of Appeal may quash any sentence passed on the defendant and, in place of it, pass such sentence as it thinks appropriate for the case and in accordance with the powers which the Crown Court had in dealing with him.

11.3 FURTHER READING

See, for example:

Archbold: Criminal Pleading, Evidence and Practice (Sweet & Maxwell, 2001);
Blackstone's Criminal Practice (Blackstone Press, 2001);
John Sprack *Emmins on Criminal Procedure* (Blackstone Press, 2000).

APPENDICES

Appendix 1

PROCEDURAL CHARTS AND DIAGRAMS

(A)   AN OVERVIEW OF CRIMINAL PROCEDURE

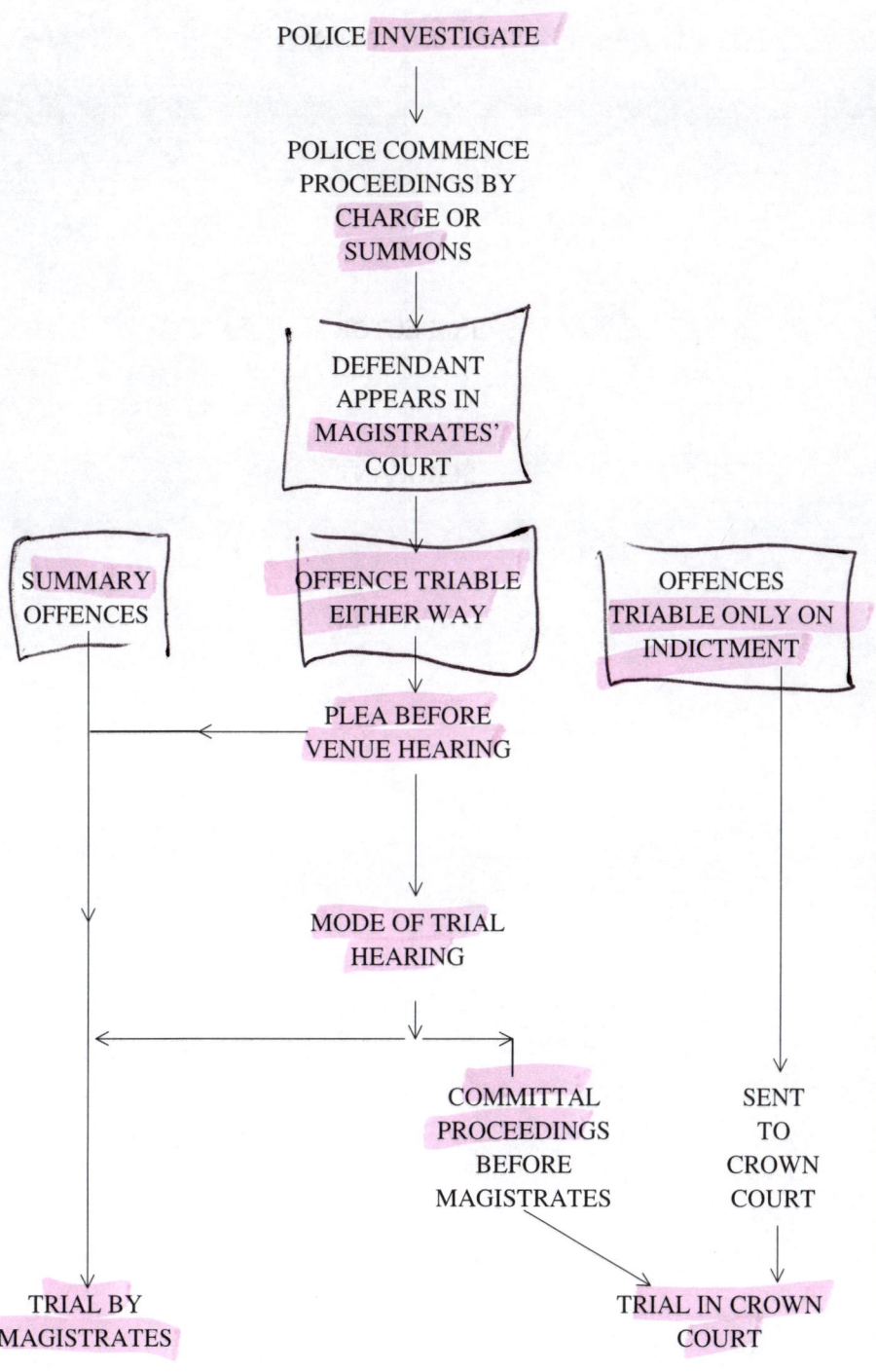

POLICE INVESTIGATE

POLICE COMMENCE
PROCEEDINGS BY
CHARGE OR
SUMMONS

DEFENDANT
APPEARS IN
MAGISTRATES'
COURT

SUMMARY
OFFENCES

OFFENCE TRIABLE
EITHER WAY

OFFENCES
TRIABLE ONLY ON
INDICTMENT

PLEA BEFORE
VENUE HEARING

MODE OF TRIAL
HEARING

COMMITTAL
PROCEEDINGS
BEFORE
MAGISTRATES

SENT
TO
CROWN
COURT

TRIAL BY
MAGISTRATES

TRIAL IN CROWN
COURT

(B)   POLICE RANKS

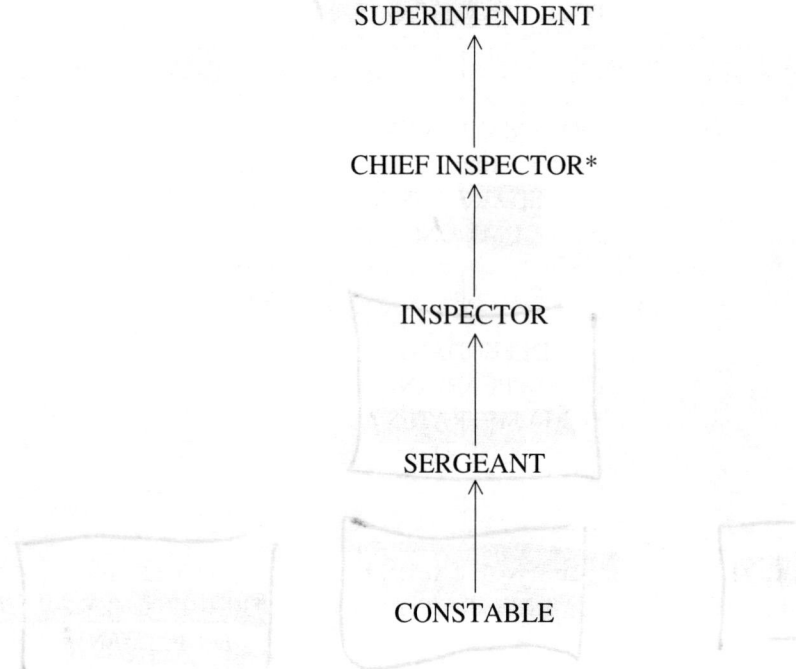

SUPERINTENDENT

↑

CHIEF INSPECTOR*

↑

INSPECTOR

↑

SERGEANT

↑

CONSTABLE

* Not a significant rank under PACE 1984

(C) POLICE STATION PROCEDURE

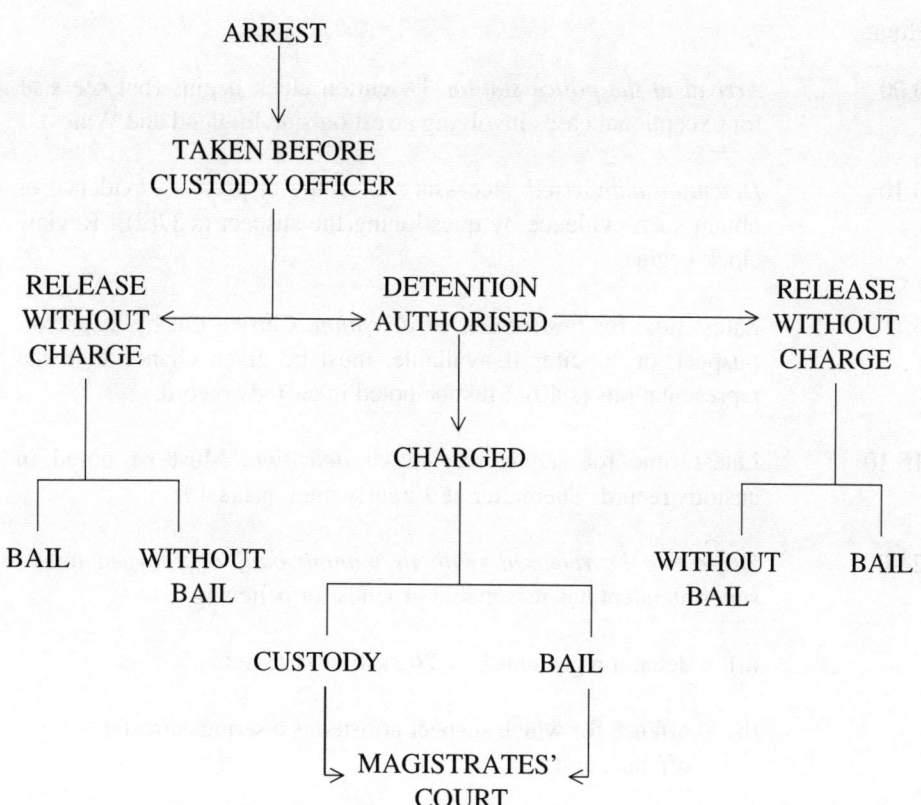

(D)   THE DETENTION PROCESS

Hours

0.00   *Arrival at the police station.* Detention clock begins (but see s 41 for exceptional cases involving arrest outside England and Wales).

0.10   *Detention authorised.* Necessary to secure or preserve evidence or obtain such evidence by questioning the suspect (s 37(2)). Review clock begins.

6.10   Latest time for *first review of detention.* Carried out by inspector. Suspect, or solicitor if available, must be given chance to make representations (s 40). Must be noted in custody record.

15.10   Latest time for *second review of detention.* Must be noted in custody record. Thereafter at 9-hourly intervals (s 40).

24.00   *Suspect to be released (with or without bail) or charged* unless superintendent has reasonable grounds for believing:

              (a)   detention grounds in s 37(2) still exist; and

              (b)   offence for which suspect arrested is a serious arrestable offence; and

              (c)   investigation conducted diligently and expeditiously.

              Authorisation cannot be granted before second review or after 24 hours (s 42).

36.00   *Superintendent's authority expires.* Suspect to be released (with or without bail) or charged unless extension of warrant of further detention obtained from magistrates' court.

72.00   *Maximum period warrant can authorise expires.* Suspect to be released (with or without bail) or charged unless extension of warrant obtained from magistrates (s 43).

96.00   *Absolute maximum period of detention.* Suspect to be released (with or without bail) or charged.

(E)   COMMENCEMENT OF CRIMINAL PROCEEDINGS

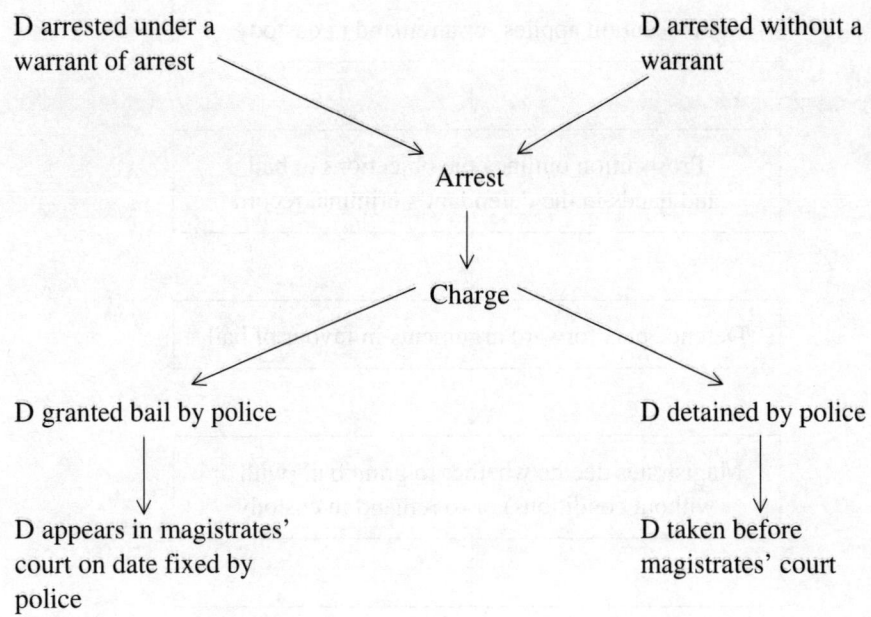

D arrested under a
warrant of arrest

D arrested without a
warrant

Arrest

Charge

D granted bail by police

D detained by police

D appears in magistrates'
court on date fixed by
police

D taken before
magistrates' court

OR

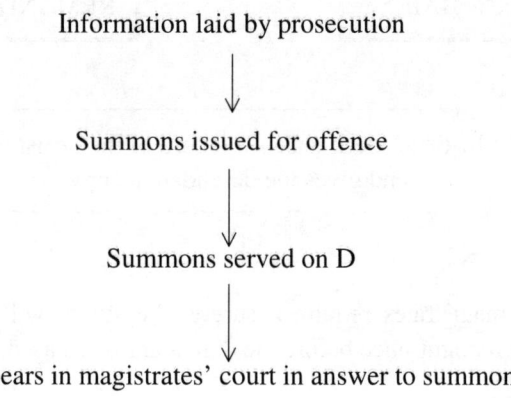

Information laid by prosecution

Summons issued for offence

Summons served on D

D appears in magistrates' court in answer to summons

(F)   CONTESTED BAIL APPLICATION PROCEDURE

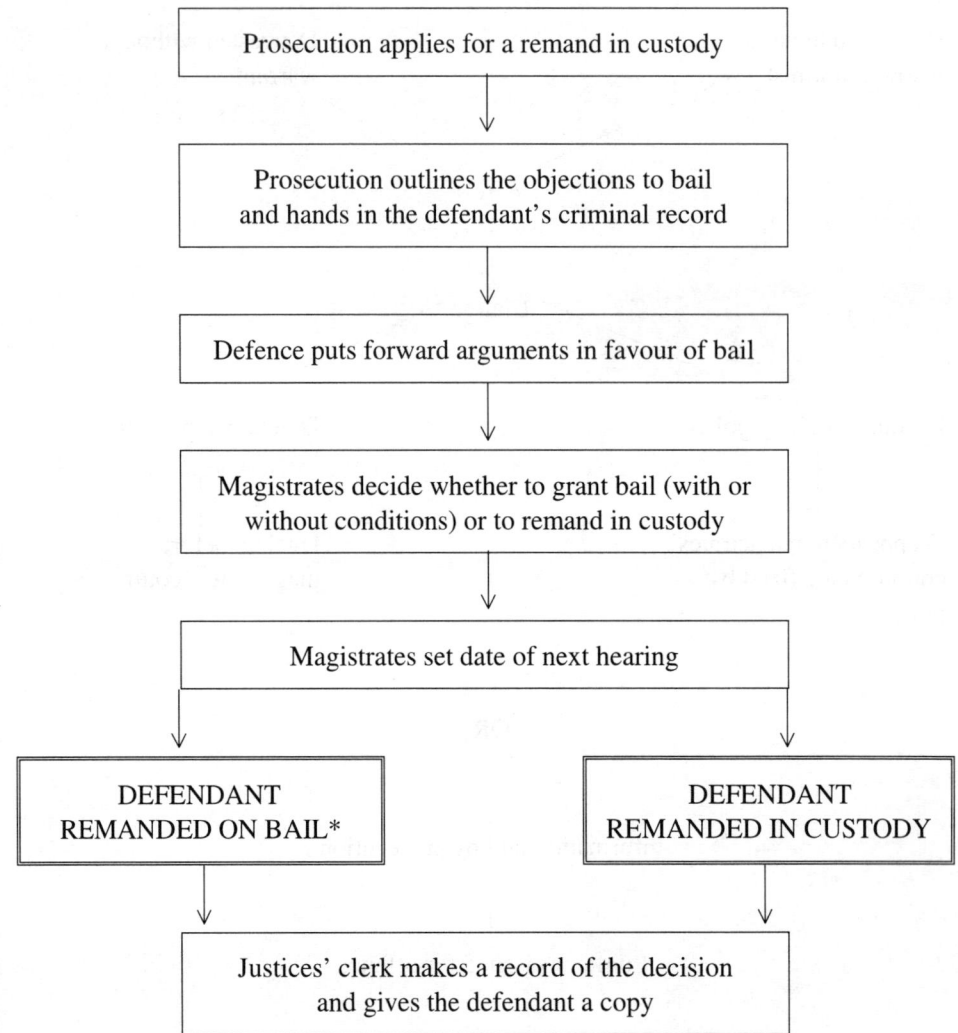

* *Note*:   If the magistrates require a surety, the surety will have to enter into his/her recognisance before the defendant is released.

(G) DOCUMENTARY HEARSAY (CRIMINAL JUSTICE ACT 1988, s 23)

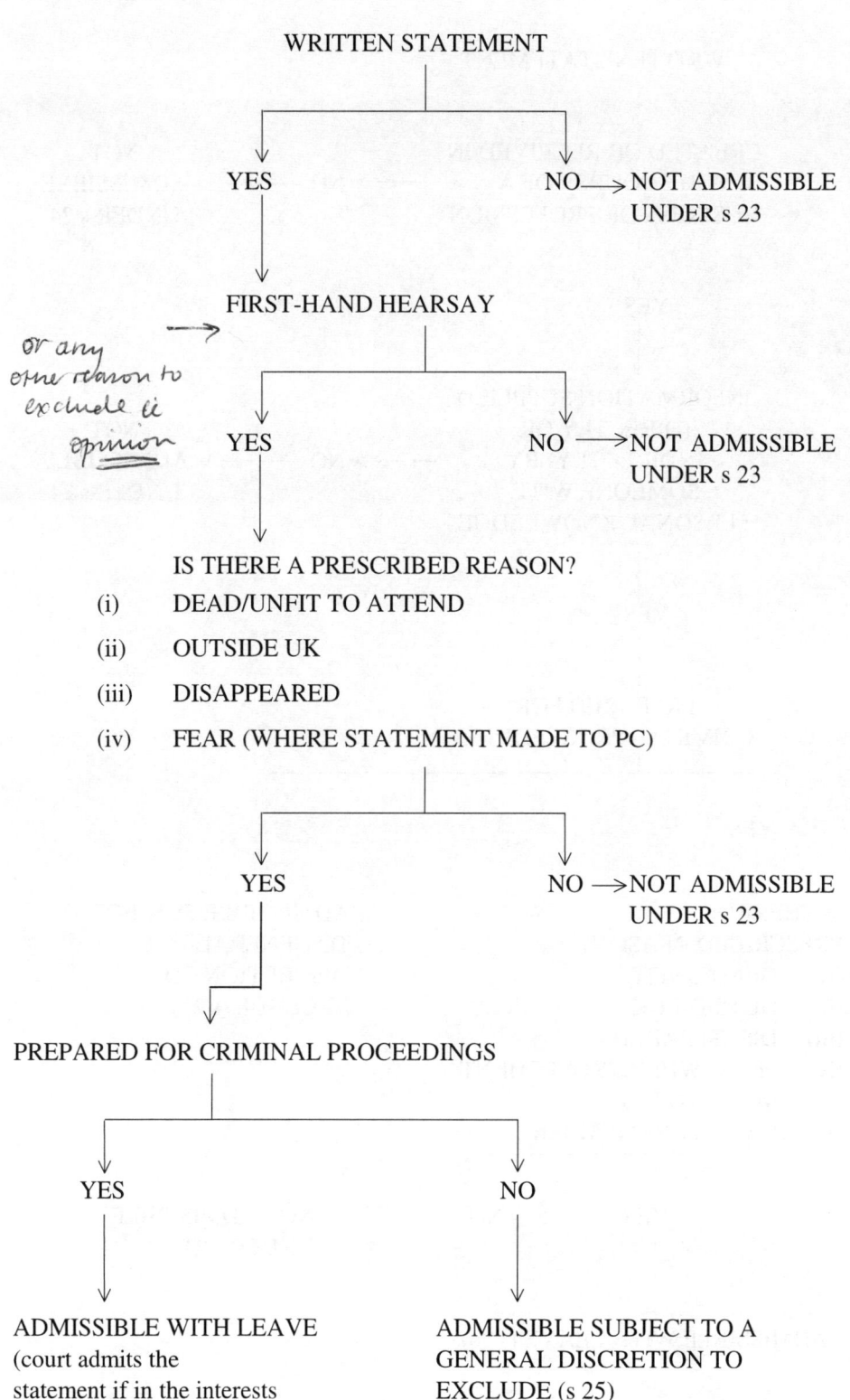

WRITTEN STATEMENT

YES   NO → NOT ADMISSIBLE UNDER s 23

FIRST-HAND HEARSAY

or any other reason to exclude ie opinion

YES   NO → NOT ADMISSIBLE UNDER s 23

IS THERE A PRESCRIBED REASON?

(i)   DEAD/UNFIT TO ATTEND

(ii)   OUTSIDE UK

(iii) DISAPPEARED

(iv)   FEAR (WHERE STATEMENT MADE TO PC)

YES   NO → NOT ADMISSIBLE UNDER s 23

PREPARED FOR CRIMINAL PROCEEDINGS

YES   NO

ADMISSIBLE WITH LEAVE
(court admits the
statement if in the interests
of justice (s 26))

ADMISSIBLE SUBJECT TO A
GENERAL DISCRETION TO
EXCLUDE (s 25)

(H)   DOCUMENTARY HEARSAY (CRIMINAL JUSTICE ACT 1988, s 24)

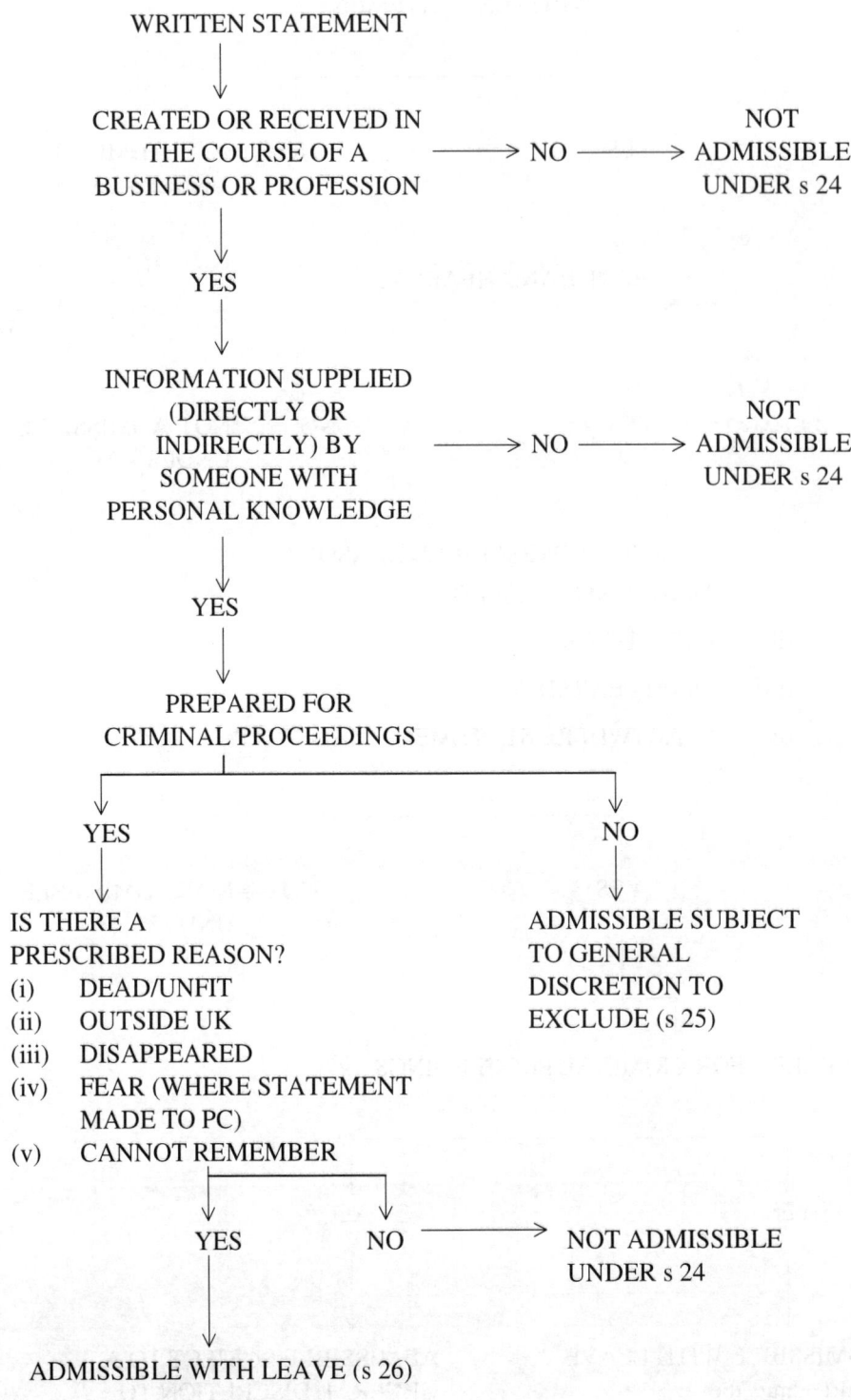

WRITTEN STATEMENT

CREATED OR RECEIVED IN
THE COURSE OF A   ⟶ NO ⟶   NOT
BUSINESS OR PROFESSION   ADMISSIBLE
                                            UNDER s 24

YES

INFORMATION SUPPLIED
(DIRECTLY OR
INDIRECTLY) BY   ⟶ NO ⟶   NOT
SOMEONE WITH   ADMISSIBLE
PERSONAL KNOWLEDGE   UNDER s 24

YES

PREPARED FOR
CRIMINAL PROCEEDINGS

YES   NO

IS THERE A   ADMISSIBLE SUBJECT
PRESCRIBED REASON?   TO GENERAL
(i)   DEAD/UNFIT   DISCRETION TO
(ii)   OUTSIDE UK   EXCLUDE (s 25)
(iii)   DISAPPEARED
(iv)   FEAR (WHERE STATEMENT
        MADE TO PC)
(v)   CANNOT REMEMBER

        YES   NO   ⟶   NOT ADMISSIBLE
                                  UNDER s 24

ADMISSIBLE WITH LEAVE (s 26)

(I) **DISCLOSURE IN THE MAGISTRATES' COURT OF MATERIAL THE PROSECUTION DOES NOT INTEND TO RELY ON**

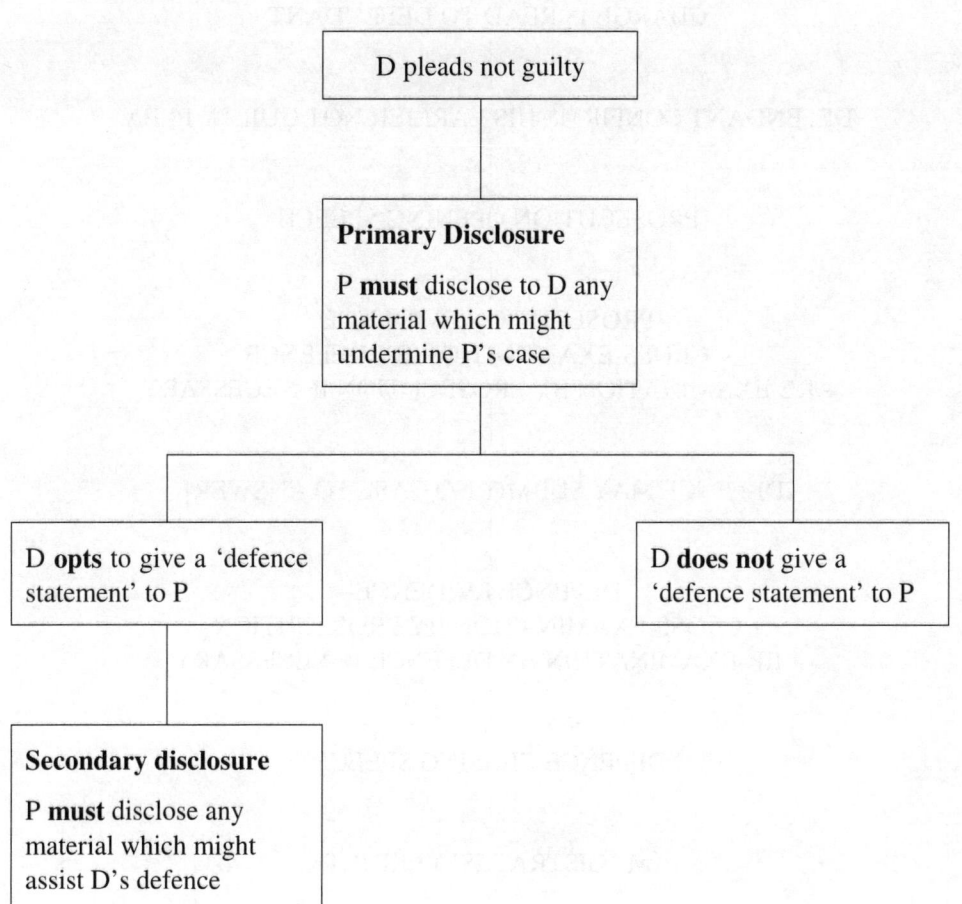

**(J) MAGISTRATES' COURT PROCEDURE –
NOT GUILTY PLEA**

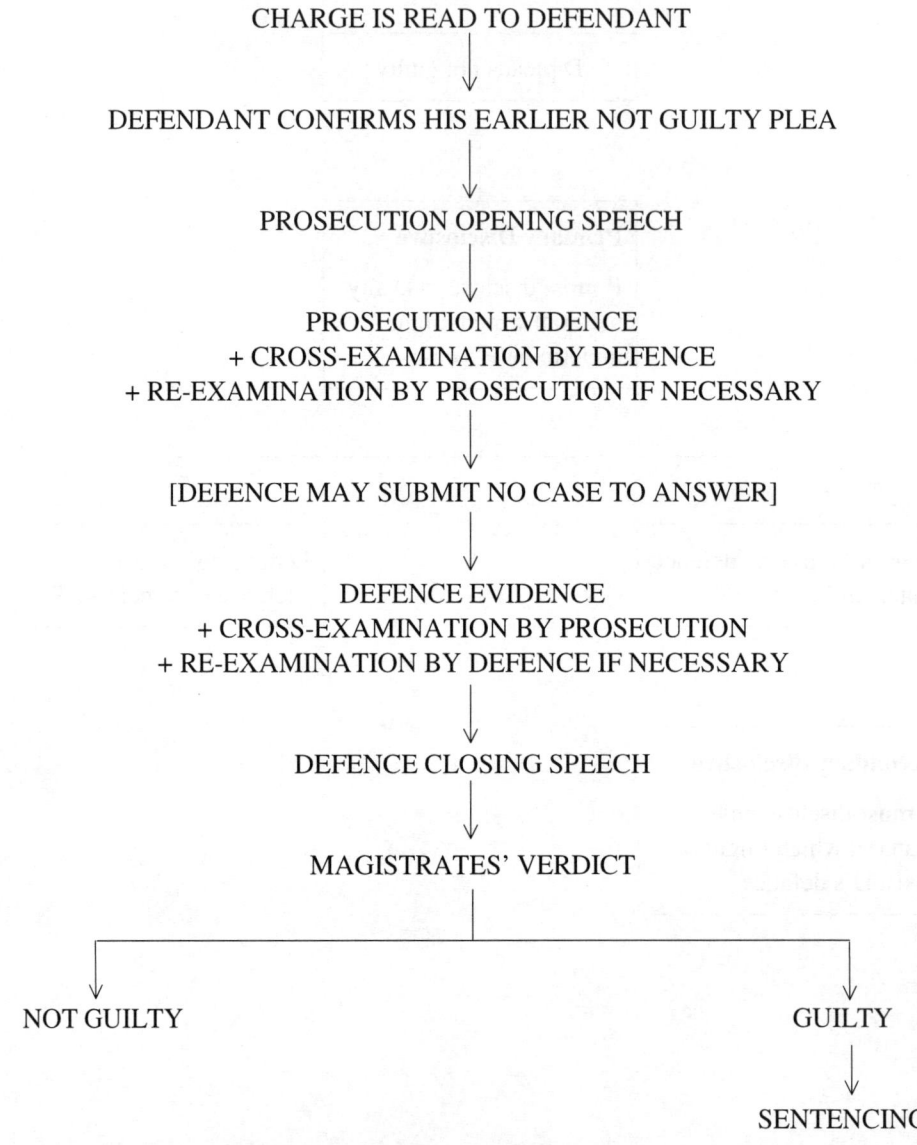

CHARGE IS READ TO DEFENDANT

DEFENDANT CONFIRMS HIS EARLIER NOT GUILTY PLEA

PROSECUTION OPENING SPEECH

PROSECUTION EVIDENCE
+ CROSS-EXAMINATION BY DEFENCE
+ RE-EXAMINATION BY PROSECUTION IF NECESSARY

[DEFENCE MAY SUBMIT NO CASE TO ANSWER]

DEFENCE EVIDENCE
+ CROSS-EXAMINATION BY PROSECUTION
+ RE-EXAMINATION BY DEFENCE IF NECESSARY

DEFENCE CLOSING SPEECH

MAGISTRATES' VERDICT

NOT GUILTY   GUILTY

SENTENCING

(K) PLEA BEFORE VENUE AND MODE OF TRIAL PROCEDURE

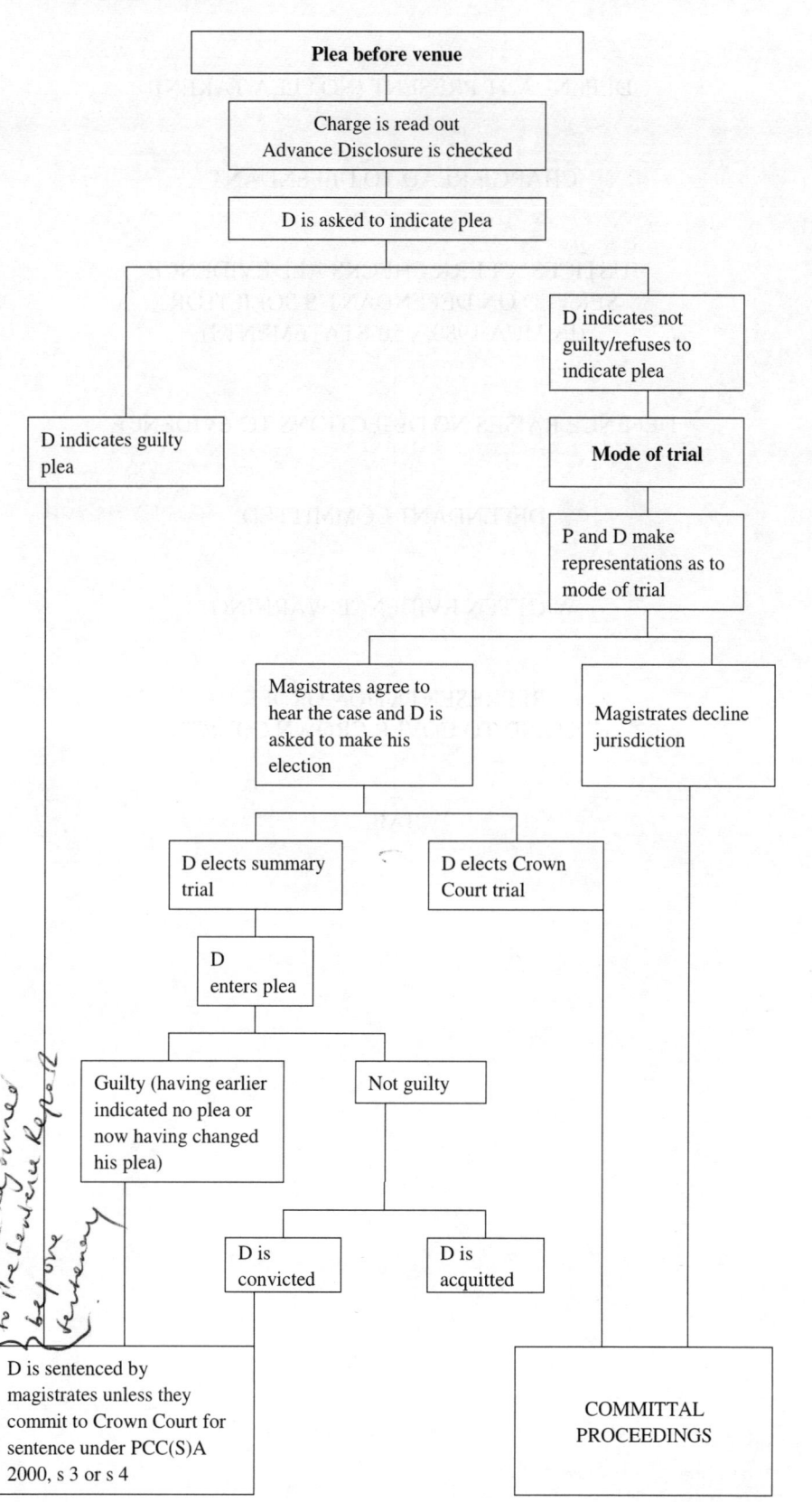

Plea before venue

Charge is read out
Advance Disclosure is checked

D is asked to indicate plea

D indicates not guilty/refuses to indicate plea

D indicates guilty plea

Mode of trial

P and D make representations as to mode of trial

Magistrates agree to hear the case and D is asked to make his election

Magistrates decline jurisdiction

D elects summary trial

D elects Crown Court trial

D enters plea

Guilty (having earlier indicated no plea or now having changed his plea)

Not guilty

D is convicted

D is acquitted

D is sentenced by magistrates unless they commit to Crown Court for sentence under PCC(S)A 2000, s 3 or s 4

COMMITTAL PROCEEDINGS

Terry Ball would adjourned to the lawyers report before sentence

(L)   COMMITTAL WITHOUT CONSIDERATION OF THE EVIDENCE (MAGISTRATES' COURTS ACT 1980, s 6(2))

DEFENDANT PRESENT (NO PLEA TAKEN)

↓

CHARGE READ TO DEFENDANT

↓

JUSTICES' CLERK CHECKS ALL EVIDENCE
SERVED ON DEFENDANT'S SOLICITOR
(IN MCA 1980, s 5B STATEMENTS)

↓

DEFENCE RAISES NO OBJECTIONS TO EVIDENCE

↓

DEFENDANT COMMITTED

↓

WRITTEN EVIDENCE WARNING

↓

REPRESENTATION ORDER
(EXTEND TO COVER CROWN COURT)

↓

BAIL

**(M)   COMMITTAL WITH CONSIDERATION OF THE
           EVIDENCE (MAGISTRATES' COURTS ACT 1980, s 6(1))**

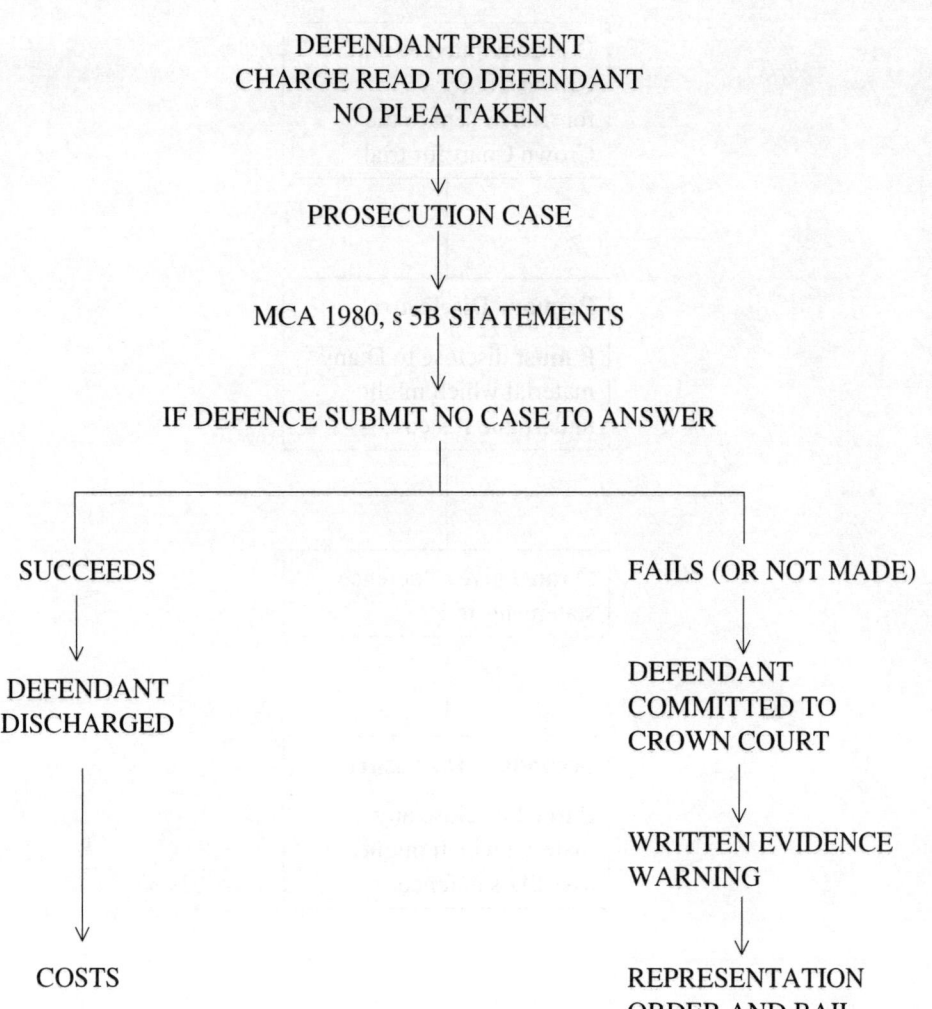

DEFENDANT PRESENT
CHARGE READ TO DEFENDANT
NO PLEA TAKEN

PROSECUTION CASE

MCA 1980, s 5B STATEMENTS

IF DEFENCE SUBMIT NO CASE TO ANSWER

SUCCEEDS

FAILS (OR NOT MADE)

DEFENDANT
DISCHARGED

DEFENDANT
COMMITTED TO
CROWN COURT

WRITTEN EVIDENCE
WARNING

COSTS

REPRESENTATION
ORDER AND BAIL

(N)   DISCLOSURE IN THE CROWN COURT OF MATERIAL THE PROSECUTION DOES NOT INTEND TO RELY ON

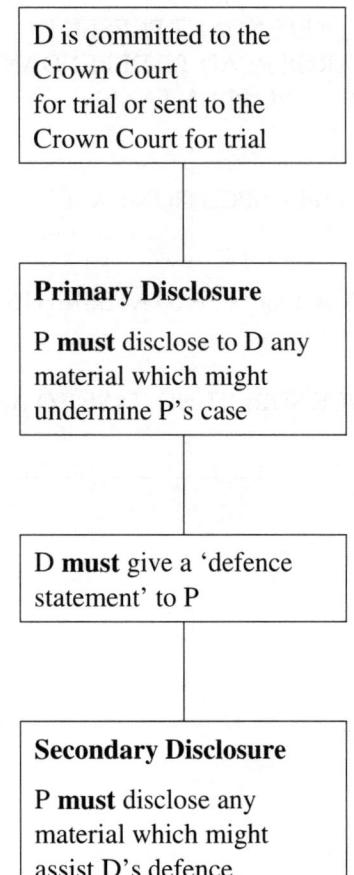

(O) CROWN COURT PROCEDURE – NOT GUILTY PLEA

DEFENDANT PLEADS NOT GUILTY

↓

PROSECUTION OPENING SPEECH

↓

PROSECUTION EVIDENCE
+ CROSS-EXAMINATION
+ RE-EXAMINATION

↓

[POSSIBLE SUBMISSION OF NO CASE TO ANSWER]

↓

DEFENCE EVIDENCE
+ CROSS-EXAMINATION
+ RE-EXAMINATION

↓

PROSECUTION CLOSING SPEECH

↓

DEFENCE CLOSING SPEECH

↓

JUDGE'S SUMMING UP
(as to law)

↓

JURY'S VERDICT
(on the facts)

↓

JUDGE SENTENCES
(if convicted)

(P) **THE POWERS OF CRIMINAL COURTS (SENTENCING) ACT 2000 SENTENCING SCHEME FOR ADULT OFFENDERS**

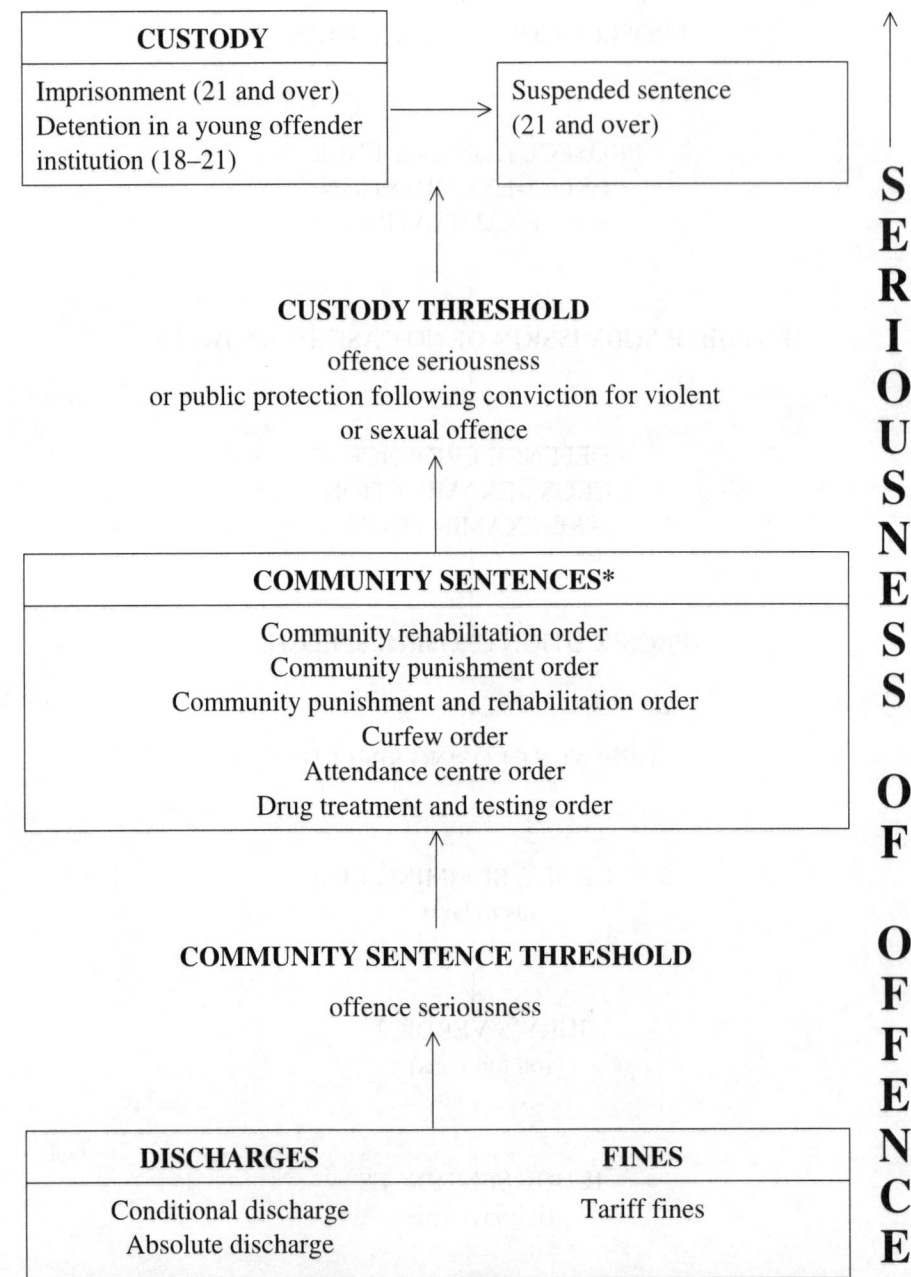

CUSTODY
Imprisonment (21 and over) Detention in a young offender institution (18–21)

Suspended sentence (21 and over)

CUSTODY THRESHOLD

offence seriousness
or public protection following conviction for violent
or sexual offence

COMMUNITY SENTENCES*
Community rehabilitation order Community punishment order Community punishment and rehabilitation order Curfew order Attendance centre order Drug treatment and testing order

COMMUNITY SENTENCE THRESHOLD

offence seriousness

DISCHARGES	FINES
Conditional discharge Absolute discharge	Tariff fines

S E R I O U S N E S S   O F   O F F E N C E

* Selection of particular community sentences requires justification in terms of both 'suitability' and 'seriousness of offence'.

(Q)   MAGISTRATES' COURT SENTENCING PROCEDURES

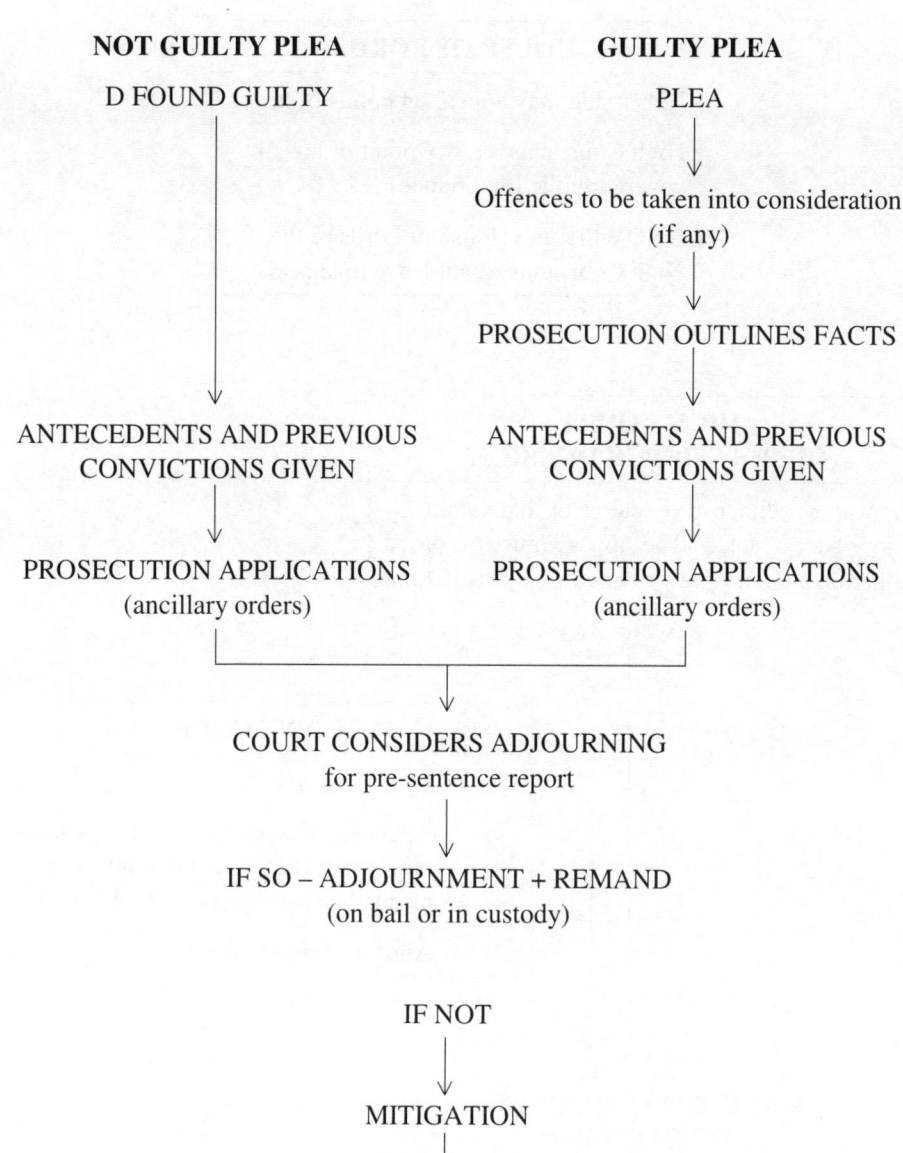

NOT GUILTY PLEA

D FOUND GUILTY

GUILTY PLEA

PLEA

Offences to be taken into consideration
(if any)

PROSECUTION OUTLINES FACTS

ANTECEDENTS AND PREVIOUS
CONVICTIONS GIVEN

ANTECEDENTS AND PREVIOUS
CONVICTIONS GIVEN

PROSECUTION APPLICATIONS
(ancillary orders)

PROSECUTION APPLICATIONS
(ancillary orders)

COURT CONSIDERS ADJOURNING
for pre-sentence report

IF SO – ADJOURNMENT + REMAND
(on bail or in custody)

IF NOT

MITIGATION

SENTENCE

(R)   SUMMARY TRIALS: APPEALS

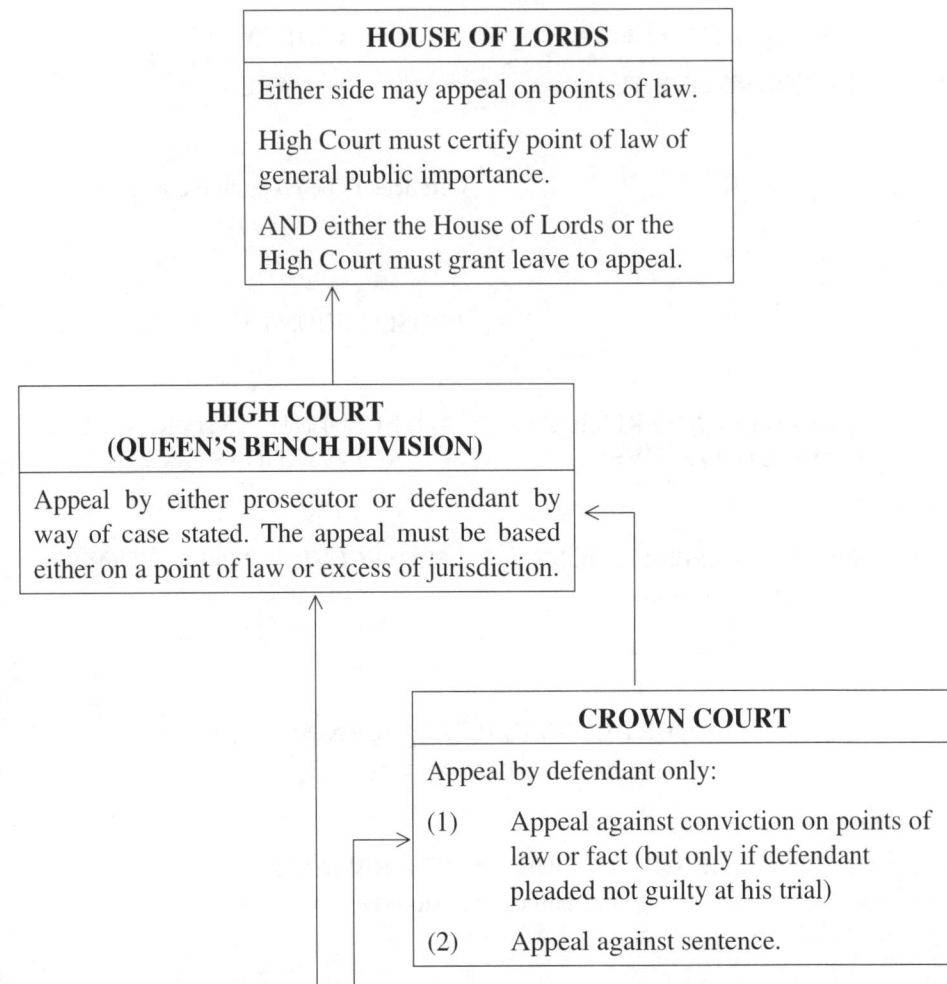

HOUSE OF LORDS

Either side may appeal on points of law.

High Court must certify point of law of general public importance.

AND either the House of Lords or the High Court must grant leave to appeal.

HIGH COURT (QUEEN'S BENCH DIVISION)

Appeal by either prosecutor or defendant by way of case stated. The appeal must be based either on a point of law or excess of jurisdiction.

CROWN COURT

Appeal by defendant only:

(1)   Appeal against conviction on points of law or fact (but only if defendant pleaded not guilty at his trial)

(2)   Appeal against sentence.

MAGISTRATES' COURT YOUTH COURT

Summary trial

(S)   TRIAL ON INDICTMENT: APPEALS

HOUSE OF LORDS

Appeal on points of law only

Court of Appeal must certify point of law of general public importance; AND Court of Appeal or House of Lords must grant leave to appeal.

Either side may appeal.

(Attorney-General's references may reach House of Lords.)

(Attorney-General's references on sentence may also reach House of Lords.)

↑

COURT OF APPEAL (CRIMINAL DIVISION)

Appeal by defendant only

(1)   against conviction – on a point of law or fact or mixed law and fact – leave required (unless trial judge has issued certificate of fitness for appeal).

(2)   against sentence – leave required (unless trial judge has issued certificate of fitness for appeal).

[Following an acquittal in the Crown Court, the Attorney-General may refer a point of law for clarification to Court of Appeal – but this does not affect the acquittal (Criminal Justice Act 1972, s 36).]

Where the Attorney-General believes that the trial judge has imposed a sentence which is unduly lenient (in certain serious offences) he may refer the case to the Court of Appeal where the sentence can be replaced by one the Court of Appeal considers to be more appropriate (Criminal Justice Act 1988, ss 35, 36).

↑

CROWN COURT

Trial on indictment before judge and jury

Appendix 2
DOCUMENTS

(A)   **Custody Record**

(B)   **Volunteer's Notice**

(C)   **Notice to Detained Person**

(D)   **Notice of Entitlements**

(E)   **Record of Tape-recorded Interview**

(F)   **Written Statement under Caution**

(G)   **Solicitor's Record of Attendance at Police Station**

(H)   **Identification Parade Record**

(I)   **Charge Sheet**

(J)   **Summons**

(K)   **Application for the Right to Representation in Criminal Proceedings: Magistrates' Court or Crown Court (Form A)**

(L)   **Representation Order: Magistrates' Court**

(M)   **Record of Decision to Grant or Withhold Bail and Certificate as to Hearing of Full Argument on Application for Bail**

(N)   **Witness Statement**

(O)   **Criminal Procedure and Investigations Act 1996 Part I: Disclosure; Rights and Duties of Accused Persons**

(P)   **Notice to Accused: Right to Object to Written Statement or Deposition**

(Q)   **Statement of means for Right to Representation in Criminal Proceedings in the Crown Court (Form B)**

(R)   **Plea and Directions Hearing – Judge's Questionnaire**

(S)   **Brief to Counsel**

(T)   **'TIC' Form**

(U)   **Notice of Appeal**

(A) CUSTODY RECORD

BLANKSHIRE POLICE
CUSTODY RECORD

| Station: WEYFORD | EM No: | | Custody No: | WE 17963 | 9 |

1. Reasons for Arrest: TAKING A CONVEYANCE — s.12(1) THEFT ACT 1968, THEFT OF £750 — s.1(1) THEFT ACT 1968

2. † Comment made by person if present when facts of arrest explained
Yes ☐   No ☑   If "Yes" record on Log of Events

3. Place of Arrest: 123 SOMERSET AVENUE, WEYFORD

4.

	Time	Date
Arrested at:	20.45	30/7/00
Arrived at Station:	21.00	30/7/00
Relevant Time:	21.00	30/7/00

Condition on Arrival: ....
Relevant time not applicable ☐ ✓ if appropriate

5. DETENTION DECISION   *Delete as appropriate*
A. Detention authorised*:
~~B. Detention not authorised*:~~
Signature: John Platt
Name: JOHN PLATT
Time: 21.10   Date: 30/7/00
REASON FOR DETENTION:
(i) To charge .... ☐
&/or (ii) Other authority (state authority) .... ☐
&/or (iii) Other secure or preserve evidence .... ☐
&/or (iv) To obtain evidence by questioning .... ☑
Record grounds for detention – MUST complete for (iii) and (iv).
ARRESTED IN POSSESSION OF PROPERTY STOLEN FROM MOTOR VEHICLE, DETENTION NECESSARY TO OBTAIN EVIDENCE BY QUESTIONING

Person present when grounds recorded: Yes ☑ : No ☐x
Person informed of grounds: Yes ☑ : No ☐x
x : If 'No', in either case, record reason(s) in Log of Events

6. † Comment made by person when informed of detention
Yes ☐   No ☑   If "Yes" record on Log of Events

7. Drugs Referral Information leaflet issued:
Time: ....   Date: ..../..................../...............

OFFICER OPENING CUSTODY RECORD
Signature: John Platt
Name: JOHN PLATT
Rank/No: SGT 3456
Time: 21.10   Date: 30/7/00

11.97

8. PERSONAL DETAILS
Surname: EVERETT
Forename(s): RONALD EDWIN
Address: 123 SOMERSET AVENUE, WEYFORD, BLANKSHIRE
Telephone No: 01730 400902   Post Code WE2 1AE
Occupation: LABOURER
Age: 43   Date of Birth: 25/6/57
Height: 1M 80   Sex: Male/Female
Ethnic Origin: GB
Place of Birth: GB

9. Arresting Officer: ALAN BROWN
Rank: DC   No: 2907   Stn: WEYFORD

10. Officer in the case: ALAN BROWN
Rank: DC   No: 2907   Stn: WEYFORD

11. DETAINED PERSON'S RIGHTS
An extract from a notice setting out my rights has been read to me and I have been given a copy. I have also been provided with a written notice setting out my entitlements while in custody.
Signature: Everett
Time: 21.10   Date: 30/7/00

LEGAL ADVICE REQUESTED
I want to speak to a solicitor as soon as practicable:
Signature: Everett
Time: 21.10   Date: 30/7/00

LEGAL ADVICE DECLINED
I have been informed that I may speak to a solicitor IN PERSON or ON THE TELEPHONE:
Signature: ....
Time: ....   Date: ..../.........../...........
I DO NOT WANT TO SPEAK TO A SOLICITOR at this time:
Signature: ....
Time: ....   Date: ..../.........../...........
† Reasons, if given, for not wanting legal advice:

Notification of named person: Requested Yes ☐ : No ☑
Nominated person: ....
Detainees signature: ....

12. APPROPRIATE ADULT   INTERPRETER
Yes ☐ : No ☑   Yes ☐ : No ☑
Notices served, rights and grounds for detention explained in presence of Appropriate Adult/Interpreter.
Signature of A/Adult: ....
Time: ....   Date: ..../.........../...........
Signature of Interpreter: ....
Time: ....   Date: ..../.........../...........

13. FOREIGN NATIONALS
Embassy/Consulate informed: Yes ☐ : Not Applicable ☑
(Record details in Log of Events)
Force Immigration Dept informed: Yes ☐ : Record on 7K

RECORD OF RIGHTS

| Surname | EVERETT | | Custody Record No. | WE | 17963 | 9 |

Interpreter present   Yes ☐   No ☑   Detained person informed of rights   Yes ☑   No ☐
                                                                 (If No, record reason on detention log)

> "You have the right to have someone informed that you have been detained. You have the right to consult privately with an independent solicitor either in person, in writing or on the telephone. Independent legal advice is available from the duty solicitor free of charge. You also have the right to consult a copy of the Codes of Practice covering police powers and procedures. You may do any of these things now, but if you do not you may still do so at any time whilst detained at the police station."

Solicitor requested   Yes ☑   No ☐
(If No, remind the person of the right to speak to a solicitor, in person, or on the telephone)

Solicitor requested   Yes ☑   No ☐
(If No, ask for and if applicable, record reason)

Name of solicitor requested   MR. ANDREW CRAWFORD

Reason, if given, for not
wanting legal advice

Notification of named person requested   Yes ☐   No ☑

Details of nominated person (if appropriate)

Name

Address

Telephone number

Details of appropriate adult (if appropriate)

Name

Address

Telephone number

> An extract from a notice setting out a detained person's rights has been read to me and I have been given a copy. I have been provided with a written notice setting out a detained person's entitlements while in custody.
>
> I ~~do~~/ do not .... want a person informed.
>
> I understand that my right to speak to a solicitor includes the right to speak on the telephone.
>
> I do /~~do not~~ want to ~~speak~~ to a solicitor at this time.
>
> Signature *~~Everett~~*   Time 21.10   Date 30|7|00

DETENTION LOG

Surname [EVERETT]   Custody Record No. [WE | 17963 | 9]

Date	Time		Signed
30/7/00	21.10	Detention authorised for questioning. Everett informed of rights. Requested access to solicitor but no notification to a third party.	J Platt
30/7/00	21.15	Search of Everett. Wallet marked 'A' containing £10 retained.	J Platt
30/7/00	21.20	Telephoned Mr. Andrew Crawford, Solicitors at Everett's request. Consultation on telephone between Everett and solicitor. Mr. Crawford asked note to be made that travelling to station to see Everett.	J Platt
30/7/00	21.30	Everett taken cup of tea and placed in cell.	J Platt
30/7/00	21.45	Mr. Crawford, Solicitor arrived to see Everett. Everett taken from cell to interview room by PC Smith. Private consultation with solicitor.	J Platt
30/7/00	22.30	Everett transferred to custody of Inspector Kingston for identification parade.	J Platt
30/7/00	23.05	Everett transferred to my custody by Inspector Kingston who confirmed all provisions of Identification Code complied with.	J Platt
30/7/00	23.15	Everett transferred to custody of DC Brown. Taken to interview room. Interviewed by DC Brown in presence of WDC Carpenter and Mr Crawford, Solicitor.	J Platt
30/7/00	23.45	Everett returned to my custody by DC Brown who stated to me that all provisions of Detention Code complied with.	J Platt
30/7/00	23.55	Sufficient evidence to charge Everett. Everett placed in cell by PC Smith while papers prepared.	J Platt
31/7/00	00.20	Everett charged. Copy charge supplied.	
31/7/00	00.25	Authorised Everett to be kept in custody on grounds I believed that he would not answer bail. Informed Everett and Mr. Crawford accordingly.	J Platt
31/7/00	00.35	Everett returned to his cell by PC Smith. Given snack and cup of tea.	J Platt
31/7/00	01.00	Visited. Asleep.	J Platt
31/7/00	02.00	Visited. Asleep.	J Platt
31/7/00	02.45	Detention reviewed. Everett asleep. No representations. Ground for detention unchanged.	J Platt
31/7/00	03.00	Visited. Asleep.	S Platt
31/7/00	04.00	Visited. Asleep.	J Platt
31/7/00	05.00	Visited. Asleep.	J Platt
31/7/00	06.00	Visited. Asleep.	J Platt

DETENTION LOG

| Surname | EVERETT | | Custody Record No. | WE | 17963 | 9 |

Date	Time		Signed
31/7/00	07.00	Everett given breakfast. Informed of result of review. No comment from Everett.	J Platt
31/7/00	08.30	Transferred to custody of PS 972 White to take to Weyford Magistrates' Court.	J Platt

(B) VOLUNTEER'S NOTICE

BLANKSHIRE POLICE

PERSON ATTENDING VOLUNTARILY AT POLICE STATION AND NOT UNDER ARREST

You can speak to a solicitor at the police station at any time, day or night. It will cost you nothing.

If you do not know a solicitor, or you cannot contact your own solicitor, ask for the duty solicitor. He or she is nothing to do with the police. Or you can ask to see a list of local solicitors.

You can talk to the solicitor in private on the telephone, and the solicitor may come and see you at the police station.

If the police want to question you, you can ask for the solicitor to be there. If there is a delay ask the police to contact the solicitor again. You can ask the police to wait for the solicitor to be at the interview.

The Law Society   **The Criminal Defence Service**

(C)   NOTICE TO DETAINED PERSON

BLANKSHIRE POLICE

Notice to Detained Person

The section in capital letters is to be read by the detained person by the custody officer before giving the notice to the detained person.

YOU HAVE THE RIGHT TO:

(1)   SPEAK TO AN INDEPENDENT SOLICITOR FREE OF CHARGE
(2)   HAVE SOMEONE TOLD THAT YOU HAVE BEEN ARRESTED
(3)   CONSULT THE CODES OF PRACTICE COVERING POLICE POWERS AND PROCEDURES.

YOU MAY DO ANY OF THESE THINGS NOW, BUT IF YOU DO NOT, YOU MAY STILL DO SO ANY TIME WHILST DETAINED AT THE POLICE STATION.

If you are asked questions about a suspected offence, you do not have to say anything. But it may harm your defence if you do not mention when questioned something which you later rely on in court. Anything you do say may be given in evidence.

Free Legal Advice

You can speak to a solicitor at the police station at any time, day or night. It will cost you nothing.

Access to legal advice can only be delayed in certain circumstances (see Annex B of Code of Practice C).

If you do not know a solicitor, or you cannot contact your own solicitor, ask for the duty solicitor. He or she is nothing to do with the police. Or you can ask to see a list of local solicitors.

You can talk to the solicitor in private on the telephone, and the solicitor may come to see you at the police station.

If the police want to question you, you can ask for the solicitor to be there.

If there is a delay, ask the police to contact the solicitor again. Normally, the police must not question you until you have spoken to the solicitor. However, there are certain circumstances in which the police may question you without a solicitor being present (see paragraph 6.6 of Code of Practice C).

If you want to see a solicitor, tell the custody officer at once. You can ask for legal advice at any time during your detention. Even if you tell the police you do not want a solicitor at first, you can change your mind at any time.

Your right to legal advice does not entitle you to delay procedures under the Road Traffic Act 1988 which require the provision of breath, blood and urine specimens.

THE LAW SOCIETY   The Criminal Defence Service

The right to have someone informed of your detention.

You may on request have one person known to you, or who is likely to take an interest in your welfare, informed at public expense as soon as practicable of your whereabouts. If the person you name cannot be contacted you may choose up to two alternatives. If they too cannot be contacted the custody officer has discretion to allow further attempts until the information can be conveyed. This right can

only be delayed in exceptional circumstances (see Annex B of Code of Practice C).

The right to consult the Codes of Practice.

The Codes of Practice will be made available to you on request. These Codes govern police procedures. The right to consult the Codes of Practice does not entitle you to delay unreasonably any necessary investigative and administrative action, neither does it allow procedures under the Road Traffic Act of 1988 requiring the provision of breath, blood or urine specimens to be delayed.

The right to a copy of the Custody Record.

A record of your detention will be kept by the custody officer. When you leave police detention or are taken before a court, you and your legal representative or the appropriate adult shall be supplied on request with a copy of the custody record as soon as practicable. This entitlement lasts for 12 months after your release from police detention.

(D)   NOTICE OF ENTITLEMENTS

BLANKSHIRE POLICE
NOTICE OF ENTITLEMENTS

This notice summarises provisions contained in Codes C and D of the Codes of Practice regarding your entitlements whilst in custody. The letters and numbers in brackets relate to the appropriate Code and paragraph references. If you require more detailed information please ask to consult the Codes.

All persons should read parts A and B of the notice. Part C explains provisions which apply to juveniles and persons suffering from mental disorder or mental handicap and Part D explains additional provisions which apply to citizens of independent commonwealth countries and nationals of foreign countries.

PART A – GENERAL ENTITLEMENTS

Whilst in custody you are entitled to the following:–

1. **Visits and contact with outside persons**
    In addition to your rights to have someone informed of your arrest, and legal advice, you may receive visits, at the custody officer's discretion. Unless certain conditions apply you may also make one telephone call, and be supplied with writing materials ('C'5.4 and 5.6).

2. **Reasonable Standards of Physical Comfort**
    Where practicable you should have your own cell ('C'8.1), which is clean, heated, ventilated and lit ('C'8.2). Bedding should be clean and serviceable ('C'8.3).

3. **Adequate Food and Drink**
    Three meals per day. Drinks with and, upon reasonable request, between meals ('C' 8.6).

4. **Access to Toilets and Washing Facilities** ('C' 8.4).

5. **Replacement Clothing**
    If your own clothes are taken from you, you must be given replacements that are clean and comfortable ('C'8.5).

6. **Medical Attention**
    You may ask to see the police surgeon (or other doctor at your own expense) for a medical examination, or if you require medication. You may also be allowed to take or apply your own medication at appropriate times, but in the case of controlled drugs the police surgeon will supervise you when doing so ('C'9.4–'C'9.6).

7. **Exercise**
    Where practicable, brief outdoor exercise every day ('C'8.7).

8. **If in 'Police Detention' to make representations when your detention is reviewed**
    When the grounds for your detention are periodically reviewed, you have a statutory right to say why you think you should be released, unless you are unfit to do so because of your condition or behaviour ('C'15.1).

PART B – CONDUCT OF INTERVIEWS

1. Interview rooms should be adequately heated, lit and ventilated ('C'12.4).

2. Persons being interviewed should not be required to stand ('C'12.5).

3. In any 24 hour period you must be allowed at least 8 hours rest, normally at night 'C'12.7).

4. Breaks should be made at recognised meal times, and short breaks for refreshments should normally be made at intervals of approximately two hours ('C'12.7)

5. Interviewing officers should identify themselves by name and rank (or by warrant number in terrorism cases) ('C'12.6).

PART C – APPROPRIATE ADULTS

If you are under 17 years of age or suffering from a mental disorder or mental handicap, you should be assisted by an 'appropriate adult' as explained in Code C, paragraph 1.7. A solicitor present at the station in a professional capacity may not act as the appropriate adult ('C' Note 1F). The appropriate adult will be present when you are:

1. informed of and served with notices explaining the rights of detained persons, and when informed of the grounds for detention ('C'3.11);

2. interviewed (except in urgent cases), or provide or sign a written statement ('C'11.14);

3. intimately searched ('C' Annex A, paragraph 4);

4. cautioned ('C'10.6);

5. given information, asked to sign documentation, or asked to give consent regarding any identification procedure ('D'1.11, 1.12, 1.13); or

6. charged ('C'16.1); or

7. when the grounds for detention are periodically reviewed ('C'15.1).

PART D – FOREIGN NATIONALS/COMMONWEALTH CITIZENS

If you are a citizen of a foreign or commonwealth country, you are entitled to the following:

1. To communicate at any time with your High Commission, Embassy or Consulate, and have them told of your whereabouts and the grounds for your detention ('C'7.1).
2. To private visits from a consular officer to talk, or to arrange for legal advice ('C'7.3).

(E) RECORD OF A TAPE-RECORDED INTERVIEW

BLANKSHIRE POLICE

RECORD OF TAPE RECORDED INTERVIEW

Name of person interviewed Ronald E. Everrett at Weyford Police Station

Date of interview 30.7.0- Time commenced 22.30 Time concluded 22.45

Interviewing Officer(s) DC 2907 Brown Tape Reference 9_/WPS/1697

Other Person(s) Present Donald Crawford Solicitor Exhibit Number AB/2

This record consisting of 2 pages is the exhibit referred to in the statement made and signed by me. The interviewee has been cautioned by me and informed that at the end of the interview a notice will be given to him/her about what will happen to the tapes

Signature *Alan Brown*

Signature of officer preparing record _____
(if different from above)

Tape Times		
0050		Introductions. Caution.
		You have been positively identified as the man who took away a Jaguar from New Street this afternoon. What do you have to say?
	R	He's wrong. It wasn't me.
	2907	Well, he's certain about it. There was £750 stolen from that car and in your flat there is very nearly £750 in cash. How do you account for that?
	R	I've saved it. We're trying to buy a house.
2.30	2907	And the leather jacket is just a coincidence?
	R	I've told you. I don't know anything about any of it - lots of people have leather jackets.
10.00	2907	Was your wife with you this afternoon?
	R	Yes.
	2907	She remembers it differently from you.
	R	How do you mean?
	2907	She told us all about it - that you and she took the car and stole the money.
	R	You're lying.
	2907	No. It's written down. Want to think again?
	R	We didn't do it.
	2907	So she's lying

CONTINUATION OF RECORD OF TAPED INTERVIEW OF   Ronald E. Everett   **PAGE**

Tape Times	
R	[No reply]
2907	Well
R	We didn't do it. It's nothing to do with us. That's final.

Signature of officer preparing record   *Alan Brown*

(F)   WRITTEN STATEMENT UNDER CAUTION

<u>**BLANKSHIRE POLICE**</u>

STATEMENT

Commenced: 12.15
Finished: 12.45

WEYFORD Division
G Station

23 August 200-

I make this statement of my own free will. I understand that I need not say anything unless I wish to do so but that it may harm my defence if I do not mention now something which I later rely on in court. I also understand that anything I do say may be given in evidence.

(Signed)   *June South*

I had run out of food this morning and as a friend was coming to tea this evening I had to go to the shops. I took the children on the bus into Weyford. I went to Tescos. The kids played in the shop and made a lot of noise. I decided to buy some salmon for tea. I picked out as well some toothpaste for everyone, and some bread and margarine and other things. I paid for everything in the basket but did not pay for the salmon and toothpaste. I must have put the other things into my bag by mistake as I meant to pay for them because I had enough money. I was stopped outside the shop by a store detective and taken back inside. I never meant to steal anything.

(Signed)   *June South*

Statement and signatures witnessed by A. Butchers DC 1007

(G)   SOLICITOR'S RECORD OF ATTENDANCE AT POLICE STATION

ATTENDING THE POLICE STATION

POLICE STATION:-   DATE:-

FEE EARNER:-

DUTY SOLICITOR/OWN SOLICITOR/REPRESENTATIVE

TIME ARRIVED:-   TIME LEFT:

CUSTODY OFFICER

NAME:

RANK:

NO:-

CUSTODY RECORD:-

SUSPECT:-

ADDRESS:-

ARREST/VOLUNTEER

TIME OF ARRIVING

OFFENCE:-

INTERVIEWS:-

OTHER MATTERS:-

INVESTIGATING OFFICER

NAME:-

RANK:-

NO:-   PAGE ONE

INFORMATION GIVEN:-

SUSPECT

NAME:-

ADDRESS:-

AGE:-

OCCUPATION:-

CONVICTIONS:-

[Instructions and advice given on separate record]

INTERVIEW

PRESENT:-

TAPED:- YES/NO

NOTES:-

PAGE TWO

OTHER MATTERS

SIGNED   --

(H)   IDENTIFICATION PARADE RECORD

Name: RONALD EDWIN EVERRETT   Age 43

Address: 123, SOMERSET AVENUE,
                      WEYFORD.

I have read this notice.

I am [willing] [not willing] to attend an identification parade.
        [My reasons for not wishing to attend are:]

I am [willing] [not willing] to attend an group identification.
        [My reasons for not wishing to attend are:]

I would like the following to attend:

        Name of solicitor: MR DONALD CRAWFORD

        Address: HERRICK-BROWN & CO, 7 HIGH STREET,
                          WEYFORD, BLANKSHIRE

        Name of friend:

        Address:

        Name of parent/guardian
        or appropriate adult:

        Address:

                        Signed: Ronald E. Everett.
                        Date: 30/7/0—   Time: 22.05
To be signed by the appropriate adult in the case of a juvenile or person
who is mentally ill or mentally handicapped.

                        Signed:
                        Date: Time:

Officer serving Notice

                        Signed: Brian Kingston
                        Date: 30/7/0—   Time: 22.06

_____

One copy should be retained and attached to the report of the
identification parade if one is held subsequently.

REPORT OF IDENTIFICATION PARADE OR GROUP IDENTIFICATION[BOTH HEREINAFTER
REFERRED TO AS "PARADE"]

(see Notes below)

Part I

Station: WEYFORD

Place held: WEYFORD POLICE STATION

Date held: 30/7/0—

Screen used: ~~YES~~/NO   Photographed: ~~YES~~/NO

If screen used: ~~[video recorded] or~~
                 ~~[solicitor] friend] appropriate adult] present~~   ~~Name:~~

Name of suspect: RONALD   EDWIN EVERRETT

Offence(s) with which charged or suspected:

TAKING A CONVEYANCE WITHOUT CONSENT CONTRARY
TO S12(1) THEFT ACT 1968

THEFT OF £750 CONTRARY TO S1 THEFT ACT 1968

Notes:

1. If the space is insufficient for the reply to any question, attach a
    continuation sheet.

2. Form C will be completed as a record of persons forming the parade
    where their names are known to the police.

3. All copies of Form C will then be attached to this report, together
    with a copy of Form A.

Part 1 (contd)   FORM B (contd)

Provision for a suspect who is mentally ill, mentally handicapped or a juvenile.

Age:

Name of appropriate adult:

Address:

Relationship:

Provision for attendance of solicitor or friend.

QUESTION TO SUSPECT:

"Do you wish to have your solicitor or any friend present at this parade?"

ANSWER:

Steps taken to comply with suspect's request (to include the name and address of solicitor/friend and the time he attended and if it was not possible for request to be complied with, the reason for this):

MR DONALD CRAWFORD, SOLICITOR, HERRICK-BROWN & CO, 7 HIGH STREET, WEYFORD, BLANKSHIRE WAS ALREADY
Note: PRESENT.

If the colicitor/friend is already present this should be recorded, with his/her name and address.

I confirm immediately before the parade that the suspect had received a Notice to the Suspect on identification parades. At 22:15 (time) on 30/7/0- (date) I again explained to him the procedures which would be followed during the parade and I advised him that he did not have to say anything unless he wished to do so but that anything he did say in the course of the parade would be recorded and might be given in evidence in subsequent court proceedings.

Identification Officer INSPECTOR   Time: 22.19
                        KINGSTON
                        Brian Kingston

Witnesses will be kept in a place where they cannot see the parade or the suspect, or hear any of the proceedings, and will be introduced one at a time. Witnesses who have previously seen a photograph etc. or desription of the suspect should not be shown the photograph etc. or description again before inspecting parade.

Part 1 (contd)   FORM B (contd)

While waiting to attend the parade they should be prevented from talking with each other.

On leaving they will not be allowed to communicate with witnesses still waiting to view.

Where was the suspect placed before the parade was held and how was he introduced?

SUSPECT HELD IN INTERVIEW ROOM BEFORE PARADE

Description of the suspect and clothing:-

1m 80cm. WHITE. CLEAN SHAVEN. SHORT BROWN HAIR. WEARING OPEN NECK BLUE SHIRT AND BLUE DENIM JEANS.

Where were the witnesses placed before the parade was held and who was posted with them?

IN THE FINGERPRINT ROOM. PC SMITH WAS POSTED WITH HIM.

SKETCH PLAN

To show rooms or areas witnesses and persons standing on the parade were kept prior to their introduction to the parade.

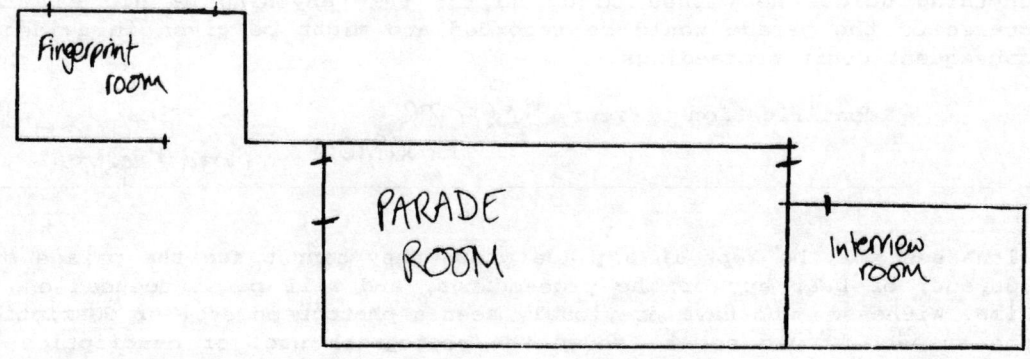

Part II   FORM B (contd)

Time parade began: 22.20

QUESTION TO SUSPECT(S)
"Do you object to any of the persons paraded?"

ANSWER (A):   NO

~~ANSWER (B):~~

State arrangements made in consequence of any objection and if any person
is replaced, cross through his name on Form C. All copies of Form C are to
be attached to the final report and not destroyed:

State names of all police officers and other persons present during the
parade showing in the case of police officers, whether under instruction or
connected with the investigation of the above offence:

INSPECTOR KINGSTON
DC BROWN
WDC CARPENTER   } SUBSEQUENTLY LEFT - SEE BELOW
DONALD CRAWFORD
PC SMITH

QUESTION TO SUSPECT(S):
"Do you object to any of the other persons being present who are not on the
parade or to any of the arrangements for the parade?"

ANSWER (A):   YES, I DO NOT WISH DC BROWN OR WDC
               CARPENTER TO BE PRESENT

~~ANSWER (B):~~

Steps taken to comply with any objection:

DC BROWN & WDC CARPENTER WERE ASKED
TO LEAVE THE ROOM WHICH THEY DID.

Explain to your suspect(s) before the witness appears "You may select any place you like among the persons paraded." Show opposite, as is facing the parade, the position of members of the parade marking the suspect(s) as X (and Y), and giving the other participants the numbers they have on Form C. Delete excess numbers.

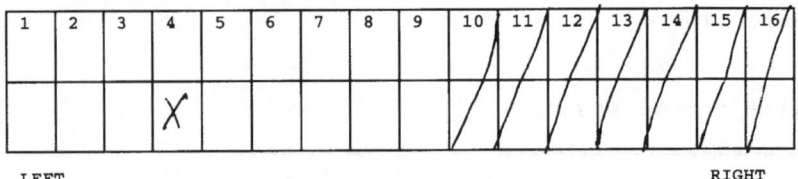

1	2	3	4	5	6	7	8	9	10	11	12	13	14	15	16
			X												

LEFT   RIGHT

Name of witness: JAMES WRIGHT

Address: 22, THE AVENUE, WEYFORD, BLANKSHIRE

Who ushered witness in?   PC 609 SMITH

(a) ADDRESS TO EACH WITNESS BY OFFICER IN CHARGE:

The officer should identify the occasion on which the witness saw the person whom he has come to identify and should explain to the witness that the person who he saw at the scene of the crime is not necessarily amongst those paraded. The following words are an example of those which might be used, adapted as necessary.

"Mr/Mrs/Miss/Ms ....

You have been asked here today to see if you can pick out the person whom you saw on .... at .... in .... (doing) ....

The person(s) you saw may or may not be amongst those on this parade and if you cannot make a positive identification you should say so.

I am going to ask you in a moment to walk along the line at least twice, taking as much time and care as you wish. When you have done so, I shall ask you whether the person(s) you saw on............. is (are) here, and that if the person(s) is (are), you should indicate to me the number of the person(s) concerned."

The conduct of each witness's inspection of the parade must be reported on Part III(c). If there is more than one witness, additional copies of Part III(c) are to be attached.

Describe what witness does and says e.g. walked L to R along front, reverse at rear. If identification made, how was it made?

WALKED L to R ALONG FRONT. WALKED R TO L ALONG REAR. WHEN ASKED IF HE COULD MAKE AN IDENTIFICATION WITNESS WALKED L TO R ALONG FRONT AND SAID "I THINK IT IS NUMBER 4."

Describe what parade was asked to do at request of witness, if applicable
e.g. walk, speak, remove hat, etc. (see Notes below)

(A) Was (Suspect) .....RONALD EDWIN EVERETT.... identified?   YES

    Did he/~~she~~ say anything? (if identified) ~~If Yes, what~~ ....NO.........

(B) Was ....* identified?

    Did he/she say anything? (if identified) If Yes, what ....

    * Insert name(s) of suspect(s)

Any comments made by suspect after witness left:

SUSPECT SAID "HE'S WRONG."

Where was the witness taken after the parade, who escorted him there and
who was posted with him?

WITNESS TAKEN BACK TO FINGERPRINT ROOM BY PC SMITH
WHO REMAINED WITH HIM THERE UNTIL PARADE
WAS CONCLUDED

                  Signed: *Brian Kingston*   Time: 22.28
                  Identification Officer

Notes:

It may sometimes happen that a witness desires to see the suspect with a
hat on or off and there is no objection to the persons paraded thereupon
being asked to wear or remove hats. If a witness asks to hear members of
the parade speak or see them move, he should be asked whether he can first
identify any persons on the parade on the basis of appearance only, and his
reply should be noted. When the request is to hear members of the parade
speak, he should be reminded that the participants in the parade have been
chosen on the basis of physical appearance only. Members of the parade may
then be asked to comply with the witness's request to hear them speak or
see them move. Full details of the incident, including the stages at which
any identification was made, should be recorded.

To be completed for each witness inspecting the parade

After the last witness has left:

QUESTION TO SUSPECT(S)

"Do you wish to make any comments on the conduct of this parade?"

ANSWER (A):   NO

~~ANSWER (B):~~

Time parade finished: 22 : 30

Remarks on any point not already covered:

I certify that the above parade took place in accordance with the code of practice. I am not involved with the investigation of the case.

Signature and rank of Identification Officer: Brian Kingston
                                                      INSPECTOR

Date signed: 30/7/0—   Time: 22:32

Attach completed Form C and a copy of Form A.

RECORD OF PERSONS FORMING IDENTIFICATION PARADE ~~OR GROUP IDENTIFICATION~~

DATE HELD: 30/7/0—

Name(s) of suspect(s): RONALD EDWIN EVERETT   Ref No:

Details of persons forming the parade
N.B. For parade not videoed or photographed include age, height, and dress.

Signature for Expenses

1. Name MICHAEL JAMES WRIGHT
   Address
   Age 35   Height 1m 85
   Dress BLUE JEANS, WHITE SHIRT

   MJ Wright

2. Name HENRY PHILIP JONES
   Address
   Age 38   Height 1m 99
   Dress BLUE JEANS, GREY SHIRT

   HP Jones

3. Name DAVID BERTRAM RICHARDS
   Address
   Age 44   Height 1m 82
   Dress BLUE JEANS, BLUE T SHIRT

   David Richards

4. Name MAURICE ALAN HARMER
   Address
   Age 41   Height 1m 85
   Dress BLUE JEANS BLUE SHIRT

   Maurice A Harmer

5. Name WAYNE JEROME BINDMAN
   Address
   Age 39   Height 1m 80
   Dress BLUE JEANS, YELLOW SHIRT

   Wayne Bindman.

6. Name CHARLES EDWARD SORWIND
   Address
   Age 32   Height 1m 83
   Dress BLUE JEANS, PINK SHIRT

   Charles Sorwinde.

7. Name DAMIAN LITTLETON
   Address
   Age 40   Height 1m 78
   Dress BLUE JEANS, WHITE SHIRT

   Damian Littleton

8. Name CHRISTOPHER EDWARD HILL
   Address
   Age 34   Height 1m 74
   Dress BLUE JEANS, YELLOW SHIRT

   C Hill

Note: (Continue overleaf if necessary)

1. If the suspect objects to any of the persons forming the parade, that person should not be used and his name and details should be crossed through.

2. If a parade is held without a solicitor or friend of the suspect being present, a colour photograph of the parade shall be taken unless any member of the parade objects. A copy of the photograph shall be supplied on request to the suspect of his solicitor within a reasonable time.

3. When a group identification is held in a public place, it will not normally be practicable to note the details of persons involved or to take a photograph.

(I) CHARGE SHEET

COURT COPY

```
Police Station    WEYFORD           Custody No       WGG/0-/33
Station Code      WFF
Charged Persons Surname   DOE        Title            MR
                Forenames  JOHN
Place of Birth  GUILDFORD            Date of Birth    01/02/34
Address        NO FIXED ABODE
               WOODBRIDGE MEADOWS
               WEYFORD WE1 1AA
```

You are charged with the offence/s shown below.
You do not have to say anything. But it may harm your defence if you do not
mention anything now something which you later rely on in court.
Anything you do say may be given in evidence.

Page 1 of 1

No: 1   Crime No: WG/0-/1234   Local Code: C203

ON MONDAY 15TH MAY 200- AT WEYFORD IN THE COUNTY OF BLANKSHIRE STOLE AN
AIRMAIL LETTER OF A VALUE UNKNOWN BELONGING TO CHARLES BLAKE

CONTRARY TO SECTION 1(1) OF THE THEFT ACT 1968

Reply to charges

None

Charged Persons Signature   *JDoe*

Person Charging Name
Signature   *[signature]*

Officer Charging Name
Signature *[signature]*   PS/333/DICKSON

Officer In Case   INSP/N/MEAD

Charged 17/6/0-

Time 10.30 am

Date ✓

CHARGE RECORD

DETAINEE COPY

Police Station	WEYFORD	Custody No	WGG/0-/33
Station Code	WFF		
Charged Persons Surname	DOE	Title	MR
Forenames	JOHN		
Place of Birth	GUILDFORD	Date of Birth	01/02/34

Address   NO FIXED ABODE
WOODBRIDGE MEADOWS
WEYFORD WE1 1AA

You are charged with the offence/s shown on the charge sheet.

You do not have to say anything. But it may harm your defence if you do not mention anything now something which you later rely on in court. Anything you do say may be given in evidence.

YOU ARE REQUIRED TO ATTEND COURT

at WEYFORD MAGS CT

on 20/06/0-   at 10.00 a.m.

If you fail without reasonable cause to surrender to the Court at the appointed place and time, you commit an offence for which you may be fined, imprisoned or both.

LEGAL AID

IF YOU REQUIRE LEGAL REPRESENTATION AT COURT AND CANNOT AFFORD A SOLICITOR YOU MAY BE ENTITLED TO LEGAL AID. IF YOU WISH TO APPLY FOR LEGAL AID A SPECIAL FORM IS OBTAINABLE FROM ANY POLICE STATION, MAGISTRATES CLERKS OFFICE, OR A SOLICITOR DEALING IN CRIMINAL LEGAL AID CASES.

YOU SHOULD MAKE YOUR APPLICATION IMMEDIATELY

THE COURT WILL NOT AUTOMATICALLY ADJOURN THE CASE WHEN THERE HAS BEEN A DELAY IN APPLYING FOR LEGAL AID.

PRODUCTION OF DRIVING LICENCE

If the offence with which you have been charged is one for which your driving licence may be endorsed (and the Inspector or Sergeant on duty at the station will advise you) you are required to have your driving licence at Court when you appear. If you are convicted you may be required to produce the licence.
FAILURE TO PRODUCE IT IS AN OFFENCE AND THE LICENCE IS AUTOMATICALLY SUSPENDED UNTIL IT IS PRODUCED.

(Section 101(4), Road Traffic Act, 1988).

Custody Officer   PS/333/DICKSON

Signature   _____

(J)   SUMMONS

In Blankshire

Petty Sessional Division of Weyford

To: James Baker   .... the Defendant

of   18 Dorset Avenue   Date of Birth: 20.8.1958

Weyford   Unemployed

Blankshire   being the last known or usual place of abode

THE INFORMATION of Barry Williams Sgt 891 of Blankshire Constabulary this day laid before me that you the Defendant, on 20th August 200–, at Station Road, Weyford in the said County drove a Ford Fiesta motor car reg. no. D 796 LWN dangerously.
Contrary to s.2 Road Traffic Act 1988

THE INFORMATION of Barry Williams Sgt 891 of Blankshire Constabulary this day laid before me that you the Defendant, on 20th August 200–, in the said County stole a Radio Cassette recorder belonging to Alfred Roberts valued at £80.
Contrary to s.1(1) Theft Act 1968

Barry Williams

YOU THE DEFENDANT ARE THEREFORE HEREBY SUMMONED to appear on 1st November 200–, at 10.00 before the Magistrates' Court sitting at The Law Courts, The Civic Centre, Weyford, Blankshire to answer the said information.

DATED this 25th September 200–

Paul French

Justice of the Peace

LEGAL AID:– If you require details you should immediately communicate with the Clerk to the Justices at the address on the notice herewith.

CERTIFICATE OF SERVICE
(Magistrates' Courts Rules, 1981, Rule 67(2))

Defendant ___JAMES   BAKER___

I HEREBY CERTIFY that I this day served the within-named defendant with a document of which this is a true copy, in the manner shown a (**a**) below.

(a)   By sending it by post to him in a prepaid recorded delivery letter posted by me on **5-10-200-**
at the **WEYFORD**   Post Office situated at **HIGH STREET, WEYFORD**
addressed as overleaf being his last known place of abode.

(b)   Delivering to him personally.

(c)   By leaving it for him with a person at the address overleaf, being the defendant's last known place of abode.

(d)   By sending it by post in a prepaid recorded delivery letter posted by me on
at the   Post Office situated at

to the registered office of the defendant company.

Dated this   **5ᵗʰ**   day of **OCTOBER**   20 **O —**

_____ Signature
J.C. Waites

(K) **APPLICATION FOR THE RIGHT TO REPRESENTATION: MAGISTRATES' COURT OR CROWN COURT**

Application for the Right to Representation in Criminal Proceedings: Magistrates' Court or Crown Court

Form A

I apply for the right to representation for the purposes of proceedings before the

Crown Court ☐   Magistrates' court ☑   Youth court ☐

1. Personal details

1a	Surname	PRESCOTT
1b	Forename(s)	JAKE
1c	Title Mr, Mrs, Miss, Ms, or another	MR

1d Date of birth   17·06·1983

1e Home address

10 AGRARIA ROAD
WEYFORD
WE2 7AF

1f Present address
If different from above

2. Case details

2a What charges have been brought against you? *Describe briefly what it is that you are accused of doing. For example, theft of £10 worth of CD's, or assault on a neighbour.*

ROBBERY OF A NINTENDO GAMES MACHINE FROM A 14 YEAR OLD BOY IN A PEDESTRIAN PRECINCT DURING THE HOURS OF DARKNESS.

2b Are there any co-defendants in this matter?

No ☐   Yes ☑ **If Yes**, give their names

NOEL ALEXANDER

2c Give reasons why you and your co-defendants cannot be represented by the same solicitors

THERE IS A CONFLICT OF INTEREST. HE CLAIMS THAT I TOOK PART IN THE ROBBERY AND FORCED HIM TO PARTICIPATE. I DENY BEING PRESENT.

3. The Court Proceedings

3a   I am due to appear before

The	**NEWTOWN**	magistrates' court ✓ youth court ☐

or

Date   **21. 01. 200–**   at **10** am / ~~pm~~

3b   I appeared before

The		magistrates' court ☐ youth court ☐
Date		at am/pm

and

Tick whichever applies

My case has been sent to the Crown Court for trial under Section 51 of the Crime and Disorder Act 1998	
My case has been transferred to the Crown Court for trial	
I was convicted and committed for sentence to the Crown Court	
I was convicted and/or sentenced and I wish to appeal against the conviction/sentence	

4. Outstanding matters

If there are any other **outstanding** criminal charges or cases against you, give details including the court where you are due to appear.

N/A

5. Reasons for wanting representation

To avoid the possiblity of your application being delayed, or publicly funded representation being refused because the court does not have enough information about the case, you must complete the rest of this form.

When deciding whether to grant publicly funded representation, the court will need to know why it is in the interests of justice for you to be represented.

If you need help in completing the form you should speak to a solicitor.

Details

Reason(s) for grant or refusal
For court use only

5a   It is likely that I will lose my liberty
You should consider seeing a solicitor before answering this question

I HAVE PREVIOUS CONVICTIONS FOR OFFENCES OF VIOLENCE AND DISHONESTY. THE VICTIM WAS A SCHOOLBOY, ALONE IN A PEDESTRIAN PRECINCT DURING THE HOURS OF DARKNESS.	

5. Reasons for wanting representation *continued*

Details

5b   I am currently subject to a sentence that is suspended or non-custodial that if breached may allow the court to deal with me for the original offence
Please give details

> PROBATION ORDER FOR THEFT, IMPOSED BY WESTVILLE MAGISTRATES' COURT FOR 2 YEARS ON _____ .

5c   It is likely that I will lose my livelihood

5d   It is likely that I will suffer serious damage to my reputation

5e   A substantial question of law is involved
You will need the help of a solicitor to answer this question

> *Please give authorities to be quoted with law reports references* CASE INVOLVES :
> • DISPUTED IDENTIFICATION (TURNBULL GUIDELINES APPLY)
> • CHALLENGING ADMISSIBILITY OF CONFESSION (SS 76 & 78 PACE)
> • ADVERSE INFERENCES (S34 CJPO ACT 1996)

5f   I shall be unable to understand the court proceedings or state my own case because:
   i)   My understanding of English is inadequate
   ii)   I suffer from a disability

5g   Witnesses have to be traced and/or interviewed on my behalf
State the circumstances

> AT THE TIME OF THE ALLEGED OFFENCE I WAS IN AN AMUSEMENT ARCADE. AS WELL AS A FRIEND WHO WAS WITH ME, THERE MAY BE OTHER WITNESSES WHO SAW ME THERE.

5h   The case involves expert cross examination of a prosecution witness
Give brief details

> THE POLICE OFFICER WHO INTERVIEWED ME AS TO BREACHES OF PACE AND THE CODES. THE VICTIM AS TO MISTAKEN IDENTIFICATION. MY CO-ACCUSED AS TO IMPLICATING ME.

5. Reasons for wanting representation *continued*

Details

Reason(s) for grant or refusal
For court use only

5i It is in someone else's interests that I am represented

> IT IS NOT APPROPRIATE THAT A SCHOOLBOY BE CROSS-EXAMINED IN PERSON BY ONE OF HIS ALLEGED ATTACKERS.

5j Any other reasons
Give full particulars

> I INTEND TO PLEAD NOT GUILTY AND THE TRIAL WILL TAKE PLACE AT NEWTOWN CROWN COURT.

6. Legal representation

a) If you do not give the name of a solicitor, the court will select a solicitor for you.

b) You must tell the solicitor that you have named him.

c) If you have been charged together with another person or persons, the court may assign a solicitor other than the solicitor of your choice.

> The solictor I wish to act for me is:
>
> JOHN SMITH

> Give the firm's name and address (if known)
>
> COLLAWS SOLICITORS, 14 THE HIGH STREET, NEWTOWN, NA17 2BA.

Declaration to be completed on behalf of the solicitor named above

i) I certify that the named solicitor above has a crime franchise contract or a general criminal contract, or an individual case contract.

ii) I understand that only firms with a general criminal contract or individual case contract may provide representation in the magistrates' court.

Signed _____ Date _____

7. Declaration

> If you knowingly make a statement which is false, knowingly withhold information, you may be prosecuted.
>
> If convicted, you may be sent to prison for up to three months or be fined or both (*section 21 Access to Justice Act 1999*)

I apply for representation for the charge(s) that are currently before the court.

I understand that should my case proceed to the Crown Court or any higher court, the court may order that I pay for some or all of the costs of representation incurred in the proceedings by way of a Recovery of Defence Costs Order.

I understand that should my case proceed to the Crown Court or any higher court, I will have to furnish details of my means to the court and/or the Legal Services Commission.

Signed _____Jake Prescott_____ Date _____14·01·0─_____

For Court use only

Any additional factors considered when determining the application, including any information given orally

Decision on Interests of Justice Test

I have considered all available details of all the charges and it /it is not in the interests of justice that representation be granted for the following reasons:

Signed _____ Appropriate officer

Date | | | | | | | |

To be completed where the right to representataion extends to the Crown Court

Statement of Means Form B given to the defendant on *(date)*_____

Indicate type of case:

Indictable only   Yes ☐   No ☐

Section 51 offence   Yes ☐   No ☐

Either-way offence and
elected/not suitable for summary trial   Yes ☐   No ☐

First date of hearing at the Crown Court _____

(L)   REPRESENTATION ORDER: MAGISTRATES' COURT

WEYFORD MAGISTRATES' COURT

Court Code: 2936
Reference: LA/2936/00/1341
Date of Hearing: –

REPRESENTATION ORDER (MAGISTRATES' COURT)

In accordance with the Access to Justice 1999 the Court now grants representation to
                                                    for the following purpose:

Delete (1) to (4) as necessary.

(1)   Proceedings before a Magistrates' Court in connection with

(2)   Appealing to Crown Court against a decision of the Magistrates' Court on
(3)   Resisting an appeal to the Crown Court against a decision of the Magistrate Court
(4)   Proceedings for (both a Magistrates' Court and *) the Crown Court in connection with
                                                    including in the event of his
         being convicted or sentenced in those proceedings, advice and assistance in regard to
         the making of an appeal to the Criminal Division of the Court of Appeal.

The representation granted shall consist of the following:-

Magistrates' Court proceedings*-

Solicitor
Solicitor and Junior Counsel

Crown Court proceedings*-

Solicitor
Solicitor and Junior Counsel
Solicitor and Queens' Counsel (only available where the offence charged is murder)
Solicitor, Junior Counsel and Queens' Counsel (only available where prosecution brought by
Serious Fraud Office)

including advice on the preparation of the case for the proceedings.

The Solicitor/Counsel assigned is
of

The assisted person has been committed to   prison/released on bail and
may be communicated with at

--(signed)   ------------------------------------(dated)

 * Delete as necessary

(M) RECORD OF DECISION TO GRANT OR WITHHOLD BAIL AND CERTIFICATE AS TO HEARING OF APPLICATION FOR BAIL

WEYFORD MAGISTRATES' COURT

Date 31/7/2000 Accused RONALD EDWIN EVERETT Date of birth 25/6/1943

Alleged offence(s) TAKING A CONVEYANCE , THEFT

BAIL

The accused is granted bail (subject to the conditions set out below) with a duty to surrender to the custody of

☑ WEYFORD Magistrates'/~~Youth~~ Court at Weyford

on Monday -day the 14ᵗʰ August at 9.45 am/~~pm~~

☐ the Crown Court at Guildford/ at 10am on or on such a day and at such a time and place as may be notified to the accused by the appropriate officer of that court

N.B. If you fail to surrender to bail or to comply with bail conditions you may be arrested and taken into custody.

Failure to surrender to bail is an offence punishable with imprisonment and/or a fine.

Conditions to be complied with

Before release

☑ To provide 1 suret(y)~~(ies)~~ in the sum of £ 500 ~~(each)~~ ☐ To surrender passport to police

☐ To provide a security in the sum of £ to be deposited with the court

After release

☐ To live and sleep each night at ☐ To abide by the rules of the hostel between the hours of

☐ To remain indoors at

☐ To report to Weyford Police Station each Wednesday and Saturday between 1900 — 2100 hours

☐ Not to go except to see solicitor by prior written appointment or to attend court

☐ To make himself available as and when required to enable pre-sentence/medical report to be prepared

☐ Not to contact directly or indirectly

☐

☐

The reasons for imposing conditions are to ensure that the accused:-

☑ surrenders to custody ☐ does not commit an offence while on bail

☐ does not interfere with witnesses or obstruct the course of justice

☐ is available to enable enquiries or a report to be made ☐ goes to see his solicitor (legal representative)

CUSTODY

The court withholds bail, having found the exception(s) to the right to bail specified in the first column of the schedule hereto (and applying the exception(s) for the reasons specified in the second column)

☐ The accused is remanded in custody for appearance before WEYFORD Magistrates'/Youth Court at Weyford at 10 am on

☐ The accused is committed in custody for appearance before the Crown Court at Weyford on at 10 am or on such a day and at such a time and place as may be notified to the accused by the appropriate officer of that court

☐ The accused has consented to the hearing and determination in his absence of future applications for remand in custody and the notice overleaf applies

SCHEDULE

EXCEPTIONS TO THE RIGHT TO BAIL - SCHED. 1	REASONS FOR APPLYING EXCEPTIONS (pt I, paras 2, 2A)
Indictable/either-way cases (Part I, para 2A)	☐ Nature and seriousness of offence and likely conclusion
☐ Alleged offence committed while on bail	☐ Character, antecedents and lack of community ties
Imprisonable (Part I, paras 2(a)-(c), 5, 7)	☐ Accused's record under previous grants of bail
☐ Belief would fail to surrender	☐ Strength of evidence against accused
☐ Belief would commit offence while on bail	☐
☐ Belief would interfere with witnesses or obstruct the course of justice	☐

REASONS FOR APPLYING EXCEPTIONS (pt I, paras 2, 2A)

☐ Insufficient information for bail decision

☐ Otherwise impracticable to complete enquiries or make report

All cases (Pt I, paras 3, 4, 6; Pt II, paras 3, 4, 5)

☐ Serving a custodial sentence

☐ For accused's (protection) (welfare) (youths only)

☐ Arrested for absconding or breaching bail conditions

Non-imprisonable (Part II, para 2)

☐ Previous failure to answer bail and belief would fail to surrender to custody

CERTIFICATE OF FULL ARGUMENT

I hereby certify that at the hearing today the court heard full argument on application for bail by or on behalf of accused and

☐ that the court has not previously heard full argument in these proceedings (except at the last hearing)

☐ that the following new considerations/change in circumstances apply

Signed Ian Gallagher Clerk of the Court present during the proceedings

| Solicitor | FEB 2000 |

(N) WITNESS STATEMENT

BLANKSHIRE POLICE

Statement or Section	WEYFORD	**Division**	G
		Date	23rd August 200-

Statement of (name of witness)   IAN GOVERN
          (In full - Block Letters)

Date and place of birth   25.8.1954   Cardiff

This statement, (consisting of   1   pages each signed by me), is true to the best of my knowledge and belief and I make it knowing that, if it is tendered in evidence, I shall be liable to prosecution if I wilfully stated in it anything which I know to be false or do not believe to be true.

          Dated the   23rd   day of   August   20 0-

          Signature ...*Ian Govern*..................................

.... being unable to read the above statement I ....
of ....read it to him before he signed it.

          Dated the   day of   20

   I am the manager of Tesco Supermarket, Oxford Street, Weyford. At
about 11.15 a.m. on Monday 23rd August I was called to my office by
Mr. Astor Teck who is employed as a security officer by Tesco Limited.
A woman I now know to be Mrs. June South was in the office with her three
children. In my presence Mr. Teck went through the cash receipt and
checked it against the items in Mrs South's shopping bag. Five items
appeared not to have been paid for, two 7 oz tins of John West Salmon and
three large tubes of Gibbs S.R. Toothpaste. These I identified as coming
from this store by the price ticket on them. The goods were recovered
from Mrs. South No one has authority to take items from this store
without payment.

Signature ...*Ian Govern*........................

Taken by ...*A Butchers PC 1007*.................

(continued overleaf)

Address...... 2A, The Parade, Weyford
...... Blankshire   WE9 6BB ......

Telephone Number ..W...686872...........   Occupation ...Retail Manager......

Dates to avoid:

18 - 12 - 0 - — 8 - 1 - 0

(O)   CRIMINAL PROCEDURE AND INVESTIGATIONS ACT 1996
PART I: DISCLOSURE
RIGHTS AND DUTIES OF ACCUSED PERSONS

1.   The Criminal Procedure and Investigations Act 1996 makes important changes to the law on prosecution and defence disclosure in criminal cases. This notice sets out your rights and duties under the relevant provisions. Please read it carefully and show it to your solicitor if you have one.

2.   Although this notice is sent to you by the prosecutor, he cannot advise you on its contents and you should not approach him for advice.

Disclosure by the accused

3.   Before the trial begins, the prosecutor must disclose to you prosecution material which he thinks might undermine the case against you. If there is no such material, he must write to you to say so. In either case, he must also send you a schedule of non-sensitive material at the same time.

4.   If your case is to be tried in the Crown Court, you must give the prosecutor and the court a 'defence statement' containing certain information about your defence. This must –

   (a)   set out in general terms the nature of your defence, ie the reasons for your intention to plead not guilty,

   (b)   state the matters on which you disagree with the prosecution, and

   (c)   state in each case the reason why you disagree.

5.   If you have an alibi, you must give details of the alibi in the defence statement, including –

   (a)   if you know it, the name and address of any witness you believe is able to give evidence in support of the alibi, or

   (b)   any information you may have which might be useful in finding any such witness.

   'Evidence in support of an alibi' means 'evidence tending to show that by reason of the presence of the accused at a particular place or in a particular area at a particular time he was not, or was unlikely, to have been at the place where the offence is alleged to have been committed at the time of its alleged commission'.

6.   You may give the defence statement within 14 days of the prosecutor making disclosure to you. The 14-day period starts on the date when the prosecutor writes to you, not the day when you receive his letter. If you cannot give a defence statement within 14 days, you may ask the court for more time. The court will want to know why you cannot do so, and how much more time you need. If you apply for more time, you must –

   (a)   do so before the 14 days are up, and

   (b)   give the prosecutor a copy of your application.

7.   Section 11 of the Act says that if you fail to comply with these requirements, certain consequences follow. You fail to comply with these requirements if you:

   (a)   do not give a defence statement, or

   (b)   give a defence statement after the end of the 14-day period, or after the end of any longer period of time allowed by the court, or

   (c)   set out inconsistent defences in the defence statement, or

   (d)   put forward a defence at trial which is different from any defence set out in the defence statement, or

   (e)   put forward evidence in support of an alibi at trial, without giving details of the alibi in the defence statement, or

   (f)   call a witness in support of an alibi at trial without giving details of the witness in the defence statement.

8.   If you fail to comply with these requirements, the court (or, if the court allows, any other party) may comment on the failure to comply, and the jury may draw such inferences as appear proper in deciding whether you are guilty.

9. If you put forward a defence at trial which is different from any defence set out in the defence statement, then (when deciding whether to comment on the failure to comply) the court must consider the extent of the difference in the defences, and whether there is any justification for it.

10. You cannot be convicted solely on the basis of an inference drawn from a failure to comply with these requirements.

11. If your case is to be tried in a magistrates' court, you may give a defence statement if you wish (for example, to get further prosecution disclosure) but you are not required to do so. If you do not give a defence statement, no inference may be drawn. If you do give a defence statement the same procedures apply as if your case was being tried in the Crown Court (paragraphs 4–10 above), except that there is no jury but the court may draw inferences from a failure to comply with the relevant requirements.

12. If you decide not to give a defence statement, your case may come to court more quickly if you tell the court and the prosecutor before the end of the 14-day period.

Right of accused person to apply for additional prosecution disclosure

13. If you give a defence statement, the prosecutor must then disclose to you any additional prosecution material which might reasonably be expected to assist the defence which you disclosed in your defence statement. If there is no such material, he must write to you to say so.

14 After this, if you have reason to believe that there is more prosecution material which has not been disclosed to you and which might reasonably be expected to assist the defence which you disclosed in your defence statement, you may apply to the court for an order to disclose it. You must –

    (a)   identify the material you need, and
    (b)   tell the court why you think it might assist your defence.

    If you apply to the court, you must give the prosecutor a copy of your application. If you contact the prosecutor first, you may be able to obtain the material you need without having to apply to the court.

Right of accused person to apply for review of a non-disclosure ruling

15. If the prosecutor has material which he ought to disclose to you, but which is sensitive for some reason, he may apply to the court for a ruling that on balance it is not in the public interest to disclose it.

16. If the court rules against disclosure, you may ask the court to review its ruling. If you do so, you must –

    (a)   say why you think the ruling should be reviewed, and
    (b)   give the prosecutor a copy of your application.

Duty to disclose material in confidence

17. You may use material disclosed to you for the purposes of your trial, or (if you are convicted) in connection with any appeal. If you want to use the material for any other purpose, you must first apply to the court for permission to do so, and say why you want to use it. You must also give a copy of your application to the prosecutor.

18. If you use the material for any other purpose without getting the permission of the court, you may be liable to proceedings for contempt of court. If the court finds you guilty of contempt, it may commit you to custody for a specified period or fine you or both.

(P)   NOTICE TO ACCUSED: RIGHT TO OBJECT TO WRITTEN STATEMENT OR DEPOSITION

FORM 14A

Notice to accused: right to object to written statement or deposition being read out at trial without further proof (CPI Act 1996, s 68, Sch 2, paragraphs 1(3)(c) and 2(3)(c): MC Rules 1981, r 4B (as inserted by MC (Amendment) Rules 1997)

To AB, of

If you are committed for trial, the Crown Court may try you in respect of the charge or charges on which you are committed or in respect of any other charge arising out of the same transaction or set of circumstances which may, with leave of the Court, be put to you.

[Written statements] [and] [depositions] have been made by the witness named below and copies of their [statements] [and] [depositions] are enclosed. Each of these [statements] [and] [depositions] will be read out at the trial without oral evidence being given by the witness who has made the [statement] [or] [deposition] unless you want that witness to give oral evidence and to be cross-examined on such oral evidence. If you want any of these witnesses to give oral evidence, and be cross-examined if necessary, you should inform the Crown Court and me in writing within 14 days of being committed for trial. If you do not do so you will lose your right to prevent the [statement] [or] [deposition] being read out without any oral evidence being given by the witness in question and to require the attendance of that witness unless the Court gives you leave to do so, but that will not prevent the prosecutor from exercising his discretion to call that witness to give oral evidence, and be cross-examined, at the trial if the prosecutor so wishes.

[* [Pre-paid] reply forms [and pre-paid envelopes] are enclosed and if you object to any [statement] [or] [deposition] being read out at the trial without oral evidence being given by the witness who made it you must let the Crown Court and myself know within 14 days of being committed for trial, and at the same time indicate which of these witnesses you want to give oral evidence at the trial.

If you have a solicitor acting for you in your case you should hand this notice and the [statements] [and] [depositions] to him at once, so that he may deal with them].

Names of witnesses whose [statements] [and] [depositions] are enclosed:–

Address any reply to:–

(Signed) ....

[On behalf of the Prosecutor]

* Omit if documents are sent to accused's solicitor.

(Q) STATEMENT OF MEANS FOR RIGHT TO REPRESENTATION IN CRIMINAL PROCEEDINGS IN THE CROWN COURT

Statement of Means for Right to Representation in Criminal Proceedings in the Crown Court

Form B

Reference

Now that you have been granted publicly funded representation in the Crown Court you must complete this form and return it to the court at least **4 days** before your first hearing at the Crown Court. If you do not comply, the judge may make a Court Order against you requiring you to pay for all costs incurred in your defence.

If you or your partner are receiving one of the following benefits, you are only required to complete Parts 1 and 2A of this form:
■ Income-based Job Seeker's Allowance
■ Income Support
■ Working Families' Tax Credit
■ Disabled Person's Tax Credit

If you indicate one of the above, and no further enquiries are made of you or your partner, only this information will go before the judge to consider whether to make a Recovery of Defence Costs Order.

A partner is a person with whom the applicant lives as a couple and includes a person with whom the person concerned is not currently living but from whom he or she is not living separate and apart.

You should inform the Court if your circumstances change once you have completed this form and returned it to the Crown Court.

See the Declaration at the end of this form for enquiries that can be made about the information you provide.

Part 1 - Personal details

1a	Surname	PRESCOTT

1b	Surname at birth *If different*	

1c	Title *Mr/Mrs/Miss/Ms/other*	MR	1d	Date of birth	17·06·1983

1e	Forename(s)	JAKE

1f	Home address *Including postcode*	10 KERIARIA ROAD WEYFORD WE2 7AF

1g	Address where we can contact you *If different from above*	

1h Marital status
Tick as appropriate

Single ☑   Cohabiting ☐   Widowed ☐

Married ☐   Married but separated ☐   Divorced ☐

Part 2 - Financial position

Part A - Benefits

If you or your partner receive Income-based Job Seeker's Allowance, Income Support, Working Families' Tax Credit or Disabled Person's Tax Credit, please provide the following details:

(i) The address of the Social Security Office or Jobcentre or Tax Credit Office that is dealing with you or your partner's claim

> I HIGH STREET
> NEWTOWN
> NE 19 2BX

(ii) National Insurance number of the person claiming benefit.

> NA 37 81 26 X

This is required so that we can verify your, or your partner's, claim with the Benefits Agency or Inland Revenue

(iii) Name of Benefit

> JOB SEEKER'S ALLOWANCE

(iv) Name of recipient of Benefit

> JAKE PRESCOTT

(v) Date of birth of recipient of Benefit

> 17 . 06 . 1983

Please go to the end of the form and sign the Declarations if you have completed this section.

Part B - Income from work

In this section you are asked to give details of the money you receive.
You should answer these questions with annual amounts. Where you are paid monthly, multiply the amount by 12 or where you are paid weekly, multiply the amount by 52.

		You	**Your partner**	**Additional details**	**Court use**
1	Provide details of gross earnings, including bonuses, overtime or commission				
	Do you or your partner receive benefits from work that are not money? *For example: luncheon vouchers, company car, free health insurance etc. Please specify*	Yes ☐ No ☐	Yes ☐ No ☐		
	Employer's name and address				
2	Are you or your partner, self-employed / in partnership?	Yes ☐ No ☐	Yes ☐ No ☐		
	Indicate nature of work for you and/or your partner			(i) Turnover (ii) Business expenses (not taken out for personal use) (iii) Net profit (Turnover minus business expenses) (iv) Period of trading	
	Indicate you and/or your partner's role in company				

Part B - Income (continued)

	You	Your partner	Additional details	Court use
3 Part-time work : gross earnings including bonuses, commission and overtime				
Employer's name and address				
4 Are you or your partner a shareholder in a private limited company, or are you or your partner a company director?	Yes ☐ No ☐	Yes ☐ No ☐	Provide details for you and/or your partner.	
5 Is anybody else, including a company or other body, supporting either you or your partner financially or making resources available to either of you?	Yes ☐ No ☐	Yes ☐ No ☐	Examples of non-financial support may include the following: Do you live in someone else's house or drive someone else's car? Indicate the nature of the support and what period this support covered. Provide details of connection to individual or company, and name the individual or company.	
6 Do you receive any other income not mentioned in any of the above questions?	Yes ☐ No ☐	Yes ☐ No ☐	Indicate the nature of this income. For example, an allowance or income from trust. Indicate how often this income is received.	
7 Do you receive any income from state benefits? *Give details of benefit received, how much and how often*	Yes ☐ No ☐	Yes ☐ No ☐		

Part C - Capital and Savings
Please provide details of all your capital and savings.

	You	Your partner	Additional details	Court use
1 Main dwelling Do you and/or your partner own the house/property that you treat as your main dwelling?	Yes ☐ No ☐	Yes ☐ No ☐	If **Yes**, please provide the following details: i) What is the out-standing mortgage on your property? ii) What is its current market value? iii) What share do you own in this property and if not shared with your partner, who do you own this property with? iv) What type of property is this? *For example, flat* v) How many bed-rooms does this property have?	
2 Other property Do you and/or your partner own any other property?	Yes ☐ No ☐	Yes ☐ No ☐	If **Yes**, provide the following details: i) What is the out-standing mortgage on this property? ii) What is its current market value? iii) What share do you own in this property and if not with your partner, who do you own this property with? iv) What type of property is this? *For example, flat* v) How many bed-rooms does this property have?	

Part C - Capital and Savings (continued)

	You	Your partner	Additional details	Court use

3 Savings

Please provide details of savings, including money in the bank, building society, or at home or in current accounts, National Savings Certificates, ISA's.

Additional details: If you have savings certificates, provide details of the issue and how many units you have

4 Do you and/or your partner own any stocks or shares? *Include Unit Trusts, PEPs or ISAs.*

You: Yes ☐ No ☐   Your partner: Yes ☐ No ☐

Additional details: If **Yes**, please provide details of the company and name of the fund if appropriate. Also provide the present value and the amount of the yearly dividend

5 Do you and/or your partner have any rights under a trust fund?

You: Yes ☐ No ☐   Your partner: Yes ☐ No ☐

Additional details: If **Yes**, what are the details of the fund and what rights do you have?

6 Articles of value
Please provide details of any articles of value that you and/or your partner own, and their approximate value.

Additional details: Include antiques, jewellery, art etc.

7 Do you or your partner have any other capital assets that you have not indicated above?

You: Yes ☐ No ☐   Your partner: Yes ☐ No ☐

Additional details: If **Yes**, please provide details of the same

Part D - Financial commitments

		You		Your partner		Additional details	Court use
1	Do you have any dependants who live with you?	Yes ☐	No ☐	Yes ☐	No ☐	If **Yes**, please provide details of how many, their relationship and their ages.	
2	Do you and/or your partner have any financial orders that this court should know about?	Yes ☐	No ☐	Yes ☐	No ☐	If **Yes**, please indicate the nature of the order(s) and the amount(s).	
3	How much do you and/or your partner pay in housing costs?					Provide details of rent or mortgage on your main dwelling. Indicate the period that this amount covers.	

Part E - Further information

		You		Your partner		Additional details	Court use
1	Has any other person been paying towards your legal costs and expenses in these or any other proceedings prior to your grant of representation?	Yes ☐	No ☐			If **Yes**, please provide details of the amount and from whom this support came. Indicate their relationship.	
2	Are any of your and/or your partner's assets subject to a mareva injunction or freezing order?	Yes ☐	No ☐	Yes ☐	No ☐	If **Yes**, please provide details of the nature of the assets, the value of the order and whose order or injunction it is.	

Part E - Further information

	You	Your partner	Additional details	Court use
3 Do you and/or your partner have interests in any business abroad?	Yes ☐ No ☐	Yes ☐ No ☐	If **Yes**, please provide details of the nature of the business, its name and address and your and/or your partner's interest in it.	
4 Are you and/or your partner currently bankrupt or subject to bankruptcy proceedings or subject to an Individual Voluntary Arrangement?	Yes ☐ No ☐	Yes ☐ No ☐	If **Yes**, please provide full details	

Is there any other information that you feel is relevant to the Court or the Legal Services Commission which should be taken into account when considering your means?

Please provide details where relevant.

Declaration

1. I declare that to the best of my knowledge and belief, I have given a complete and correct statement of my income and/or savings and/or capital and those of my partner.

2. I understand I may be required to provide evidence to support the information I have supplied on this form.

3. I authorise such enquiries as are considered necessary to enable the Court or the Legal Services Commission to ascertain mine and/or my partner's income, outgoings, savings, business interests.

4. I consent to the disclosure of any information by other parties that may assist in their enquiries.

5. I authorise the Court or the Legal Services Commission to make such enquiries to the Benefits Agency, Tax Credit Office or Inland Revenue as they feel necessary and I consent to the disclosure of information to confirm that I am in receipt of such benefits as I have stated.

6. I understand that the Court and the Legal Services Commission can provide a report on my financial position to the trial judge and my representative, with a view to a Recovery of Defence Costs Order being made for up to the full amount of the costs incurred in defending me in the proceedings, in this and any other court.

7. I understand that if I knowingly make a statement which is false or knowingly withhold information I may be prosecuted. If convicted of such an offence I may be sent to prison for up to three months or fined or both (section 21 Access to Justice Act 1999).

8. I understand that I must co-operate fully and immediately with any enquiry into my financial circumstances by the Court or Legal Services Commission, and that if the information I have provided is not correct or complete, then an Order may be made against me requiring me to pay all costs incurred in defending me in the proceedings, in this and any other court.

Signature: *Jake Prescott*   Date: 14-01-01

Full name in Block Capitals: JAKE PRESCOTT

Declaration and authority by person receiving the benefit

This additional declaration should be signed by the person receiving the benefit if they are not the person applying for publicly funded representation.

I consent to the Court or Legal Services Commission disclosing information about me to the Department of Social Security and making such enquiries as may be necessary to check the information provided in this application. The Department of Social Security may carry out such processing as is necessary to check this information remains correct and may inform the Court or Legal Services Commission of any relevant changes.

Signature: Date:

(R)   PLEA AND DIRECTIONS HEARING – JUDGE'S QUESTIONNAIRE

Plea and Directions Hearing

Judge's Questionnaire

In accordance with the practice rules issued by the Lord Chief Justice.

A copy of this questionnaire, completed as far as possible with the agreement of both advocates, is to be handed in to the court prior to the commencement of the Plea and Directions Hearing.

The Crown Court at

Case No. **T**

PTI URN

R v

Date of PDH

Name of Prosecution Advocate at PDH

Name of Defence Advocate at PDH

1	a	Are the actual/proposed not guilty pleas definitely to be maintained through to a jury trial?	Yes ☐ No ☐
	b	Has the defence advocate advised his client of section 152 Powers of Criminal Courts (Sentencing) Act 2000? *(Reductions in sentence for guilty pleas)*	Yes ☐ No ☐
	c	Will the prosecution accept part guilty or alternative pleas?	Yes ☐ No ☐
2		How long is the trial likely to take?	
3	a	Are there Human Rights issues to be relied upon?	Yes ☐ No ☐
		If **Yes**, what are the Human Rights issues?	
	b	What are the other issues in the case?	
4		Issues as to the mental or medical condition of any defendant or witness.	
5		Prosecution witnesses whose evidence will be given. Can any statement be read instead of calling the witnesses?	To be read (number) ☐ To be called (number) ☐ Names:

6   a   Number of Defence witnesses whose
          evidence will be placed before the Court.   Defendant +   [   ]

     b   Any whose statements have been served
          which can be agreed and accepted
          in writing.

7   Is the prosecution intending to serve any   Yes ☐   No ☐
          further evidence?

          If **Yes**, what area(s) will it cover?

          What are the witnesses' names?

8   Facts which are admitted and can be
          reduced into writing.
          (s10(2)(b) CJA 1967)

9   Exhibits and schedules which are to be
          admitted.

10   Is the order and pagination of
          the prosecution papers agreed?

11   Any alibi which should have been   Yes ☐   No ☐
          disclosed in accordance with CJA 1967?

12   a   Any points of law likely to arise at trial?

     b   Any questions of admissibility of
          evidence together with any authorities it
          is intended to rely upon.

13   a   Has the defence notified the prosecution   Yes ☐   No ☐
          of any issue arising out of the record of
          interview?
          *(Practice Direction Crime: Tape Recording of
          police interview 26 May 1989)*

     b   What efforts have been made to agree
          verbatim records or summaries and
          have they been successful?

14	Any applications granted / pending for:	
	(i) evidence to be given through live television links?	Yes ☐ No ☐
	(ii) evidence to be given by pre-recorded video interviews with children?	Yes ☐ No ☐
	(iii) screens?	Yes ☐ No ☐
	(iv) the use of video equipment during the trial?	Yes ☐ No ☐
	(v) use of tape playback equipment?	Yes ☐ No ☐

15	Any other significant matter which might affect the proper and convenient trial of the case? *(e.g. expert witnesses or other cases outstanding against the defendant)*	

16	Any other work which needs to be done. *Orders of the Court with time limits should be noted on page 4.*	Prosecution
		Defence

17	a	Witness availability and approximate length of witness evidence.	Prosecution
			Defence
	b	Can any witness attendance be staggered?	Yes ☐ No ☐
		If **Yes**, have any arrangements been agreed?	Yes ☐ No ☐

18	Advocates' availability?	Prosecution
		Defence

Case listing arrangements

Name of Trial Judge:

Custody Cases *Fix or warned list within 16 weeks of committal*

Fixed for trial on

Place in warned list for trial   for week beginning

Further directions fixed for

Not fixed or put in warned list within
16 weeks because:

Date of expiry of custody time limit

Application to extend custody time limit?   Yes ☐   Extended to

                                                No ☐

Bail Cases

Further directions fixed for

Fixed for trial on

Fixed as a floater / backer on

Place in a reserve/warned list for trial   for week beginning

List officer to allocate   ☐ within [＿＿＿＿] days / weeks

                                     ☐ before

Sentence

Adjourned for sentence on

(to follow trial of R v

Other directions, orders, comments

Signed: *Judge*   Date:

(S)   BRIEF TO COUNSEL

IN THE CROWN COURT   REPRESENTATION ORDER

AT GUILDFLEET   Case No.0–/1732

REGINA

v

ALAN TRIP

**BRIEF TO COUNSEL ON BEHALF OF THE DEFENDANT
TO APPEAR AT THE PDH ON 7 NOVEMBER 200– AT 10.30 AND
AT
THE TRIAL ON A DATE TO BE FIXED**

Counsel has copies of the following –

1. Statements of Alan Trip (including comments on prosecution statements)
2. Bundle of prosecution witness statements
3. Custody record of Alan Trip
4. List of Alan Trip's previous convictions
5. Representation Order
6. Indictment
7. Bail notice
8. Primary disclosure by the prosecution under the Criminal Procedure and Investigations Act 1996 ('the 1996 Act')
9. 'Defence statement' under the 1996 Act
10. Secondary disclosure by the prosecution under the 1996 Act

INTRODUCTION

Counsel is instructed on behalf of Alan Trip of 1 Oakwell Terrace, Guildfleet. The defendant is on bail and charged with theft of a gold ring to the value of £225, the property of Cedric Mane, contrary to s 1 Theft Act 1968. The defendant will plead not guilty. He was committed under s 6(2), Magistrates' Courts Act 1980 to Guildfleet Crown Court for trial by Guildfleet Magistrates on 30th September 199–. All prosecution witnesses should attend the trial to give oral evidence. There are no defence witnesses other than the defendant.

The prosecution and defence have complied with the disclosure provisions of the 1996 Act. The prosecution has confirmed in writing that there is no material which might undermine the prosecution case; instructing solicitors have set out in the 'defence statement' the general nature of the defence and the matters on which the defence takes issue with the prosecution and the reasons for doing so; the prosecution has confirmed in writing that there is no prosecution material which assists in the defendant's defence.

THE PROSECUTION CASE

The prosecution case is that the defendant took the ring from 6 Marchant Cresecent, Guildfleet, a property belonging to Mr. Mane, on 3rd May 200–. The defendant was a lodger at 6 Marchant Crescent from 2nd January 200– to 3rd May 200–. On the morning of 3rd May, following a row with Mr. Mane, the defendant was asked to leave. Mr. Mane will say that he left the ring on the coffee table in the lounge when he left for work on 3rd May at approximately 8.30 a.m. At this time the defendant was still packing his bags prior to leaving. When Mr. Mane returned home from work at 5.30 p.m. both the defendant and the ring had gone. There was no sign of a forcible entry into the property and nothing else had been taken. Peter Plant, a friend of Mr. Mane's will say that the defendant offered him a gold ring for £50 in the Cat and Lion Public House, Guildfleet, on the evening of 3rd May. Plant allegedly refused the offer but informed Mr. Mane on hearing of the theft. The defendant was arrested on 6th May. Counsel will note from the custody record that he did not, on arrival at the police station, ask for a solicitor. The defendant was interrogated by D.C. Blakeway and D.C. Hind and made both oral and written confessions of guilt.

THE DEFENCE CASE

The defendant denies all knowledge of the ring. He claims that Mr. Mane is making allegations of theft against him to 'get even' following their row. The defendant admits talking to Peter Plant in the Cat and Lion Public House but denies offering him a ring. Whilst the defendant cannot put forward any real motive for Plant lying, he suspects that Mane has some 'hold' over Plant and is forcing him to give false testimony. There is no dispute that the defendant confessed his guilt but he claims that he did so only after being denied access to a solicitor and being threatened with physical violence.

EVIDENCE

Counsel's attention is particularly drawn to the following points of evidence:–

The confession – the admissibility of the defendant's confession should be challenged under s.76 and s.78 Police and Criminal Evidence Act 1984. The threats of violence, if accepted by the judge, may constitute oppression and Counsel will be aware of a number of recently reported cases in which denial of access to a solicitor has led to exclusion of a confession under s.78. Although the defendant did not request a solicitor on arrival at the police station he claims that he did so prior to being interrogated. Under the Code of Practice dealing with detention and interrogation the defendant is entitled to request a solicitor at any time. The custody record is silent on the issue and it would appear that the police will deny all knowledge of the request.

The defendant's previous convictions – Counsel will note that the defendant has six previous convictions for theft. In view of the allegations being made against Mr. Mane and the police (if the confession is admitted) it would seem likely that the defendant will be cross-examined on the convictions under s.1(3)(ii) Criminal Evidence Act 1898. Instructing solicitors have explained this to Mr. Trip.

MITIGATION

Instructing solicitors have considered the question of a plea in mitigation if the defendant is convicted. Mr. Trip is a single man, aged 23, and has been unemployed since leaving school at 16. Counsel will note that the present offence was allegedly committed three months into the operational period of a suspended sentence imposed for theft. If the defendant is convicted, a custodial sentence would seem to be inevitable.

Counsel is requested to advise in conference, attend the PDH, the represent the defendant at the trial on a plea of not guilty and, if necessary, to make a plea in mitigation and advise on the prospects of an appeal.

(T)   'TIC' FORM

BLANKSHIRE POLICE

WEYFORD	STATION
G	DIVISION
23/8/0–	DATE

OTHER OFFENCES

To: Jayne Jones

charged with)   Theft
indicated   )

for   (hearing)   at Weyford Magistrates' Court   on   27th August 200–
      (trial)

MEMORANDUM FOR THE INFORMATION OF THE ACCUSED

(1)   The list on the back hereof gives particulars of _____ FIVE _____
other offences with which you are charged.

      In the event of you(r) **being found guilty / conviction** of any offence of which you are **charged /
indicted** it will be open to you, before **the court makes an order / sentence is passed,** to admit all or
any of the other offences, and you may thereupon ask that any of these other offences which you have admitted
may be taken into consideration in any   **order the court may make / sentence the court may pass upon you.**

(2)   Please sign the receipt below, and retain for your own information the copy of this document.

(3)   If you wish now to volunteer any statement concerning any of these other offences, or to ask
for any further information in respect thereto, you may do so in writing, either in the space at the foot of this
document or in a separate letter. Or, if you prefer, you may ask for a Police Officer to take any statement you
may wish to give.

FORM OF RECEIPT TO BE SIGNED BY THE ACCUSED

I have received a copy of this document.

Signed   *J Jones*
Date   23–8–0–
In the presence of   *A Butchers* £ 1007

SPACE FOR ANY STATEMENT THE ACCUSED MAY WISH TO VOLUNTEER

Signed   _____
Date   _____
In the presence of   _____

CHARGES OUTSTANDING AGAINST   Jane Jones

No.	Crime Ref.	Place of Offence	Date of Offence	Details of Offence	Name and Address of Victim	Remarks
1		Weyford	6.6.0–	Stole a packet of frozen peas valued a £1.77 Contrary to s.1(1) Theft Act 1968	Tesco Ltd. 88 High Street, Weyford	
2		Weyford	6.6.0–	Stole a tube of toothpaste valued at £0.70 Contrary to s.1(1) Theft Act 1968	Boots Ltd 84 High Street, Weyford	
3		Weyford	6.6.0–	Stole some writing paper valued at £1.50 Contrary to s.1(1) Theft Act 1968	W.H. Smith Ltd 86 High Street, Weyford	
4		Weyford	10.7.0–	Stole coffee, butter, sardines, and chocolate valued at £5.50 Contrary to s.1(1) Theft Act 1968	Tesco Ltd 88 High Street, Weyford	
5		Weyford	24.7.0–	Stole toothpaste, baked beans and tea valued at £2.10 Contrary to s.1(1) Theft Act 1968	Keymarkets Ltd 98 High Street, Weyford	

A. Butchers DC 1007

Signature and Rank of Officer in Charge of Case

(U)   NOTICE OF APPEAL

MAGISTRATES' COURT

NOTICE OF APPEAL TO CROWN COURT, AGAINST CONVICTION

To the Justices' Clerk of the Magistrates' Court sitting at Weyford

AND TO the Crown Prosecution Services, Weyford Branch Office, 9 Guildfleet Road, Weyford, Blankshire WE7 5XX

TAKE NOTICE THAT I, Barry Jones of 42 Murdstone Close Weyford, Blankshire WE4 2AF

intend to appeal to the Crown Court at Weyford against my conviction on 11 November 200– by Weyford Magistrates' Court for the offence of driving a Ford Escort motor car Reg. No L207 LBP on Hamilton Avenue, Weyford without due care and attention Contrary to Section 3 Road Traffic Act 1988.

The basis of my appeal is that the magistrates' decision was wrong and contrary to the evidence. I am not guilty of the offence.

Dated 18 November 200–   **Signed** Barry Jones

Case Reference Number WE 24105

Appendix 3

MAGISTRATES' ASSOCIATION
SENTENCING GUIDELINES

Note: These Guidelines refer to community service orders, probation orders and combination orders.

Community service orders are renamed 'community punishment orders' by the Criminal Justice and Court Services Act 2000, s 44.

Probation orders are renamed 'community rehabilitation orders' by the Criminal Justice and Court Services Act 2000, s 43.

Combination orders are renamed 'community punishment and rehabilitation orders' by the Criminal Justice and Court Services Act 2000, s 45.

IMPORTANT: THIS USER GUIDE IS AN INTEGRAL PART OF THE GUIDELINES – PLEASE READ IT

Introduction

These Sentencing Guidelines cover offences with which magistrates deal regularly and frequently in the adult criminal courts. They provide a sentencing structure which sets out how to:

- establish the seriousness of each case
- determine the most appropriate way of dealing with it

The Sentencing Guidelines provide a method for considering individual cases and a Guideline from which discussion should properly flow; but **they are not a tariff and should never be used as such.**

Using the sentencing structure

The sentencing structure used for these Guidelines was established by the Criminal Justice Act 1991. This reaffirms the principle of 'just deserts' so that any penalty must reflect the seriousness of the offence for which it is imposed and the personal circumstances of the offender. Magistrates must always start the sentencing process by taking full account of all the circumstances of the offence and making a judicial assessment of the seriousness category into which it falls.

In every case, the Criminal Justice Act 1991 requires sentencers to consider:

- Is discharge or a fine appropriate?
- Is the offence serious enough for a community penalty?
- Is it so serious that only custody is appropriate?

If the last, in either way cases, justices will also need to consider if magistrates' courts' powers are appropriate.

The format of the Sentencing Guidelines

1.

CONSIDER THE SERIOUSNESS OF THE OFFENCE

Magistrates must always make an assessment of seriousness following the structure of the Criminal Justice Act 1991. However, the Sentencing Guidelines do give a starting point guideline for each offence.

Where this guideline is discharge or fine, a suggested starting point guideline fine is also given. Refer to the guidance on pages 69, 70 and 85.

Where the starting point guideline is a community penalty, refer to the guidance on pages 72 and 73.

Where the starting point guideline is custody, think in terms of weeks or months and discount as appropriate for a timely guilty plea. Refer to page 66 for further guidance.

For some either way offences the guideline is **'are magistrates' sentencing powers appropriate?'**. This indicates that magistrates should be considering whether the seriousness of the offence is such that six months (or twelve months in the case of two or more offences) is insufficient, so that the case must be committed to the Crown Court (consult the clerk with regard to Crown Court sentencing and guideline cases). If the case is retained in the magistrates' court a substantial custodial sentence is likely to be necessary.

It should be noted that if magistrates consider (say) nine months to be the appropriate sentence, to be reduced for a timely guilty plea to six months, then the case falls within their powers and must be retained. Subject to offender mitigation, six months would appear to be the appropriate sentence.

2.

CONSIDER AGGRAVATING AND MITIGATING FACTORS

Make sure that all aggravating and mitigating factors are considered. The lists in the Sentencing Guidelines are neither exhaustive nor a substitute for the personal judgment of magistrates. Factors which do not appear in the Guidelines may be important in individual cases.

If the offence was racially aggravated, the court must treat that fact as an aggravating factor under statute (s.82 Crime and Disorder Act 1998).

If the offence was committed while the offender was on bail, the court must treat that as an aggravating factor under statute (s. 29 Criminal Justice Act 1991, as amended).

Consider previous convictions, or any failure to respond to previous sentences, in assessing seriousness. Courts should identify any convictions relevant for this purpose and then consider to what extent they affect the seriousness of the present offence.

3.

TAKE A PRELIMINARY VIEW OF SERIOUSNESS, THEN CONSIDER OFFENDER MITIGATION

When an initial assessment of the seriousness of the offence has been formed, consider the offender.

The Guidelines set out some examples of offender mitigation but there are frequently others to be considered in individual cases. Any offender mitigation that the court accepts must lead to some downward revision of the provisional assessment of seriousness, although this revision may be minor.

A previous criminal record may deprive the defendant of being able to say that he is a person of good character.

4.

CONSIDER YOUR SENTENCE

The law requires that the court reduces the sentence for a timely guilty plea but this provision should be used with judicial flexibility. A timely guilty plea may attract a sentencing discount of up to one third but the precise amount of discount will depend on the facts of each case and a last minute plea of guilty may attract only a minimal reduction.

Discount may be given in respect of the amount of a fine or periods of community service or custody. Periods of mandatory disqualification or mandatory penalty points cannot be reduced for a guilty plea.

5.

DECIDE YOUR SENTENCE

Remember that magistrates have a duty to consider the award of compensation in all appropriate cases, and to give reasons if compensation is not awarded. See page 75 to 77, Section Three.

Agree the form of words that the Chairman will use when announcing sentence. See the Magistrates' Association *Pronouncements in Court* for examples.

Aggravated Vehicle-Taking	Theft Act 1968 s. 12A as inserted by Aggravated Vehicle-Taking Act 1992 Triable either way – but in certain cases summarily only – consult clerk. Penalty: Level 5 and/or 6 months Must endorse and disqualify at least 12 months

CONSIDER THE SERIOUSNESS OF THE OFFENCE
(INCLUDING THE IMPACT ON THE VICTIM)

IS DISCHARGE OR FINE APPROPRIATE?

IS IT SERIOUS ENOUGH FOR A COMMUNITY PENALTY?

GUIDELINE: → IS IT SO SERIOUS THAT ONLY CUSTODY IS APPROPRIATE?

ARE MAGISTRATES' SENTENCING POWERS APPROPRIATE?

 ## CONSIDER AGGRAVATING AND MITIGATING FACTORS

for example	for example
Competitive driving: racing, showing off	No competitiveness/racing
Disregard of warnings eg from passengers or others in vicinity	Passenger only
Group action	Single incident of bad driving
Police chase	Speed not excessive
Pre-meditated	Very minor injury/damage
Serious injury/damage	*This list is not exhaustive*
Serious risk	
Trying to avoid detection or arrest	
Vehicle destroyed	
This list is not exhaustive	

If racially aggravated, or offender is on bail, this offence is more serious
If offender has previous convictions, their relevance and any failure to respond to previous sentences must be considered – they may increase the seriousness

TAKE A PRELIMINARY VIEW OF SERIOUSNESS, THEN CONSIDER OFFENDER MITIGATION

for example
    Health (physical or mental)
    Co-operation with police
    Voluntary compensation
    Evidence of genuine remorse

CONSIDER YOUR SENTENCE

Compare it with the suggested guideline level of sentence and reconsider your reasons carefully if you have chosen a sentence at a different level. Consider a discount for a timely guilty plea.

DECIDE YOUR SENTENCE
NB. COMPENSATION – Give reasons if not awarding compensation

Remember: These are GUIDELINES only

Assault – Actual Bodily Harm	Offences Against the Person Act 1861 s.47 Triable either way – see Mode of Trial Guidelines Penalty: Level 5 and/or 6 months

CONSIDER THE SERIOUSNESS OF THE OFFENCE
(INCLUDING THE IMPACT ON THE VICTIM)

IS DISCHARGE OR FINE APPROPRIATE?

IS IT SERIOUS ENOUGH FOR A COMMUNITY PENALTY?

IS IT SO SERIOUS THAT ONLY CUSTODY IS APPROPRIATE?

GUIDELINE: → *ARE MAGISTRATES' SENTENCING POWERS APPROPRIATE?*

 CONSIDER AGGRAVATING AND MITIGATING FACTORS

for example	for example
Deliberate kicking or biting Extensive injuries (may be psychiatric) Headbutting Group action Offender in position of authority On hospital/medical premises Premeditated Victim particularly vulnerable Victim serving the public Weapon *This list is not exhaustive*	Minor injury Provocation Single blow *This list is not exhaustive*

If offender is on bail, this offence is more serious

If offender has previous convictions, their relevance and any failure to respond to previous sentences must be considered – they may increase the seriousness

TAKE A PRELIMINARY VIEW OF SERIOUSNESS, THEN CONSIDER WHETHER THE CASE SHOULD BE COMMITTED FOR SENTENCE, THEN CONSIDER OFFENDER MITIGATION

for example

> Age, health (physical or mental)
> Co-operation with police
> Voluntary compensation
> Evidence of genuine remorse

CONSIDER COMMITTAL OR YOUR SENTENCE

Compare it with the suggested guideline level of sentence and reconsider your reasons carefully if you have chosen a sentence at a different level. Consider a discount for a timely guilty plea.

DECIDE YOUR SENTENCE
NB. COMPENSATION – Give reasons if not awarding compensation

Remember: These are GUIDELINES only

Breach of a community order	Criminal Justice Act 1991 sch. 2 A fine – maximum £1,000 A Community Service Order (up to 60 hours) A Curfew Order In certain circumstances, an Attendance Centre Order Revocation of Order and re-sentence for original offence Commit a Crown Court Order to be dealt with at Crown Court

CONSIDER THE SERIOUSNESS OF THE OFFENCE

 ## CONSIDER AGGRAVATING AND MITIGATING FACTORS

for example No attempt to start the sentence Unco-operative *This list is not exhaustive*	**for example** Completed a significant part of the order *This list is not exhaustive*

CONSIDER OFFENDER MITIGATION
(including timely admission)

DECIDE IF THE ORDER SHOULD CONTINUE

IF THE ORDER SHOULD CONTINUE

    Is a fine appropriate? (Starting Point B)

    Is a community service order appropriate?

    Where the order is a probation order, is an attendance centre order appropriate?

    Is a curfew order appropriate?

IF THE ORDER SHOULD NOT CONTINUE AND IT IS A MAGISTRATES' COURT ORDER:

    Revoke and re-sentence for original sentence (see relevant guideline)

NB. IF THE ORDER WAS MADE BY THE CROWN COURT, MAY FINE AND ALLOW ORDER TO CONTINUE, OR COMMIT TO CROWN COURT TO BE DEALT WITH (CONSULT CLERK)

For further guidance, refer to the summary National Standards guide, and to the booklet, *Community Penalties and the Court – Towards Good Practice.*

Remember: These are GUIDELINES only

Theft Act 1968 s.9 Triable either way – see Mode of Trial Guidelines Penalty: Level 5 and/or 6 months	**Burglary (Dwelling)**

CONSIDER THE SERIOUSNESS OF THE OFFENCE
(INCLUDING THE IMPACT ON THE VICTIM)

IS DISCHARGE OR FINE APPROPRIATE?

IS IT SERIOUS ENOUGH FOR A COMMUNITY PENALTY?

IS IT SO SERIOUS THAT ONLY CUSTODY IS APPROPRIATE?

GUIDELINE: → ARE MAGISTRATES' SENTENCING POWERS APPROPRIATE?

CONSIDER AGGRAVATING AND MITIGATING FACTORS

for example At night Forcible entry Group offence People in house Occupants frightened Professional operation Repeat victimisation Soiling, ransacking, damage *This list is not exhaustive*	**for example** Low value Nobody frightened No damage or disturbance No forcible entry Opportunist *This list is not exhaustive*

If racially aggravated, or offender is on bail, this offence is more serious

If offender has previous convictions, their relevance and any failure to respond to previous sentences must be considered – they may increase the seriousness

TAKE A PRELIMINARY VIEW OF SERIOUSNESS, THEN CONSIDER WHETHER THE CASE SHOULD BE COMMITTED FOR SENTENCE, THEN CONSIDER OFFENDER MITIGATION

for example
Age, health (physical or mental)
Co-operation with police
Voluntary compensation
Evidence of genuine remorse

CONSIDER COMMITTAL OR YOUR SENTENCE

Compare it with the suggested guideline level of sentence and reconsider your reasons carefully if you have chosen a sentence at a different level. Consider a discount for a timely guilty plea.

DECIDE YOUR SENTENCE
NB. COMPENSATION – Give reasons if not awarding compensation

Remember: These are GUIDELINES only

Burglary (Non-dwelling)

Theft Act 1968 s.9
Triable either way – see Mode of Trial Guidelines
Penalty: Level 5 and/or 6 months

CONSIDER THE SERIOUSNESS OF THE OFFENCE
(INCLUDING THE IMPACT ON THE VICTIM)

IS DISCHARGE OR FINE APPROPRIATE?

GUIDELINE: →   *IS IT SERIOUS ENOUGH FOR A COMMUNITY PENALTY?*

IS IT SO SERIOUS THAT ONLY CUSTODY IS APPROPRIATE?

ARE MAGISTRATES' SENTENCING POWERS APPROPRIATE?

 CONSIDER AGGRAVATING AND MITIGATING FACTORS

for example	**for example**
Forcible entry	Low value
Group offence	Nobody frightened
Harm to business	No damage or disturbance
Night time	No forcible entry
Occupants frightened	*This list is not exhaustive*
Professional operation	
Repeat victimisation	
School premises	
Soiling, ransacking, damage	
This list is not exhaustive	

If racially aggravated, or offender is on bail, this offence is more serious
*If offender has previous convictions, their relevance and any failure to respond to previous
sentences must be considered – they may increase the seriousness*

TAKE A PRELIMINARY VIEW OF SERIOUSNESS, THEN CONSIDER OFFENDER MITIGATION

for example
Age, health (physical or mental)
Co-operation with police
Voluntary compensation
Evidence of genuine remorse

CONSIDER YOUR SENTENCE

*Compare it with the suggested guideline level of sentence and reconsider
your reasons carefully if you have chosen a sentence at a different level.
Consider a discount for a timely guilty plea.*

DECIDE YOUR SENTENCE

NB. COMPENSATION – Give reasons if not awarding compensation

Remember: These are GUIDELINES only

Failure to surrender to bail

Bail Act 1976 s.6
Triable only summarily
Penalty: Level 5 and/or 3 months

CONSIDER THE SERIOUSNESS OF THE OFFENCE

GUIDELINE: → *IS DISCHARGE OR FINE APPROPRIATE?*
IS IT SERIOUS ENOUGH FOR A COMMUNITY PENALTY?
IS IT SO SERIOUS THAT ONLY CUSTODY IS APPROPRIATE?

GUIDELINE FINE – STARTING POINT B

➕ CONSIDER AGGRAVATING AND MITIGATING FACTORS ➖

for example	**for example**
Leaves jurisdiction	Appears late on day of hearing
Wilful evasion	Genuine misunderstanding
Appears after arrest	Voluntary surrender
This list is not exhaustive	*This list is not exhaustive*

Previous convictions for this offence increase the seriousness

TAKE A PRELIMINARY VIEW OF SERIOUSNESS, THEN CONSIDER OFFENDER MITIGATION

for example
Age, health (physical or mental)
Co-operation with police
Evidence of genuine remorse

CONSIDER YOUR SENTENCE

*Compare it with the suggested guideline level of sentence and reconsider
your reasons carefully if you have chosen a sentence at a different level.
Consider a discount for a timely guilty plea.*

DECIDE YOUR SENTENCE

Remember: These are GUIDELINES only

Offences Against the Person Act 1861 s.47 Crime and Disorder Act 1998 s.29 Triable either way – see Mode of Trial Guidelines Penalty: Level 5 and/or 6 months	**Racially Aggravated Assault – Actual Bodily Harm**

CONSIDER THE SERIOUSNESS OF THE OFFENCE
(INCLUDING THE LEVEL OF RACIAL AGGRAVATION AND THE IMPACT ON THE VICTIM)

IS DISCHARGE OR FINE APPROPRIATE?

IS IT SERIOUS ENOUGH FOR A COMMUNITY PENALTY?

IS IT SO SERIOUS THAT ONLY CUSTODY IS APPROPRIATE?

GUIDELINE: → *ARE MAGISTRATES' SENTENCING POWERS APPROPRIATE?*

CONSIDER AGGRAVATING AND MITIGATING FACTORS

for example
- Deliberate kicking or biting
- Extensive injuries (may be psychiatric)
- Headbutting
- Group action
- Offender in position of authority
- On hospital/medical premises
- Premeditated
- Victim particularly vulnerable
- Victim serving the public
- Weapon
- *This list is not exhaustive*

for example
- Minor injury
- Provocation
- Single blow
- *This list is not exhaustive*

If offender is on bail, this offence is more serious

If offender has previous convictions, their relevance and any failure to respond to previous sentences must be considered – they may increase the seriousness

TAKE A PRELIMINARY VIEW OF SERIOUSNESS, THEN CONSIDER WHETHER THE CASE SHOULD BE COMMITTED FOR SENTENCE, THEN CONSIDER OFFENDER MITIGATION

for example
- Age, health (physical or mental)
- Co-operation with police
- Voluntary compensation
- Evidence of genuine remorse

CONSIDER COMMITTAL OR YOUR SENTENCE

Compare it with the suggested guideline level of sentence and reconsider your reasons carefully if you have chosen a sentence at a different level. Consider a discount for a timely guilty plea.

DECIDE YOUR SENTENCE
NB. COMPENSATION – Give reasons if not awarding compensation

Remember: These are GUIDELINES only

Taking Vehicle without Consent	**Theft Act 1968 s.12** **Triable only summarily** **Penalty: Level 5 and/or 6 months** **May disqualify**

CONSIDER THE SERIOUSNESS OF THE OFFENCE
(INCLUDING THE IMPACT ON THE VICTIM)

IS DISCHARGE OR FINE APPROPRIATE?

GUIDELINE: → *IS IT SERIOUS ENOUGH FOR A COMMUNITY PENALTY?*

IS IT SO SERIOUS THAT ONLY CUSTODY IS APPROPRIATE?

 ## CONSIDER AGGRAVATING AND MITIGATING FACTORS

for example	**for example**
Group action Premeditated Related damage Professional hallmarks Vulnerable victim *This list is not exhaustive*	Misunderstanding with owner Soon returned Vehicle belonged to family or friend *This list is not exhaustive*

If offender is on bail, this offence is more serious

If offender has previous convictions, their relevance and any failure to respond to previous sentences must be considered – they may increase the seriousness

TAKE A PRELIMINARY VIEW OF SERIOUSNESS, THEN CONSIDER OFFENDER MITIGATION

for example
Health (physical or mental)
Co-operation with police
Voluntary compensation
Evidence of genuine remorse

CONSIDER YOUR SENTENCE

Compare it with the suggested guideline level of sentence and reconsider your reasons carefully if you have chosen a sentence at a different level. Consider a discount for a timely guilty plea.

DECIDE YOUR SENTENCE
NB. COMPENSATION – Give reasons if not awarding compensation

Remember: These are GUIDELINES only

Theft Act 1968 s.1 Triable either way – see Mode of Trial Guidelines Penalty: Level 5 and/or 6 months May disqualify where committed with reference to the theft or taking of the vehicle	**Theft**

CONSIDER THE SERIOUSNESS OF THE OFFENCE
(INCLUDING THE IMPACT ON THE VICTIM)

IS DISCHARGE OR FINE APPROPRIATE? **GUIDELINE:** → **IS IT SERIOUS ENOUGH FOR A COMMUNITY PENALTY?** *IS IT SO SERIOUS THAT ONLY CUSTODY IS APPROPRIATE?* *ARE MAGISTRATES' SENTENCING POWERS APPROPRIATE?*

CONSIDER AGGRAVATING AND MITIGATING FACTORS

for example
    High value
    Planned
    Sophisticated
    Adult involving children
    Organised team
    Related damage
    Vulnerable victim
    This list is not exhaustive
	for example
	    Impulsive action
	    Low value
	    This list is not exhaustive

If racially aggravated, or offender is on bail, this offence is more serious *If offender has previous convictions, their relevance and any failure to respond to previous sentences must be considered – they may increase the seriousness*

TAKE A PRELIMINARY VIEW OF SERIOUSNESS, THEN CONSIDER OFFENDER MITIGATION

for example
    Age, health (physical or mental)
    Co-operation with police
    Voluntary compensation
    Evidence of genuine remorse

CONSIDER YOUR SENTENCE

Compare it with the suggested guideline level of sentence and reconsider your reasons carefully if you have chosen a sentence at a different level. Consider a discount for a timely guilty plea.

DECIDE YOUR SENTENCE
NB. COMPENSATION – Give reasons if not awarding compensation

Remember: These are GUIDELINES only

43 *Issue September 2000*

Theft in Breach of Trust	Theft Act 1968 s.1 Triable either way – see Mode of Trial Guidelines Penalty: Level 5 and/or 6 months

CONSIDER THE SERIOUSNESS OF THE OFFENCE
(INCLUDING THE IMPACT ON THE VICTIM)

IS DISCHARGE OR FINE APPROPRIATE?

IS IT SERIOUS ENOUGH FOR A COMMUNITY PENALTY?

IS IT SO SERIOUS THAT ONLY CUSTODY IS APPROPRIATE?

GUIDELINE: → *ARE MAGISTRATES' SENTENCING POWERS APPROPRIATE?*

 ## CONSIDER AGGRAVATING AND MITIGATING FACTORS

for example
    Casting suspicion on others
    Committed over a period
    High value
    Organised team
    Planned
    Senior employee
    Sophisticated
    Vulnerable victim
    This list is not exhaustive

for example
    Impulsive action
    Low value
    Previous inconsistent attitude by employer
    Single item
    Unsupported junior
    This list is not exhaustive

If racially aggravated, or offender is on bail, this offence is more serious
If offender has previous convictions, their relevance and any failure to respond to previous sentences must be considered – they may increase the seriousness

TAKE A PRELIMINARY VIEW OF SERIOUSNESS, THEN CONSIDER WHETHER THE CASE SHOULD BE COMMITTED FOR SENTENCE, THEN CONSIDER OFFENDER MITIGATION

for example
    Age, health (physical or mental)
    Co-operation with police
    Voluntary compensation
    Evidence of genuine remorse

CONSIDER COMMITTAL OR YOUR SENTENCE

Compare it with the suggested guideline level of sentence and reconsider your reasons carefully if you have chosen a sentence at a different level. Consider a discount for a timely guilty plea.

DECIDE YOUR SENTENCE
NB. COMPENSATION – Give reasons if not awarding compensation

Remember: These are GUIDELINES only

Offences Against the Person Act 1861 s.20 Triable either way – see Mode of Trial Guidelines Penalty: Level 5 and/or 6 months	**Wounding – Grievous Bodily Harm**

CONSIDER THE SERIOUSNESS OF THE OFFENCE
(INCLUDING THE IMPACT ON THE VICTIM)

IS DISCHARGE OR FINE APPROPRIATE?

IS IT SERIOUS ENOUGH FOR A COMMUNITY PENALTY?

IS IT SO SERIOUS THAT ONLY CUSTODY IS APPROPRIATE?

GUIDELINE: → *ARE MAGISTRATES' SENTENCING POWERS APPROPRIATE?*

CONSIDER AGGRAVATING AND MITIGATING FACTORS

for example
- Deliberate kicking/biting
- Extensive injuries
- Group action
- Offender in position of authority
- On hospital/medical premises
- Premeditated
- Victim particularly vulnerable
- Victim serving the public
- Weapon
- *This list is not exhaustive*

for example
- Single blow
- Minor wound
- Provocation
- *This list is not exhaustive*

If offender is on bail, this offence is more serious
If offender has previous convictions, their relevance and any failure to respond to previous sentences must be considered – they may increase the seriousness

TAKE A PRELIMINARY VIEW OF SERIOUSNESS, THEN CONSIDER WHETHER THE CASE SHOULD BE COMMITTED FOR SENTENCE, THEN CONSIDER OFFENDER MITIGATION

for example
- Age, health (physical or mental)
- Co-operation with police
- Voluntary compensation
- Evidence of genuine remorse

CONSIDER COMMITTAL OR YOUR SENTENCE

Compare it with the suggested guideline level of sentence and reconsider your reasons carefully if you have chosen a sentence at a different level.
Consider a discount for a timely guilty plea.

DECIDE YOUR SENTENCE
NB. COMPENSATION – Give reasons if not awarding compensation

Remember: These are GUIDELINES only

| Road Traffic Act 1988 s.3
Triable only summarily
Penalty: Level 4
Must endorse (3-9 points OR may disqualify) | **Careless Driving** |

CONSIDER THE SERIOUSNESS OF THE OFFENCE

GUIDELINE: → *IS DISCHARGE OR FINE APPROPRIATE?*
IS IT SERIOUS ENOUGH FOR A COMMUNITY PENALTY?

(PROBATION AND CURFEW ORDERS ARE THE ONLY AVAILABLE COMMUNITY PENALTIES FOR THIS OFFENCE)

GUIDELINE FINE – STARTING POINT B

 ## CONSIDER AGGRAVATING AND MITIGATING FACTORS

for example	**for example**
Excessive speed	Sudden change in weather conditions
High degree of carelessness	Minor risk
Serious risk	Momentary lapse
Using a hand-held mobile telephone	Negligible/parking damage
This list is not exhaustive	*This list is not exhaustive*

Death, serious injury or damage is capable of being aggravation

If offender is on bail, this offence is more serious
If offender has previous convictions, their relevance and any failure to respond to previous sentences must be considered – they may increase the seriousness

TAKE A PRELIMINARY VIEW OF SERIOUSNESS, THEN CONSIDER OFFENDER MITIGATION

for example
Co-operation with police
Voluntary compensation
Evidence of genuine remorse

CONSIDER YOUR SENTENCE

Endorse (3-9 points OR period of disqualification)
Consider other measures (including disqualification until test passed if appropriate –
for example, age, infirmity or medical condition)
Compare it with the suggested guideline level of sentence and reconsider
your reasons carefully if you have chosen a sentence at a different level.
Consider a discount for a timely guilty plea.

DECIDE YOUR SENTENCE

Remember: These are GUIDELINES only

Dangerous Driving

Road Traffic Act 1988 s.2
Triable either way – see Mode of Trial Guidelines
Penalty: Level 5 and/or 6 months
Must endorse and disqualify at least 12 months
Must endorse (3-11 points) if not disqualified
Must order EXTENDED re-test

CONSIDER THE SERIOUSNESS OF THE OFFENCE
(INCLUDING THE IMPACT ON THE VICTIM)

IS DISCHARGE OR FINE APPROPRIATE?

IS IT SERIOUS ENOUGH FOR A COMMUNITY PENALTY?

IS IT SO SERIOUS THAT ONLY CUSTODY IS APPROPRIATE?

GUIDELINE: → *ARE MAGISTRATES' SENTENCING POWERS APPROPRIATE?*

CONSIDER AGGRAVATING AND MITIGATING FACTORS

for example
- Avoiding detection or apprehension
- Competitive driving, racing, showing off
- Disregard of warnings eg. from passengers or others in vicinity
- Evidence of alcohol or drugs
- Excessive speed
- Prolonged, persistent, deliberate bad driving
- Serious risk
- Using a hand-held mobile telephone
This list is not exhaustive

for example
- Emergency
- Single incident
- Speed not excessive
This list is not exhaustive

Serious injury or damage is capable of being aggravation

If offender is on bail, this offence is more serious
If offender has previous convictions, their relevance and any failure to respond to previous sentences must be considered – they may increase the seriousness

TAKE A PRELIMINARY VIEW OF SERIOUSNESS, THEN CONSIDER WHETHER THE CASE SHOULD BE COMMITTED FOR SENTENCE, THEN CONSIDER OFFENDER MITIGATION

for example
- Co-operation with police
- Voluntary compensation
- Evidence of genuine remorse

CONSIDER COMMITTAL OR YOUR SENTENCE

Endorse licence and disqualify at least 12 months unless special reasons apply.
Order EXTENDED re-test.
Compare it with the suggested guideline level of sentence and reconsider your reasons carefully if you have chosen a sentence at a different level.
Consider a discount for a timely guilty plea.

DECIDE YOUR SENTENCE

Remember: These are GUIDELINES only

Road Traffic Act 1988 s.143 Triable only summarily Penalty: Level 5 Must endorse (6-8 points OR may disqualify)	No insurance

CONSIDER THE SERIOUSNESS OF THE OFFENCE

GUIDELINE: → *IS DISCHARGE OR FINE APPROPRIATE?*

IS IT SERIOUS ENOUGH FOR A COMMUNITY PENALTY?

(PROBATION AND CURFEW ORDERS ARE THE ONLY AVAILABLE COMMUNITY PENALTIES FOR THIS OFFENCE)

GUIDELINE FINE – STARTING POINT B

 ## CONSIDER AGGRAVATING AND MITIGATING FACTORS

for example
    Deliberate driving without insurance
    Gave false details
    LGV, HGV, PCV, PSV or minicabs
    No reference to insurance ever having
      been held
    This list is not exhaustive

for example
    Accidental oversight
    Genuine mistake
    Responsibility for providing insurance
      resting with another – the parent/
      owner/lender/hirer
    Smaller vehicle, eg. moped
    This list is not exhaustive

If offender is on bail, this offence is more serious
If offender has previous convictions, their relevance and any failure to respond to previous sentences must be considered – they may increase the seriousness

TAKE A PRELIMINARY VIEW OF SERIOUSNESS, THEN CONSIDER OFFENDER MITIGATION

for example
    Difficult domestic circumstances
    Evidence of genuine remorse

CONSIDER YOUR SENTENCE

Endorse licence.
Carefully consider the option of disqualification, suggested starting point
– two months.
Compare your decision with the suggested guideline level of sentence and reconsider
your reasons carefully if you have chosen a sentence at a different level.
Consider a discount for a timely guilty plea.

DECIDE YOUR SENTENCE

Remember: These are GUIDELINES only

Seriousness

Establishing the Seriousness of the Offence

In establishing the seriousness of the case before them, courts should:

- make sure that all factors which aggravate or mitigate the offence are considered. The lists in the *Guidelines* are neither exhaustive nor a substitute for the personal judgment of magistrates. Factors which do not appear in the *Guidelines* may be important in individual cases;
- consider the various seriousness indicators, remembering that some will carry more weight than others;
- note that, by statute, racial aggravation increases the seriousness of any offence – s.82 Crime and Disorder Act 1998 – but see the note on specific racially aggravated offences created under ss.29-32 of the same Act;
- always bear in mind that, by statute, the commission of an offence on bail aggravates its seriousness;
- consider the effect of using previous convictions, or any failure to respond to previous sentences, in assessing seriousness. Courts should identify any convictions relevant for this purpose and then consider to what extent they affect the seriousness of the present offence;
- note that, when there are several offences to be sentenced, the court must have regard to the totality principle;

When the court has formed an initial assessment of the seriousness of the offence(s), consider any offender mitigation.

Impact on the victim

The impact of the offence upon the victim should be taken into account as a seriousness factor.

Reduction in sentence for guilty pleas

(Section 48 Criminal Justice and Public Order Act 1994)

In deciding what sentence to pass on a person who has pleaded guilty the court has to take into account the stage in the proceedings at which that plea was indicated and the circumstances in which the indication was given. If the court imposes a less severe penalty than it would have given, it must state this in open court.

The principles of 'discount' apply as much to magistrates' courts as they do to Crown Courts. A timely guilty plea may attract a sentencing discount of up to a third but the precise amount of discount will depend on the facts of each case. A change of plea on the day set down for trial may attract only a minimal reduction in sentence; the court must still consider whether discount should be given.

Discounts apply to fines, periods of community sentences and custody. Mandatory periods of disqualification and mandatory penalty points cannot be reduced for a guilty plea. Reasons should be given for decisions.

Pre Sentence and Specific Sentence Reports

The purpose of a Pre-Sentence report (PSR) is to provide information to the sentencing court about the offender and the offences charged so that the court has sufficient relevant information to enable it to decide a suitable sentence.

The revised National Standards require a PSR to contain:

- an assessment of the offending behaviour
- an assessment of the risk to the public
- a clear and realistic indication of the action which can be taken by the court to reduce re-offending

When adjourning a case for receipt of a PSR the court should indicate to the officer preparing the report (preferably in writing)

- the court's preliminary view of the level of seriousness
- the aim of the sentence
- any particular issues to be addressed in the report

The court must make it clear to all that the sentencing bench is not bound by the preliminary indication of seriousness.

A PSR must be provided within a maximum of 15 working days of the court's request or any shorter time agreed. Any delay must be explained in writing.

The Specific Sentence Report (SSR) has a similar purpose to the PSR but, while still in writing, is in an expedited form. The SSR is intended for the more straightforward cases where the required information is readily available from the probation officer in court. The SSR is designed to be available on the same day on which the court's request is made, unless there are exceptional circumstances or the probation officer preparing the report considers further investigation and a full PSR to be necessary.

Giving reasons

Magistrates should normally give reasons for their findings and decisions; this is obligatory under the Human Rights Act.

- The offender should be told the reasons for the decision.
- The victim will want to know the reasons for the decision.
- The public are entitled to know what is going on in the criminal justice system, and to have confidence in it.
- If a sentence is unusual the case for reasons is doubly important.
- Ill-informed criticism in the media may be reduced if reasons have been given in public and recorded.
- In preparing an SSR or a PSR, or in implementing a community sentence, the probation service must know what the magistrates had in mind.
- If a case has to be adjourned, and a differently constituted bench sits next time, the later bench must know the reasons for the decisions of the earlier bench.

And:

- The reasons will be necessary if there is an appeal by way of case stated.

There are now many instances where the giving of reasons is required by law:

- Why bail is refused.
- Why the offence is so serious as to justify prison.
- Why a defaulter is being sent to prison.
- If a compensation order is not awarded.
- If a sentence discount is given.
- If the court does not disqualify the driver or endorse his licence for 'special reasons'.

Having reached their findings and reasons, it is perfectly proper for the magistrates to seek the advice and assistance of the legal adviser in how best to formulate and articulate those reasons for the purpose of the pronouncement.

Financial penalties

Fining

Fines are suitable as punishment for cases which are not serious enough to merit a community penalty, nor so serious that a custodial sentence must be considered.

The aim should be for the fine to have equal impact on rich or poor and before fixing the amount of a fine, the court must enquire into the offender's financial circumstances, preferably using a standard means form.

A fine must not exceed the upper statutory limit. Where this is expressed in terms of a 'level' the maxima are:

Level 1	£200
Level 2	£500
Level 3	£1,000
Level 4	£2,500
Level 5	£5,000

The fine must reflect the seriousness of the offence and must be proportionate both to the offence and the offender.

A reduction must be considered for a guilty plea – up to a third if the plea was timely (see page 66), and the appropriate announcement made.

Where compensation is awarded this must take priority over fines or costs (see pages 75-77).

The suggested fines in these Guidelines are given as either A, B or C and some example fines are given on page 85. This guidance should not be used as a tariff and every offender's means must be individually considered.

Where a defendant is to be fined for several offences and his means are limited it may be better to fix the relevant fine level for the most serious offence and order 'no separate penalty' on the lesser matters.

It is useful if the defendant can be given a document which sets out the total fines, rate of payment, date of first payment and place of payment before leaving the court.

Assessing means

Before fixing the amount of any fine the Criminal Justice Act 1991 s.18 requires the court to inquire into the financial circumstances of the offender so far as they are known.

The means form is the starting point, then any necessary further questioning about income and expenditure can be done by the clerk and/or the magistrates.

The first figure needed is net income – the guideline fines on the chart on page 85 are based on income net of tax and national insurance contributions. An assessment should then be made of the disposable or spare income left to the offender after unavoidable ordinary living expenses, such as food, housing, clothing, council tax and essential services have been deducted.

The court should discover whether the offender has savings or other disposable or realisable capital assets.

The financial circumstances of third parties, eg. other members of the family, are irrelevant, save insofar as the offender derives income or benefit from such persons.

Before the actual fine has been announced, enquiry should be made to establish the extent of any outstanding fines and consideration as to the appropriate course of action, which may be to transfer the fine to be collected by the local court.

If for any reason the magistrates are not satisfied with the information they have received, and they feel they cannot sentence until they have such information, they may adjourn the case for further information to be supplied, and they may make a financial circumstances order requiring a statement of means to be provided, Criminal Justice Act 1991 s.20.

The fine is payable in full on the day and the defendant should always be asked for immediate payment. If periodic payments are allowed, the fine should normally be payable within a maximum of twelve months. It should be remembered however, that for those on very low incomes it is often unrealistic to expect them to maintain weekly payments for as long as a year.

The fine should be a hardship, depriving the offender of the capacity to spend the money on 'luxuries', but care should be taken not to force him or her below a reasonable 'subsistence' level.

Fining in the defendant's absence

If, having been given a reasonable opportunity to inform the court of his means, the offender refuses or fails to do so, the magistrates may draw such inference as to means as they think just in the circumstances. It is inappropriate simply to fine the maximum level.

Costs

The following guidance was given by the Court of Appeal in R. v. Northallerton Magistrates' Court ex parte Dove:

1. An order for costs to the prosecutor should never exceed the sum which, having regard to the defendant's means and any other financial order imposed upon him, he is able to pay and which it is reasonable to order him to pay.

2. Such an order should never exceed the sum which the prosecutor had actually and reasonably incurred.

3. The purpose of the order is to compensate the prosecutor and not to punish the defendant.

4. The costs ordered to be paid should not in the ordinary way be grossly disproportionate to the fine imposed for the offence. If the total of the proposed fine and the costs sought by the prosecutor exceeds the sum which the defendant could reasonably be ordered to pay, it was preferable to achieve an acceptable total by reducing the sum of costs ordered than by reducing the fine.

5. It is for the defendant to provide the justices with such data relevant to his financial position as would enable them to assess what he could reasonably afford to pay, and if he fails to do so the justices are entitled to draw reasonable inferences as to his means from all the circumstances of the case.

6. It is incumbent on any court which proposed to make any financial order against a defendant to give him a fair opportunity to adduce any relevant financial information and to make any appropriate submissions.

Community penalties

The purpose of a community penalty is to provide a rigorous and effective punishment for an offender whose offence requires more than a financial penalty but is not so serious as to necessitate imprisonment. A community penalty has three principal elements: restriction of liberty, reparation and prevention of re-offending.

Community sentences include:

- attendance centre orders
- probation orders with or without special requirements
- community service orders
- combination orders
- curfew orders

The restrictions on liberty imposed by the sentence must be commensurate with the seriousness of the offence and the order must be the one most suitable for the offender.

It is generally good practice to require a Pre Sentence or Specific Sentence Report when considering whether to impose a community penalty. In ordering such a report the court should indicate its view of the level of seriousness and the aim of the sentence. In pronouncing sentence the court should stress the need of the offender to co-operate and the consequences of breach.

Penalties for breach of a community sentence are:

- a fine of up to £1,000, the order to continue
- community service of up to 60 hours, the order to continue
- revocation and re-sentencing for the original offence (in which case the probable sentence will be custody)
- attendance centre order

See the revised National Standards and the new inter-agency publication *Towards Good Practice – Community Sentences and the Courts.*

The court may ask to be kept informed of the offender's progress under the order.

Electronic monitoring of curfew orders

Curfew orders enforced by electronic monitoring are available for offenders aged sixteen and over.

The curfew order is a community sentence requiring an offender to remain at a specified place from two to twelve hours a day on from one to seven days a week, for a maximum period of six months. The court must obtain and consider information about the proposed curfew address including the attitude of others affected by the order. The order must take account of religious beliefs, employment, education and the requirements of other community orders.

The offender's consent is not required.

The aims of the order are:

- to restrict liberty in a systematic controlled way
- to make it harder for the offender to commit further crimes
- to interrupt the pattern of offending by removing the offender from the circumstances of his/her offending
- provide clear evidence of curfew compliance

The order can be used as a stand alone order, in combination with any other community order, or can be added to a pre-existing community order.

When considering whether to impose an order the offence must be assessed by the court to be 'serious enough' – and the level of punishment appropriate. When ordering a Pre-Sentence Report the court must specifically ask the probation service to carry out a curfew assessment even if an 'all options open' report is specified.

Breach of court orders

The breach of court orders should never be treated lightly. They should be rigorously enforced. In making any pronouncement on sentence the breach should be given special mention.

A failure by the court to respond effectively to a breach can:

- erode public confidence in the courts
- undermine the work of the agency supervising the order
- allow the offender to feel he has 'got away with it'

The offender should be clearly told of the seriousness of the offence and, if the court decides to allow an order to continue, be told what is expected of him/her and the likely consequence of any further breach.

In the case of community sentences there are National Standards revised in April 2000 which lay down strict enforcement requirements for the probation service.

The seriousness of any offence should be matched not just by the severity of the sentence but also by the intensity of the enforcement.

Compensation Orders

The Legal Framework

Having assessed the seriousness of the offence, including the impact on the victim, and any aggravating and mitigating factors affecting the offender, the court is under a duty to consider compensation in every case involving death, personal injury, loss or damage (Powers of the Criminal Courts Act 1973 s.35), whether or not an application has been made.

Priorities

If the sentence is to be financial, then the order of priorities is compensation, fine, costs. Compensating the victim is more important than paying money to the state. If the sentence is to be a community penalty, the court should consider carefully the overall burdens placed on the offender if a compensation order is to be made too. If the sentence is to be custody, then a compensation order will be unlikely unless the offender has financial resources available with which to pay.

Giving Reasons

If, having considered making a compensation order, the court decides that it is not appropriate to make one, it has a statutory duty to give its reasons for not ordering compensation.

Limitations on Powers

Magistrates have the power to award compensation for personal injury, loss or damage up to a total of £5,000 for each offence. An exception is where the injury, loss or damage arises from a road accident: a compensation order may not be made in such a case unless there is conviction of an offence under the Theft Act or if the offender is uninsured and the Motor Insurers' Bureau will not cover the loss. If in doubt, seek advice from the clerk. Compensation should only be awarded in fairly clear, uncomplicated cases: if there are disputes and complications, the matter should be left to the civil courts.

No Double Compensation

Any victim may bring a civil action for damages against the offender: if that action is successful, the civil court will deduct the amount paid by the offender under a compensation order. In this way, there should be no double compensation. The same applies where the victim receives a payment under the Criminal Injuries Compensation Scheme. The magistrates' court should therefore take no account of these other possibilities.

Criminal Injuries Compensation Board

The Criminal Injuries Compensation Scheme provides state compensation for the victims of crimes of violence, particularly those who are seriously injured. The minimum award is currently £1,000. Courts are encouraged to make compensation orders, whether or not the case falls within the Criminal Injuries Compensation Scheme, in order to bring home to offenders themselves the consequences of their actions.

The Purpose of Compensation Orders

The purpose of making a compensation order is to compensate the victim for his or her losses. The compensation may relate to offences taken into consideration, subject to a maximum of £5,000 per charge. Compensation for personal injury may include compensation for terror, shock or distress caused by the offence. The court must have regard to the means of the offender when calculating the amount of the order. Up to three years can be allowed for the compensation to be paid in certain cases.

The Approach to Compensation

In calculating the gross amount of compensation, courts should consider compensating the victim for two types of loss. The first, sometimes called "special damages", includes compensation for financial loss sustained as a result of the offence – e.g. the cost of repairing damage, or in cases of injury, any loss of earnings or dental expenses. If these costs are not agreed, the court should ask for evidence of them. The second type of loss, sometimes called "general damages", covers compensation for the pain and suffering of the injury itself and for any loss of facility.

Calculating the Compensation

The amount of compensation should be determined in the light of medical evidence, the victim's sex and age, and any other factors which appear to the court to be relevant in the particular case. If the court does not have sufficient information, then the matter should be adjourned to obtain more facts.

The Table on the next page gives some general guidance on appropriate starting points for general damages.

Once the court has made a preliminary calculation of the appropriate compensation, it is required to have regard to the means of the offender before making an order. Where the offender has little money, the order may have to be scaled down significantly. However, even a compensation order for a fairly small sum may be important to the victim.

Type of injury	Description	Starting point
Graze	Depending on size	Up to £75
Bruise	Depending on size	Up to £100
Black eye		£125
Cut: no permanent scar	Depending on size and whether stitched	£100-£500
Sprain	Depending on loss of mobility	£100-£1,000
Finger	Fractured little finger, recovery within month	£1,000
Loss of non-front tooth Loss of front tooth	Depending on cosmetic effect	£500-£1,000 £1,500
Eye	Blurred or double vision	£1,000
Nose Nose Nose	Undisplaced fractured of nasal bone Displaced fracture of bone requiring manipulation Not causing fracture but displaced septum requiring sub-mucous resection	£1,000 £1,500 £2,000
Facial scar	However small, resulting in permanent disfigurement	£1,500
Wrist Wrist	Simple fracture, recovery within month Displaced fracture, limb in plaster, recovery in 6 months	£3,000 £3,500
Leg or arm	Simple fracture of tibia, fibula, ulna or radius, recovery within month	£3,500
Laparotomy	Stomach scar 6-8 inches (resulting from operation)	£3,500

Racially Aggravated Offences

The present position on sentencing for racial harassment and racially aggravated offences has been substantially clarified by the Crime and Disorder Act 1998. As previously stated, the new offences have been created by s.29-s.32 which carry increased maximum sentences when compared with the basic offences from which they are derived. The increase in maximum sentence must lead sentencers to reach a provisional sentence in excess of the appropriate one for the basic offence. Parliament has given a specific message to sentencers that it expects those who have been convicted of offences which are defined as having a racial element to receive higher tariff penalties. Conversely, as indicated, if there is a conviction for one of the non-aggravated offences, the sentence must be on the basis that the offence was not racially aggravated otherwise the decision would amount to sentencing for a more serious offence than the one for which the offender has been convicted.

Road Traffic Offences

Disqualification

Some offences carry mandatory disqualification. This mandatory disqualification period may be automatically lengthened by the existence of certain previous convictions and disqualifications.

Sentencers should not disqualify in the absence of the defendant but should take steps to ensure the defendant attends the court.

Penalty points and disqualification

All penalty points offences carry also as an alternative discretionary power to disqualify for a selected period and also discretionary power to disqualify until a test is passed.

The number of variable penalty points or the period of disqualification is targeted strictly at the seriousness of the offence and in either case must not be reduced below the statutory minimum, where applicable.

Penalty points and (non-totting) disqualification cannot be awarded for the same offence, or even for offences being convictions on the same occasion.

Disqualifications for less than 56 days

A disqualification for less than 56 days is also more lenient in that it does not revoke the licence and cannot increase subsequent mandatory periods unless it is imposed under the points provisions.

Discount for guilty plea

The precise amount of discount for a timely guilty plea will depend on the facts of each case. It should be given in respect of the fine or periods of community penalty or custody, but does not apply to mandatory periods of disqualification.

The multiple offender

Where an offender is convicted of several offences committed on one occasion, it is suggested that the court should concentrate on the most serious offence, carrying the greatest number of penalty points or period of disqualification.

The application of the totality principle may then result in less than the total of the suggested amounts of fines for the remaining individual offences, or the court may decide to impose no separate penalty for the lesser offences.

Totting

Repeat offenders who reach 12 points or more within a period of three years become liable to a minimum disqualification for 6 months, and in some instances 12 months or 2 years – but must be given an opportunity to address the court and/or bring evidence to show why such disqualification should not be ordered or should be reduced. Totting disqualifications, unlike other disqualifications, erase all penalty points.

Totting disqualifications can be reduced or avoided for exceptional hardship or other circumstances. No account is to be taken of non-exceptional hardship or circumstances alleged to make the offence(s) not serious. No such ground can be used again to mitigate totting, if previously taken into account in totting mitigation within the three years preceding the conviction.

Driver – not supplying details

This offence is now prevalent and must be regarded more seriously.

New drivers

From June 1997, newly qualified drivers who tot up 6 points or more during a two year probationary period from the date of passing the driving test will automatically have their licence revoked and will have to apply for a provisional licence until they pass a repeat test. The totting must also include any points imposed prior to passing the test provided they are within three years.

Goods Vehicles over 3.5 tonnes, buses and coaches

Owners and drivers of such vehicles are often in the average or high income scale. If, exceptionally, low income is applicable, seek documentary evidence and reduce the fine as appropriate.

Fixed penalties

If a fixed penalty was offered, consider any reasons for not taking up and, if valid, fine the amount of the appropriate fixed penalty and endorse if required, considering whether costs should be waived.

EXAMPLE GUIDELINE FINES

Based on weekly income net of Tax and National Insurance

Decrease/ increase according to income	NET WEEKLY INCOME – £s																			
	100		130		160		190		220		250		300		350		400			
FINE A	50		65		80		95		110		125		150		175		200			
FINE B	100		130		160		190		220		250		300		350		400			
FINE C	150		195		240		285		330		375		450		525		600			

If the offence is aggravated, but not serious enough for a community penalty, INCREASE the fine.
If there are mitigating elements, REDUCE the fine

REDUCE IF GIVING SOME DISCOUNT FOR A TIMELY GUILTY PLEA – SEE PAGE 66

IF THERE IS INSUFFICIENT INCOME TO PAY A FINE AND COMPENSATION,
CONSIDER ORDERING ONLY THE COMPENSATION – SEE PAGE 75

                  Issue September 2000

Stating the reasons for sentence

1. We are dealing with an offence of:

   ....

2. We have considered the impact on the victim which was ....

3. We have taken into account the following aggravating features of the offence:

   ....

   ....

4. And the following mitigating features of the offence:

   ....

   ....

5. (*where relevant*) We have taken into account that the offence was:
   racially aggravated
   committed on bail

6. We have taken into account your previous record, specifically the offences of...........................
   and your failure to respond to the sentences imposed.

7. We have taken into account the following matters in mitigation:

   ....

   ....

8. We have taken into account the fact that you pleaded guilty [at an early stage] [but not
   until ....] and we have reduced the sentence accordingly.

9. And, as a result, we have decided that the most appropriate sentence for you is:

   ....

10. (*where relevant*) We have decided not to award compensation in this case because:

    ....

Appendix 4

POLICE STATION ADVICE: ADVERSE INFERENCES AND WAIVING PRIVILEGE

POLICE STATION ADVICE: ADVERSE INFERENCES AND WAIVING PRIVILEGE

Guidelines from the Criminal Law Committee of the Law Society
1 July 1997

Introduction

The operation of section 34 of the Criminal Justice and Public Order Act 1994 is complex. To help solicitors to understand the circumstances in which a court is likely to draw an adverse inference from silence and when evidence can be given of the circumstances leading to advice to remain silent without waiving privilege, the Criminal Law Committee has issued the following guidance.

Silence on its own will not prove guilt

Essential components of a judge's direction to the jury highlighted by the Court of Appeal include: *(1)*

- the burden of proof remains with the prosecution throughout;
- an inference alone cannot prove guilt;
- the court must be satisfied that the prosecution has established a case to answer on the prosecution before drawing any inferences.

Sufficiency of evidence

It follows that if you are unsure whether the police have sufficient, or sufficiently strong, evidence for:

- the police to charge; or
- the CPS to continue with a prosecution; or
- a court to convict;

the safest advice will often be that your client should remain silent.

Even if the suspect is likely, in due course, to be advised to plead guilty to the allegation, you must be satisfied that there is a significant mitigation advantage to him/her admitting guilt which is verifiable at this early stage in the proceedings.

Strategies available if your client does not answer questions

You should always consider whether the risk of the suspect being wrongfully convicted might be less if he/she remains silent instead of answering police questions. In formulating your advice, you should also consider the strategies available if your client does not answer questions. These include:

- explaining to the police that the suspect is not answering questions on your advice (but without explanation of that advice);
- explaining to the police that the suspect is not answering questions on your advice, giving reasons for that advice;
- asserting innocence and/or giving a brief explanation of facts consistent with innocence, without answering further police questions;
- handing in a statement either at the end of or after the police interview;

- handing in a statement at the time of charge (as the alleged failure to answer questions must occur before the suspect was charged, an inference cannot be drawn from silence during questioning about the statement after the charge *(2)*);
- taking a statement from the suspect to be used, if necessary, to rebut inferences of recent fabrication at trial.

Balancing the risk

Talking to the police may pose a greater risk of wrongful conviction than remaining silent if, for example:

- the suspect is in an emotional, highly suggestible, state of mind at the time of the interview;
- the suspect is confused and liable to make mistakes which could be interpreted – incorrectly – as deliberate lies at any subsequent trial;
- the suspect is likely to forget important details, distrusts his/her memory, is likely to respond inappropriately to negative feedback by the police, or is likely to go along with their suggestive questioning;
- the suspect uses loose expressions, unaware of the possible adverse interpretations which could be placed upon them at trial;
- there is some other reason, particularly psychological, why s/he might be expected to perform badly during the interview and not to do justice to his/her case;
- the behaviour of the police officers dealing with the case leads you to believe that the conduct of the interview may be unfair or may place undue pressure on the suspect.

A client who is disadvantaged

A court will not always allow comment to be made about a suspect's silence:

- the less articulate a suspect is;
- the less capable s/he is of understanding and making a reasoned choice about whether to remain silent or not;
- the less able, by reason of intellectual disadvantage, s/he is to give a good account in interview;

the more likely that a court will not allow comment to be made.

The questioning must be relevant

The alleged failure must occur during questioning under caution prior to charge, or on being charged or officially informed about the possibility of prosecution. With regard to the former, the questioning must be directed to trying to discover whether or by whom the alleged offence was committed. *(2)*

This means that an inference cannot be drawn from a failure to reply to questions:

- which are irrelevant or are not related to the immediate investigation; or
- which are put after the police believe that they already have sufficient evidence for a successful prosecution.

There should be no adverse comment at court about the suspect's silence when it was not reasonable to expect him/her to mention a fact when questioned under s 34

Examples of this are:

(i) The suspect was psychologically vulnerable. The Court of Appeal has stated that matters such as the following might all be relevant: *(1)*

- the time of day
- the suspect's
  - age
  - experience
  - mental capacity
  - state of health
  - sobriety
  - tiredness
  - personality

Advice on assessing a suspect's vulnerability is given on pages 203–213 of A Pocket Reference. *(3)*

(ii) The police have disclosed to the solicitor little or nothing of the nature of the case against the suspect, so that: *(4)*

- the solicitor cannot usefully advise the suspect; *(4)*
- the suspect's lack of knowledge is such that the suspect did not understand the reason for or the basis of the police questions;
- it was not apparent to the suspect at the time that the fact which s/he failed to mention would later become relevant to his or her defence.

(iii) The nature of the offence, or the material in the hands of the police is so complex that no sensible immediate response is feasible. *(4)*

(iv) The questioning relates to matters so long ago, that no sensible immediate response is feasible. *(4)*

The significance of legal advice

The fact that the suspect was given legal advice to remain silent will not normally be enough to prevent the issue of inference being left to the jury. In most cases, legal advice not to answer questions will be merely one factor (amongst others) for the court to take into account in deciding whether or not the defendant acted reasonably in not mentioning facts on which s/he now relies.

The court is not concerned with the correctness of the solicitor's advice, nor whether it complies with the Law Society's guidelines, but with the reasonableness of the suspect's conduct in all the circumstances which the court have found to exist. *(2)*

Neither the Law Society by its guidance, nor the solicitor by his/her advice can prevent the court considering whether an inference should be drawn. *(2)*

The circumstances relate to the individual accused

The fact must be one which in the circumstances existing at the time the suspect could reasonably have been expected to mention when questioned.

Reference to the 'accused' is to the actual accused with such qualities, apprehensions, knowledge and advice as s/he is shown to have at the time 'not to some hypothetical, reasonable accused of ordinary phlegm and fortitude'. *(2)*

The need to keep proper records

If the suspect remains silent on your recommendation, the court may still infer guilt. Therefore it may be necessary to make sure that the court understands the circumstances which led you to advise the suspect to remain silent.

This means you have to keep full, clear contemporaneous notes of the prevailing circumstances and the advice which you gave so that you can:

(i)   refer to them;
(ii) produce them in court if necessary.

keep a careful note of –

- the physical and mental state of the suspect;
- the general conduct of the police and the 'atmosphere' in which the investigation is being conducted;
- what the police allege has been said by the suspect prior to your attendance;
- what the police assert has been said to the suspect by the police eg a request to account for an object etc, and what reply, if any, was made;
- what information is made available by the police to you;
- what requests for information are made of the police by you;
- what information is given to you by the suspect;
- the suspect's apparent understanding of the significance of the allegation, and the significance of his/her replies or failure to respond;
- the advice given by you to the suspect, and the reasons for that advice;
- the wording of any caution or explanation under Code C para. 10.5B, and any responses by the suspect;
- what was said at the time of charge/report for summons.

Providing an evidential basis for inviting the court not to draw an adverse inference from silence because of the prevailing circumstances

The Court of Appeal has made it clear that a judge may direct a jury that they may draw an adverse inference where, despite any evidence relied upon to explain his/her failure to mention facts relied upon at trial, or in the absence of any evidence, the jury conclude that this can only be sensibly attributed to the defendant having no answer to the police questions, or none that would stand up to interrogation.*(5)*

Evidence that may explain a failure to mention facts relied upon at trial may be put before the court by any or all of the following:

- asking the custody officer to insert relevant information in the custody record, or attaching to the custody record a memorandum provided by you;
- explaining at the beginning of the tape recorded police interview the reasons for the advice;
- adducing a s 9 CJA 1967 statement made by you;
- the suspect and/or you giving evidence at trial;

- adducing a statement made by the suspect to you, normally whilst still at the police station, to rebut an allegation of recent fabrication (see below).

In each case, however, you must consider both the admissibility of such evidence, and whether it amounts to a waiver of privilege.

Waiving privilege

If the suspect, as a reason for not answering questions, merely asserts that s/he has been advised by you not to do so, that does not amount to a waiver of privilege. *(5)* However, that bare assertion is unlikely to be regarded as a sufficient reason for not answering questions. *(5)*

The Court of Appeal has held that in order for a jury to be able to consider whether the suspect acted reasonably in not telling the police of facts subsequently relied on at trial, it will normally be necessary for the court to hear the basis on which the advice was given. *(5)*

The test which the court should apply is not how reasonable your advice was but how reasonable it was for the suspect to behave as s/he did in the circumstances, which include the fact that you advised silence.

If you or the suspect explain the advice to remain silent by reference to a privileged conversation between you, that may amount to waiver of privilege which would allow you or the suspect to be asked whether there were any other reasons for that advice.

If the basis or reason for that advice can be explained without making reference to a privileged conversation with the suspect, this should not amount to a waiver of privilege. This may be the case where the reason for the advice is external to the suspect's instructions (eg psychological vulnerability which is apparent from your observations rather than what the suspect said to you; or lack of police disclosure).

At the police station you can put these circumstances on record (in the custody record or on tape), although in order to avoid the possibility of it being regarded as a waiver of privilege it must be done in such a way that avoids reference to a privileged conversation with your client (eg by stating at the commencement of a police interview 'I now advise my client not to answer questions because …': in these circumstances privilege should not be waived because you are not giving advice in a privileged situation and no reference is being made to a privileged conversation).

It is not possible for you to give an account of the basis of or reasons for your advice to remain silent without being in danger of waiving privilege if the basis of or reason for advising silence is derived from the instructions which the suspect has given by to you, eg the suspect's instructions are unclear, contradictory or incomplete or they relate to an alibi, or self-defence.

Use of the considered statement

The Court of Appeal have stated that the purpose of s 34 is to encourage speedy disclosure of a genuine defence or of facts which may go towards establishing a genuine defence – to permit adverse inferences to be drawn where there has been late fabrication.*(4)*

The inference which the prosecutor is likely to invite the court to draw from a failure to mention facts in an interview is that they have been subsequently fabricated ie the defence did not exist at the time when it should have been disclosed.

It is only when the court find that the only sensible explanation for the suspect's decision to remain silent is that s/he has no answer to the case against him/her, or none that could have stood up to cross-examination, that it is open to the court to hold the suspect's failure to give evidence against him/her. *(6)*

This means that whatever your reasons for advising the suspect to remain silent in interview, you could subsequently inform the police and the prosecutor of facts not mentioned in interview, although this would normally have to be done promptly to prevent adverse inferences from being drawn.

This would rebut an inference of recent fabrication and would not waive privilege in relation to other matters discussed with the suspect because you are, for this purpose, in the same position as any other third party to whom the fact is communicated. *(5)*

You may decide to take a statement from the suspect immediately prior to the police interview, have the suspect sign and date this and then hand it in to the custody officer at the time of charge.

Alternatively, the statement may not be handed in at the time of charge, but could be adduced at trial in order to rebut an inference of recent fabrication. This may be more suitable where there are reasons why it would not be appropriate to hand in a statement to the police whilst your client is in the police station. *(5)*

What is of significance to the court is whether and when, in the sequence of pre-trial events, the accused mentions matters relevant to his/her defence. If such evidence was not disclosed or was disclosed at a late stage in the sequence of interview, charge and trial, adverse inferences can be drawn by the court. *(4)*

References

(1) *R v Cowan, R v Gayle and R v Ricciardi* [1995] 4 All ER 939.
(2) *R v Argent* (1996) *The Times*, December 19.
(3) *A Pocket Reference* is published by the Law Society and available from Marstons Book Services, tel: 01235 465656, price £17.50.
(4) *R v Roble* [1997] Crim LR 449.
(5) *R v Condron* [1997] 1 Cr App R.
(6) The specimen Judicial Studies Board direction to be given by the Judge to a jury, approved by the Court of Appeal.

INDEX

References are to paragraph and Appendix numbers.